MARTIN HEIDEGGER:
IN EUROPE AND AMERICA

MARTIN HEIDEGGER
b. September 26, 1889 in Messkirch, Baden, Germany

MARTIN HEIDEGGER:

IN EUROPE AND AMERICA

edited by

EDWARD G. BALLARD

AND

CHARLES E. SCOTT

MARTINUS NIJHOFF / THE HAGUE / 1973

Most of the articles appearing in this volume first appeared in *The Southern Journal of Philosophy*, Volume 8, number 4, 1970 and are reprinted here by permission of the editors of *The Southern Journal* and Department of Philosophy, Memphis State University, Memphis, Tennessee, U.S.A.

ISBN 90 247 1534 2

PRINTED IN THE NETHERLANDS

TABLE OF CONTENTS

Martin Heidegger Is Eighty-Years Old

by

ROBERT COOPER*

Here: in this clearing: the evening falls
in ragged smiles around the standing stones.

In diminished light
we do not ask,

Why do stones stand?

Things lie
about us
under random
hands.

The language of the light
tilts the horizon to the monochrome
center of dusk.

A broken kaleidoscope is   at hand.

* Robert Cooper is the Episcopalian Chaplain at Vanderbilt University where he is also a teaching assistant in the department of philosophy. Having received the M.A. degree in philosophy from Louisiana State University, he is working toward the D.Div. degree at Vanderbilt. His poems have appeared in numerous periodicals, including *The Sewanee Review, The Southern Review,* and *The Christian Century.*

FOREWORD

When Heidegger's influence was at its zenith in Germany from the early fifties to the early sixties, most serious students of philosophy in that country were deeply steeped in his thought. His students or students of his students filled many if not most of the major chairs in philosophy. A cloud of reputedly Black Forest mysticism veiled the perspective of many of his critics and admirers at home and abroad. Droves of people flocked to hear lectures by him that most could not understand, even on careful reading, much less on one hearing. He loomed so large that *Being and Time* frequently could not be seen as a highly imaginative, initial approach to a strictly limited set of questions, but was viewed either as an all-embracing first order catastrophy incorporating at once the most feared consequences of Boehme, Kierkegaard, Rilke, and Nietzsche, or as THE ANSWER.

But most of that has past. Heidegger's dominance of German philosophy has ceased. One can now brush aside the larger-than-life images of Heidegger, the fears that his language was creating a cult phenomenon, the convictions that only those can understand him who give their lives to his thought. His language is at times unusually difficult, at times simple and beautiful. Some of his insights are obscure and not helpful, others are exciting and clarifying. One no longer expects Heidegger to interpret literature like a literary critic or an academic philologist. His purposes and interests are different from representatives of those disciplines. After a period of extraordinary influence, both negative and positive, Heidegger has returned to life-size, to a creative philosopher from whom one can learn, whose thought makes no absolute, systematic demands, who is, in fact, remarkably open to differences, disagreements, and criticism.

Yet Heidegger's writings are surely the strangest, the most unheimlich, upon the contemporary philosophic horizon. Since the way beyond this horizon not improbably lies through this philosophy, it holds a particular interest for us. In Heidegger's figure, his writings happen within the long evening of the spirit which intervenes between the time of the departure of the gods and the time of those not yet come. But in such a twilight it is difficult to know just how his writings are to be read in order that their significance for us be determined. Happily, Heidegger himself seems to respond to this difficulty in his letter to Professor Arthur H. Schrynemakers upon the occasion of the Heidegger symposium at Duquesne University in 1966.[n]

There he recommends, not that his books be made the topic of analyses and commentary in the spirit of exact modern scholarship, but rather that they induce the reader to raise once again the question (or *one* of the questions) of Being. He seems to indicate that his books are intended to be a means for leading each individual reader to investigate and to experience on his own the same questioning which inspired this philosophy.

Let us ask, then: what is the question of Being? What is the meaning of this question? What is the *Sinn von Sein*?

We think it at least clear that the decision to raise this question is intended as the initiation of the way to philosophy. Thus, some grasp of the sense of the question is essential. In pursuing this grasp, it is not inappropriate to seek first to understand the meaning it has for Heidegger in his capacity as a participant in the philosophic conversation. Here it is reasonable to suppose that careful scholarly analyses are indeed a valuable instrument for determining his role in this conversation. Also, it is well to remind oneself from time to time that penetration into the *meaning* of Being is not necessarily demonstrated by novelty of statement. A number of essays in this collection exemplify this spirt. They raise the basic philosophic question in the terms used by Heidegger but are solicitous to preserve the philosophic intention by repeating in their own thought and expression the same way of which he has already

---

[n] The letter is published in *Heidegger and the Path of Thinking*, ed. John Sallis (Pittsburgh: Duquesne University Press, 1970), pp. 9–11.

made trial. They engage Heidegger more or less directly in dialogue. Other essays appear to be more remote from immediate concern with his published writings. Nevertheless, they are of the same genus and differ only superficially in their effort to turn radically back to the source of their being and of their culture or world. Among the continental essays, for example, Gadamer's and Volkmann-Schluck's constructive discussions, though deeply influenced by him, hardly mention Heidegger or his works. They are thematic reflections which, like a German *novella,* center on a point of focus that grows and develops through the attention created by the discussion. The essay as a whole, rather than an isolatable part, constitutes its idea or insight. Professor Löwith's paper grows out of long-standing disagreements with Heidegger and reflects some of the major critical responses that have been made against Heidegger's thought. Pöggeler's discussion is concerned with direct interpretation as well as basic interpretative principles which Pöggeler finds most helpful. Beaufret, whose name has long been associated with Heidegger as the recipient of the *Letter on Humanism* in 1946, "sees" Heidegger through his essay in a way that one must admire as beautifully and utterly French.

The discussions reflect some of the ways that Heidegger's philosophy lives in Europe. Their diversity of approach, their independence of style and intelligence, point to the philosophical importance of Heidegger: he has influenced and stimulated an enormous number of thinkers, helping them to think with intensity and persistence, encouraging them to use their own ways of expression and to work on the problems and questions that seem most pressing to them, appearing to them as a philosopher who knows that most of what is worthy of thought has yet to be thought well.

The genus of these writings is suggested, we believe, by a historical analogy already intimated by those commentators who regard Heidegger's philosophy as a kind of secularized theology. Recall that spiritual power, once held to be mediated through the church and its hierarchy, was—after the movement of the Reformation —supposedly brought into direct contact with each individual believer. Likewise, poetic life and humanistic values were once mediated by the cultured and talented few, whose insights, given beautiful form, became an education and the medium whereby meaning was given to the life of the many. Heidegger, we suggest, is in this respect something of a protestant in philosophy. By persuading each reader to experience for himself the questioning of Being, he seems to invite each to a kind of reformation intended to yield something of the gift of poetical life and some personal share in this freedom. His radical reinterpretation of the history of philosophy reinforces this conviction. It is as if he sought to open the way to a new self-consciousness by means of a return to sources.

This renewed self-consciousness is initially an awareness of the self within a world which it nurtures and by which it is nurtured. Subsequently, it moves to an awareness of this nourishing interchange as the gift of a power which, like the gods, can be indicated only indirectly. This is the movement to a level of reflection by which the life of a world may be discovered. In such a manner might the courage be found to relinquish customs and beliefs now fallen away from their function and to renew the ethos of our time. The essays of this collection are all devoted, in their several ways, to discovering and setting forth some aspect of this movement of reflection. No doubt each would be most appropriately read if it, too, were to become an incitement to its readers to turn back to fundamental questioning.

We should like to express our appreciation to the Heidelberg Akademie der Wissenschaften, which first published the essays by Gadamer, Volkmann-Schluck, Löwith, and Beaufret, for permission to publish the essays in translation, to Kiepenheuer und Witsch Verlag for permission to publish Pöggeler's essay, to the Vanderbilt University Research Council for help in defraying the expenses of translation, to the Vanderbilt Department of Philosophy for help in defraying secretarial expenses, and particularly to Professor Gadamer for his help and cooperation in securing the Akademie essays for this publication.

EDWARD G. BALLARD
CHARLES E. SCOTT

HEIDEGGER TODAY*

OTTO PÖGGELER

University of Bochum

The name of Martin Heidegger is thoroughly connected with what has been carried on in intellectual discussion in the last fifty years. Just as, for example, the name of Max Planck or Kafka, Martin Buber or Rilke, Max Weber or Gropius, Karl Barth or Klee is a signal which immediately arouses the most varied emotions and provokes points of view, so also is the name 'Heidegger.' The discussion over Heidegger is carried on not only in the quiet of reflection and reasonable dialogue, but also in the noisy business of mass media and in university politics, even in pamphlets, comedies and novels. In such discussions, however, the name 'Heidegger' is often nothing more than a shibboleth which is handled only too superficially. Presently, however, the discussion of Heidegger is to be understood as the interpretation of the work of a philosopher who in our time was able to further the classical, philosophical tradition. Thus we are not discussing here Heidegger the man. (He was born in 1889 in Messkirch, north of the Lake of Constance. In Freiburg i. Br. he studied first Roman Catholic theology and then philosophy and the natural sciences and there became recognized as academic lecturer in philosophy under Rickert and taught under Husserl. In 1923 he went to Marburg and worked together with the Protestant theologian Rudolf Bultmann. With one blow, by means of his book *Sein und Zeit,* he became one of the leading philosophers and was called to Freiburg as successor to his teacher, Husserl. In 1933 after the coup d'état of the National Socialists, he, as Rector of the University of Freiburg, surprisingly declared himself for Hitler—

for a short time—and then soon joined the opposition and went into solitude. After the Second World War he once more came forward with an apparently new philosophical starting point and again achieved wide acclaim. Today, eighty years old, he lives in Freiburg in Breisgau.) We shall not speak primarily of the man Heidegger or especially of the university professor, or of his political or theological views and opinions. We shall deal, rather, solely with his philosophy and with all other issues only in relation to this philosophy. The name 'Heidegger' stands for the philosophical task which attached itself to this name.

As right as it is that Heidegger's name is attached to the intellectual discussion of the fifty years and that this name stands for a philosophical task, the title "Heidegger Today" does not ring true. One could be of the opinion that the emphatic way of relating Heidegger's philosophizing and 'today' was not always wrong, but has become so in the meantime: that the sudden success of *Sein und Zeit* and the surprising, new impact of Heidegger after the Second World War belong conclusively to the past, that Heidegger's thought has become a side issue. The fact is that the image from the first fifteen years after the last World War, when police had to be employed in order to control the masses streaming to lectures by Heidegger,

Otto Pöggeler is Ordentlicher Professor at the recently established University of Bochum and director of the Hegel-Archiv at that university. He has written Der Denkweg Martin Heideggers *and is the editor of* Heidegger: Perspektiven zur Deutung seines Werks *and* Hegel-Studien.

---

* This article first appeared in *Heidegger: Perspektiven zur Deutung seines Werks,* ed. O. Pöggeler, Neue Wissenschaftliche Bibliothek 34, Kiepenheuer und Witsch, Köln und Berlin, 1969. Translated by R. Phillip O'Hara.

Ortega y Gasset or Sartre, has been replaced by other images. Heidegger's philosophy no longer belongs to the philosophical currents which are fashionable and topical (even the interest which Heidegger's thought has encountered outside of Germany does not alter this assertion). And it is not only the philosophical currents that have changed, but also the relationship between philosophical or philosophically inspired ideas and a wider public has changed (thereby also the relation between these ideas and the police). When our time attempts to free itself from the claim which Heidegger's thought has made upon its thought, however, it accomplishes, in accord with Heidegger, that separation by which he himself attempted to free himself from the 'today' and its actualities. To be sure, Heidegger's thought remained very concretely related to the decisive questions and endeavors of our time. Heidegger did not develop his thoughts about "Building, Dwelling, Thinking," for example, in an esoteric circle, nor among technical philosophers. He developed those thoughts, rather, in that circle, which in Darmstadt — fifty years after the first exhibition of the Darmstadt Art Colony of 1901, this milestone in the architectural development of the 20th century — attempted to make clear (through retrospect and prospect, Jubilee exhibition, and discussion) to which tradition contemporary construction is indebted and how a city, after the destruction of the Second World War, could aspire to a future of construction and habitation. Such proximity to the questions of the times, however, did not for Heidegger include the proximity to the efforts by which this period itself attempted to decide its questions philosophically and scientifically. It proved more and more to have been a misunderstanding still to want to encounter Heidegger on the way of his later thought by attempting to honor him by documenting "Heideggers Einfluss auf die Wissenschaften." Even if Heidegger himself provided a series of works under the title *Unterwegs zur Sprache,* he did not have in mind to refer to all of those paths on which our time believes itself to be on the way to language, whether that be the diverse ways of philology or the philosophy of language, or even the paths of those philosophies which designate themselves as 'linguistic.' Heidegger treads the narrow edge of the path of one question which for him is the only one, and whoever wanders such a narrow way — a way which involves the heavens above, the abyss beneath, the narrow line of the path in front—looks neither to the right nor to the left.

The title "Heidegger Today," however, does not therefore sound false because Heidegger's thought and the actualities of today have gone separate ways in the meantime, or because the appearance of proximity has been abolished. Indeed, the title could have been intended to express precisely this divergence. The title already has a false ring because Heidegger's thought makes the claim that it cannot be understood at all from that foreground which we denominate with the word "today." To be sure this thought, like hardly any other, refers to the moment, the *kairos.* But this moment, for his thought, is not that which is offered publicly as the 'today' of the Twenties and Thirties or Fifties and Sixties of the Twentieth Century. Should we speak of a 'today' in Heidegger's sense — of us contemporaries, of today's thought, of today's conceptual task — then this 'today' of thought would have to be determined by the fact that in it the thought and conduct of 2000 years wait to be made public in their questionableness and wait to enter into a history of which we know only the most initial beginnings. In this 'today' an Aristotle or an Augustine, a Heraclitus or a Hölderlin, a Greek eyeglass or a result of research in physics or a vague, intimated possibility of future biological research and technology could be more modern than that which

2

serves as the most modern, perhaps more modern than what is philosophically most topical. Would not therefore Heidegger be related to today in the right way if he were taken as a classical philosopher? He would be a classicist because, in an adequate way, he would have been able to carry on in our time that thought which stretches from Anaximander to Nietzsche. Whatever a classical philosopher may be according to the more exact sense of the word, the classicist is able to carry through his concern with efficacious force and with epoch making significance, whether this significance accrues to him in his lifetime or not till later. Further, the classicist is able to measure himself with the tradition and to enlist the 'greats' of the tradition for his cause. His work is able to surmount all historical relativities, i.e., appeal to what is important only today, and to arrive at a lasting validity, even though this validity may be interpreted differently at different times. If the task of philosophy is to understand itself in dialogue with the philosophical tradition, then philosophy in a period of a developed historical consciousness can not dismiss the task of interpreting the classics. To interpret Heidegger today would mean, then, to interpret him as a classical philosopher. That, however, would also mean for philosophy: to acquire in this interpretation an understanding of itself.

Such a process of interpretation can be accomplished in various ways. Let us consider, for example, Kant interpretation. Already in Kant's lifetime, the number of works about Kant reached into the thousands, and the type of speculative idealism in which one aspired to realize fully the Kantian philosophy and thus to surpass it was also already developed. Then, a half century after Kant's death, Kantian philology and Kantian research came into play to the greatest extent and Kant's works were historically and philologically prepared after decades of work, the attendance to Kant stood

under systematic directives. For Neo-Kantianism, Kant's critical works functioned as the criterion for the precritical work as well as for that philosophy which constituted the contest in which Kant had begun his thinking. The historical-philological discoveries were undertaken on the firm foundation of a systematic adaptation, and only gradually did Kantian research learn to relativize its point of departure. Hegel-interpretation was completely different: for it too the aspired "system" seemed to be the firm foundation from which every interpretation had to proceed, and which was first to be secured and developed through the editing, interpretation and continuation of Hegel's work. The *Phänomenologie des Geistes*, however, could be fitted into this system only with difficulty. In it the system obviously reached a "crisis." When the actual Hegelian philology and research began via the works of Dilthey, the discovery of the young Hegel permanently undermined the apparent secure footing of the system. The task of Hegel-editing as well as Hegel-interpretation was therefore to win anew the unity of Hegel's work.

As far as the discussion of Heidegger is concerned, it is not possible by means of a systematic accommodation of a selected part of Heidegger's work to find that position, which could function for the discussion (as Kant's critical philosophy functioned for Kant-research) as a secure starting point for a philological-historical elaboration of the complete works. It is not even the case that (as in the Hegel-interpretation) the antagonism between a system and a crisis of the system, or between a system and its developmental history could be the motor of research. The confrontation of the early and later works of Heidegger exposes itself all too quickly as an insufficient motive for a finished Heidegger-interpretation. Is that aggregate, designated by the name Heidegger, in any way a coherent whole? Does not Heidegger's work, in which every position which is gained is immediately surpassed, disintegrate into larger segments for systematic or historical work, as well as into individual essays, addresses, lectures, and letters? Is his work most closely comparable to the work of Schelling, in which titles like "Ideas concerning . . . ," "Aphorisms regarding . . . ," "Investigations of . . . ," "First outline of a . . . ," "Introduction to the outline . . ." already indicate the continual act of self-surpassing and state of fragmentation? Schelling's works, however, are circumscribed by a unified frame, and are formed by the attempt to carry through and continue speculative idealism. It is, however, characteristic of Heidegger's work that it again and again eludes every affixed frame: Heidegger's thought as a whole cannot be ascribed to a philosophy of existence or to a renovation or critique of metaphysics, or even to a retrogression into myth. Indeed Heidegger as object of the discussion disintegrates into a "Heidegger, insofar as . . ." and numerous other "Heidegger's, insofar as . . .": the interpreter of Aristotle and the one politically engaged, the programmatitian of a science of Being and the one who conceives the world as a fourfold polyvalence, the transcendental philosopher and the interpreter of Hölderlin, appear to have little in common and appear to belong together only by an accident, which is to be disregarded.

In so far as one does not want to dispute altogether Heidegger's right to be understood as a thinker of one single thought, the task of Heidegger- interpretation should be to reverse the mentioned disintegration and to make clear the uniformity of a *process* of thought. Rightly to interpret Heidegger "historically," to present perhaps an historical development of his thought, would be the step due now. It would be illusory, however, to want to take this step before the study of Heidegger has made it possible to arrive at clarity over the guiding starting point or guiding starting points of Heideg-

ger's thought. Moreover, a presentation of the historical development of Heidegger's thought is not yet possible, because Heidegger's work has been published only in a very fragmentary and accidental or arbitrary manner. Heidegger's early thought, the way to *Sein und Zeit,* is known almost exclusively from hear-say. *Sein und Zeit* is the only larger, strictly systematic work which has been published, but the part of *Sein und Zeit* which is in print and accessible is only a fragment. The philosophical-systematic background, perchance the Nietzsche lectures and essays, is not comprehensible in any cohesive publication. Discoveries like those which the edition of Hegel's early writings brought for Hegel-interpretation or which the edition of Parisian manuscripts brought for the appropriation of Marx, are by all means possible in Heidegger's case. When, nevertheless, the contemporary critique already tends to distinguish this or that presentation of Heidegger as "historically" more correct, it overlooks the fact that an "historical" presentation of Heidegger is still not at all possible . . . What once stood in the foreground of interest and was discussed — for example, Heidegger's influence upon anthropological research — is not to be covered anew. It should become clear, however, that the hitherto existing discussion of Heidegger has produced an abundance of perspectives for Heidegger's work. When these perspectives are placed alongside each other, they mutually relativize each other; the hitherto existing Heidegger-interpretation led on its own to the question, as to which estimate would allow for a sufficient interpretation of Heidegger's work.

I

What are the decisive perspectives from which Heidegger's work has been viewed up the present? Which points of view made understandable the task before which Heidegger saw himself standing?

If we glance at the customary presentations of contemporary thought or of the history of philosophy in general, we see immediately that there is no agreement at all as to which philosophical task Heidegger's thought is to be referred, or under which title Heidegger's thought is to be presented. Heidegger's thought is first classed among the philosophies of existence. As philosophy of existence it is viewed as both different as well as together with the existential philosophy of a Jaspers and with the existentialism of a Sartre. On the other hand, however, the assertion is advocated with full energy that Heidegger's thought, as Heidegger himself has said and as one may demonstrate easily from his works, is not a philosophy of existence, that Heidegger's question is the question of Being, that his thought is an ontology or a fundamental ontology, or in any case a discussion with the way of conceiving Being inherent in Western metaphysics. Perhaps one may contend that Heidegger's thought is an attempt to replace the traditional way of conceiving Being by another, new-fashioned way of conceiving Being, or even to change over from a contemplation of "Being" to a contemplation of the "World." Such judgments show that Heidegger's thought twice had a great impact, once as a philosophy of existence immediately after the appearance of Sein und Zeit, and then as a conception of Being or World in the years after the Second World War. One attempted to combine both interpretations together by ascribing to Heidegger his own expression of "turning" ("Kehre"), a turning from existence as Dasein to Being itself.

Heidegger's work Sein und Zeit (or the first and only published section of the planned work) appeared in 1927 in the Jahrbuch für Philosophie und Phänomenologische Forschung, which was edited by Edmund Husserl and in which other significant philosophical works have also appeared, for example Husserl's Ideen zu einer reinen Phänomenologie und phänomenologischen Philosophie or Max Scheler's inquiry, Der Formalismus in der Ethik und die materiale Wertethik. Since Heidegger's work appeared here, it was immediately clear that Heidegger aligned himself with the phenomenological movement which emanated from Husserl. The question remained, what significance would fall to Heidegger in this movement? In spite of the great success as a teacher which Heidegger had already experienced in Freiburg, as well as in Marburg in a smaller circle, it was not at all clear from the beginning what the verdict would be with regard to Sein und Zeit. At that time Heidegger was teaching in Marburg as Professor of Philosophy, and he had been proposed by the faculty for the first Marburg Professorship, which had opened due to Nicolai Hartmann's departure. But the ministry in Berlin was not prepared to appoint Heidegger. It based its rejection on the fact that Heidegger had not published anything for a long time. Heidegger had the audacity to allow the first 15 fascicles (thus the first 240 pages) of his work Sein und Zeit, which he had sent to the publisher, to be presented to the ministry. The ministry returned [1] the fascicles with the comment: "inadequate." Nevertheless, the majority of those who were philosophizing at that time (or at least the majority of those who began to philosophize) did not have the same opinion as the ministry and its assessor (the ministry also finally had to retract its decision). What one thought of and how one judged Heidegger's work, Sein und Zeit, was at that time very explicitly formulated by Georg Misch. Misch, a pupil and son-in-law of Wilhelm Dilthey, and principal editor of Dilthey's Gesammelten Schriften, carried on a discussion from Dilthey's perspective with phenomenological philosophy,

---

[1] As Heidegger himself relates in his contribution to the Festschrift Hermann Niemeyer zum achtzigsten Geburtstag am 16. April 1963 (private publication).

above all with that part of *Sein und Zeit* [2] which had at that time been published. At the beginning of his work he writes that Heidegger's book, *Sein und Zeit,* had "struck like lightening," but that Heidegger, unlike Scheler, was not a typical expression of the times, that he has endurance, the craftman's ability, that Heidegger is the right master craftsman who wishes to make philosophy a science. He asserted that the helm of the Husserlian *Jahrbuch* had been turned in another direction as if with one blow.

In which direction did Heidegger now so direct the phenomenological movement that after the appearance of *Sein und Zeit* one could see in him, and no longer in Husserl or Scheler, the leading mind of this direction of philosophical work? Husserl's freeing act was that he placed philosophy under the demand, "to the thing itself," by conceiving it as phenomenology and phenomenological research. The phenomenon was supposed to be brought into view undisguised and uncovered. All traditional bias and ideological prejudices, all presuppositions such as those which can enter into the act of philosophizing through a metaphysical tendency or the inclination to a system, were to be eliminated. The logical phenomena, for example, should not be reconstrued surreptitiously into psychical realities. They should rather be taken as themselves in their self-reliant, logical sense, and thus all "psychologism" was supposed to be exorcised from logic. Phenomenology, which desires to bring the thing itself uncovered into view, seeks to extrapolate that which remains invariable in every variation on the phenomena, the *Eidos* or Being. Thus phenomenology is not only descriptive phenomenology — unbiased description—but also eidetic or ontological phenomenology, an extrapolation of that which is the *Eidos* or Being in a being. A phenomenon in its *Eidos,* a being in its Being, however, does not emerge unless a consciousness, by means of its distinct abilities, appropriates a being *as* a particular being, i.e., constitutes it in its *Eidos* or Being. Phenomenology, which asks how a being is constituted in its Being by the accomplishments of the consciousness, is constitutive or transcendental phenomenology.

The new direction in which Heidegger guided phenomenology appeared to his fellow philosophers to be characterized above all by the fact that Heidegger conceived the transcendental ego as "Existenz." Whoever reads Husserl's phenomenological analyses and raises the question, from which basic position does the one analyzing undertake his analyses, comes to see clearly (above all if he disregards Husserl's later works): for Husserl the transcendental ego is consciousness, a pure seeing; consequently the Being of a being is *Eidos,* the universal of that view which constantly endures, which as the invariable accrues in the same way to different variations. The greatness of Husserl rests in the fact that with ever new urgency he challenges those who are philosophizing to use their eyes and not to allow the sight of the phenomena to be obstructed. The question remains: is it permissible to conceive in terms of seeing the mode of Being of the pure ego, which yet has to constitute concrete existence? May one conceive of the Being of beings in every sphere in terms of a view which remains invariable? Do not Husserl's analyses show the one analyzing to be an ego which is only real in so far as it sits at some desk, brings things into view, looks at them from various angles, turns them first one way and then another—an ego which perhaps even once — and that is already a great deal —gets up from the desk in order to view something from an angle which is turned away from view, but even then only so as to be able to "look"? When Heidegger designates this ego as ex-

[2] Misch, Georg: "Lebensphilosophie und Phänomenologie," *Philosophischer Anzeiger,* 3. Jg. Bonn 1928/29, 4 Jg. Bonn 1929/30 also as a separate publication.

istence, he means that this ego is not pure vision which is actualized in someone who is sitting at a desk philosophizing. He means that his ego is the man who can indeed also commit himself to pure theory, but who usually associates with things in working *praxis,* who has to get along with other people, who is touched by the call of the conscience, and who, always, as long as he lives, stands before his death. He means a man who is concerned and afraid and who has dread, a finite and transient man, an historical, living man, a man in a very definite situation. And all of this—concern, *praxis,* conscience, dread, death, historicality, situation — is according to *Sein und Zeit* nothing which is to be abandoned because it belongs to the mere personal anxieties of humanity, but is rather something which, philosophically speaking as well, is of the utmost significance. The transcendental ego is not another world which is separated from concrete existence, an existence which itself is even constituted by this other world, but it is rather present as that which is constitutive only in this concrete existence; and it is to be appropriated in the fullness of its concretion. The further insight is: phenomenology can therefore only grasp the transcendental ego as self-evident with the guidance of one of the powers of existence (seeing), because since the beginning of Greek thought, the philosophical tradition has allowed this self-evidence to be developed. To criticize Husserl's point of departure, therefore, means, for Heidegger, to come to terms with the point of departure of the philosophical tradition in general.

In that Heidegger's thought accomplished this change in phenomenological philosophy and research, he was in competition with the efforts of Scheler in determining the character of human spirit from the "personal," from the effective character of the spirit, in pointing to the connection between knowledge and 'seeing' and emotional and interest-accruing acts — in gen-

eral, in drawing anthropology into the midst of philosophy and referring it to the profusion of knowledge about man as it had been achieved by the most diverse sciences. The attempt of Neo-Kantianism to supplement Kant's critical concept of nature by a critical concept of culture found in Heidegger's thought its radicalization just as it found its critique. Decisive was the reference to Dilthey's research which reached its peak in the effort not to interpret the transcendental ego as pure consciousness in general, but rather as historical life. Above and beyond that, Heidegger's protest against Husserl appeared in its own way to repeat the protest which almost a hundred years earlier was directed against speculative idealism, against Hegel's attempt to perfect the classical philosophical tradition. Herbert Marcuse in the years following the appearance of *Sein und Zeit* was therefore able to present Heidegger's point of departure and the starting point of the young Marx, as was illustrated in the just edited *Parisian Manuscripts,* in such a way as to bring to the fore the points of agreement. Above all, Heidegger was understood from his affinity with that critical spirit who incited the period of that time, i.e., with Kierkegaard, who in a decisive way had instigated the attempt to understand man as "existence" and to cancel an almost two thousand year foreign influence of philosophy on faith and existence. On the philosopher's side it was above all Karl Jaspers who gained new attention for Kierkegaard's concern, and thus Heidegger and Jaspers could be presented as the leading philosophers of existence, whose intellectual origin is characterized by names like Kierkegaard, Pascal, Augustine. Since the new—at that time—"dialectical" theology received its decisive incentive from Kierkegaard, it too had to seek to approach Heidegger (as Rudolf Bultmann did above all).

Concern, praxis, conscience, dread, death, historicality, situation: that Heidegger analysed all of these, incited people and drew them to Heidegger and to his philosophy. The questions concerning one's own life reoccurred in Heidegger's philosophy. A consequence that followed from this kind of attention to Heidegger was that one wished to discuss with Heidegger or with a misunderstood if not a misused Heidegger, questions of an ideological nature as well as such questions as whether man as a finite creature is completely self-dependent or whether he can rely on a God. But Heidegger's own philosophical concern—the question of how a being reveals itself in its Being — was left in the background, or even lost sight of, or not taken up as a question and further developed. His question, rather, was too hastily answered. Heidegger was again taken as a "typical expression of his time." The "endurance," the "craftsman's ability," which alone is able to make philosophy "a science," had less of an impact on Heidegger's reception. During the years of National Socialism and the Second World War philosophy, as it was, had as its only chance to be a solitary reflection and was no longer an effective task that was carried out and accomplished. To be sure, Heidegger was able to exercise an influence on those studying philosophy through his teaching in Freiburg, especially through his lectures on Schelling, Nietzsche and Hölderlin, above all on a few students who later became prominent with works on Schelling, Nietzsche, and Hölderlin. But even the simple possibility of publishing new works was no longer his.

After the Second World War the unexpected happened, namely that once again Heidegger exercised a world-wide influence. Heidegger succeeded Heidegger. Germany had destroyed itself through the National Socialistic "Revolution." The attempt to create a Great German Reich and to acquire world supremacy came to an end not only with the downfall of this German Reich, but also with the European nations conclusively eliminated from that

circle of powers which make the decisions concerning the further course of world history. Millions died—those criminally murdered and those killed in war — as the result of the politics of that day. After the war the total extent of destruction and crime came at first only gradually into the view of those who themselves had been drawn into this destruction and crime. The end of the war against Japan was gained by the introduction of a totally new mode of destruction, the atom bomb! The single, guiding question for those who were still capable of reflection, was: how could all that had taken place, happen? How could men gifted with reason arrive at this false path of self-destruction? How can humanity once again arrive at a path which does not lead anew directly or indirectly into the abyss? How can man live with the means of destruction which he now has in his hands?

At that time "Existentialism" gained ground in France. It was a radicalization of the philosophy of existence, the likes of which had developed in Germany after the First World War. The people, who half unconsciously had suffered this outburst of history, were reminded that they were the perpetrators of their deeds and that they, as *Existenz,* were a relationship which, according to Kierkegaard's formulation, must relate itself to itself and is determined by freedom. This existentialism radicalized as well the ideological tendency already present in existence-philosophy: Sartre sought proximity to theism and Marxism; Camus and Merleau-Ponty raised the question of the relationship between Communism and terror; Marcel understood himself to be a Christian thinker. Heidegger himself was viewed as forerunner, indeed as founder of this Existentialism. The tide of Existentialism once more elevated him, along with his earlier works, and thus precisely from the French side one was prepared to overlook Heidegger's temporary political entanglement with National Socialism for the sake of his fundamental philosophical departure.

Heidegger had to come to terms with this new turn toward his thought. He did this in a major letter to a young Frenchman, Jean Beaufret. This *Brief über den Humanismus* was published in 1947 along with an essay *Platons Lehre von der Wahrheit,* which had already been published. In this letter he says, for example: "Man, before he speaks, must first allow himself to be addressed again by Being, with the danger that in the light of this claiming address he will have little or seldom anything to say. Only in this way is the preciousness of its essence to be returned to the word, and to man, the dwelling where he lives in the truth of Being." One found at that time, in expressions like this one, what moved the heart, namely the question: how does someone who has wandered in such a horrible way onto a false path again come under a claim which engages him, which points him again to the right path? Man, so Heidegger appeared to want to say, can only cope with his freedom when this freedom, i.e., *"Existenz,"* submits itself to a demanding claim and is not simply a caprice which stumbles through history and seizes again and again what is false, but is rather sustained by a new obligation. That which binds and obliges is "Being." But what is Being? It can be said of Being only that in our present situation of error we are not yet able to say what is decisive. One must, nevertheless, go the way, the way of the question of Being. . . .

In this letter on humanism, Heidegger at least indicated the focus in which he wanted his own thought to be viewed. He asserted that existence was not the basic theme of his thought, rather that it was only Being and that right from the start. If man should be spoken of as existence, then this existence must be seen as ek-sistence, as man's 'standing out' in Being. Man who deals with a being does not determine that being in its Being. Rather, what a being is and what man himself is as a being, i.e., as who he is, is determined by how Being discloses itself. Traditional Western thought, which in its classical form is "metaphysics," attempts basically in its "forgetfulness of Being" simply to state principles for the capacity to comprehend and to control, even to produce a being. It attempts to place every being at man's disposal. In this sense traditional Western thought, the thought of Plato as well as of Descartes, Hegel or Nietzsche, is "humanism," in which man revolves about himself. Christianity is also such a circling of man about himself in which God is only viewed as the one who bestows upon man salvation of the soul, and in which, finally, God is granted a place in man's thought only for the sake of man (for example, in Kant's doctrine of postulates). The most crass self-circling on the part of man is found in the existentialism of a Sartre, for this existentialism recognizes truth and meaning only insofar as man designs it himself. In *Sein und Zeit* Heidegger had already conceived man's relation to Being in another way. Being was not placed at the disposal of man, but rather man was placed at the disposal of Being. Man is only the "shepherd of Being," so Heidegger writes in the letter to Jean Beaufret as a demarcation of his thought from every humanism and existentialism.

Heidegger himself speaks in the humanism-letter of the "turn," which thought must carry out from "Sein und Zeit" to "Zeit und Sein." We must not only interpret *Dasein* (man insofar as he understands Being) with respect to its being or the being of *Dasein* with respect to time. We must also ask how "Being," which is to be investigated, is already understood in light of time.

A being is open for man when, as a being, it is open in its being. Philosophically speaking, we know of no creature, which, like man, says to a being that it is and thereby expressly interprets the being according to its "it is." Nevertheless, how a being is open in its being is not simply determined by man and can not be fixed by man and his possibilities, which are presented with certainty. How a being becomes open in its being depends rather on how Being from time to time reveals itself. That I accept the desk upon which I write as a piece of furniture, as a usable object which was mechanically manufactured and which is there to be used and expended, is not so self-evident. In our profane period there are perhaps such desks for the first time ever. In any case the desk was not simply a usable object in earlier times (it was possibly, via symbolism, combined with the totality of a mythical-religious meaning of world). There may even have been periods in the human era in which man's world had no desks at all. When the desk appears today as a "profane," usable object, it is open to us in its mode of Being, which conceals other possibilities, perhaps modes of Being which have already existed. The being of man, too, (as *Sein und Zeit* attempts to grasp it in its "existentials") could be in a similar way the being of man in a certain epoch and not determine him once and for all. In any case, the history of Being's unveiling and concealing does not at all rest simply in the hands of man. Man rather rests in the hands of this history. Only when thought turns to this history in which not only a desk is revealed as what it can be, but also in which man is revealed as what he can be— even what man can address as "divine" is revealed— only in such a "turn" can man again learn to accept what is according to its being. Only then can he "allow it to be," as Heidegger expresses it in an illuminating phrase.

With his talk about turning, Heidegger attempts to develop further what he mentioned in *Sein und Zeit* as the hermeneutical circle of his investigation. This investigation was supposed to pave the way for the question about the meaning of Being by asking about the being of a distinct being (of the being which understands Being). But this question presupposed what was sought— an understanding of Being in general. Dynamic, historical moment was supposed to be introduced now into the static-geometric notion of the circle; but this new talk about turning, taken externally, itself collapsed again into an ambiguity. This expression could be understood first as a summons to put the accent in the relationship "Man (*Dasein*)–Being" on the other pole, i.e., the pole of Being. In this expression, however, one could also perceive a summons to an "historical reflection on Being"— the summons that thought should especially turn toward it's omission of the question of Being, that it should consider the estrangement of Being and thus help prepare for a new turning-toward, and that it thus should attempt to turn the basic tendency of Western history. The whole letter concerning humanism represents an understanding which draws a conclusion too quickly in such an ambiguity. Heidegger appears to be speaking of "Being," but actually he wants to put an end to the metaphysical hypostasis of Being. He speaks of the Being of beings, of Being itself, of the sense of Being, of the truth of Being, even of the clearing of Being, of the destiny of Being, of event. He speaks as a thinker who had found these words to be basic for his thought on a contemplative, previously undiscovered path. He seems to think that by means of this one discourse he surpassed the other language, but that now he must make his mode of questioning understandable to those who did not accompany him along his way, who know nothing of his distinctions, and to whom he must consequently explain his cautious allusions in an inappropriate manner. The way which Heidegger took was at that time so little in the view of his readers that on the one hand they approached him as a matter of course with the expectation and demand that he should as quickly as possible supplement the lacking part of *Sein und Zeit*. On the other hand, they misused the expression of 'turning' in a crude schematization in order to divide Heidegger's path into a phase before the turning and a phase after the turning. Thus the motives by which Heidegger was led along his path remained concealed, and one did not even arrive at a superficial, chronologically correct arrangement of his various works. At a time when one spoke in politics and philosophy of the "young people" and meant those who were fifty and sixty years old, one reckoned works like the lectures and essays on Nietzsche which Heidegger had worked up as a man between 47 and 52 years old, as the "late work" of this thinker. Above all, one did not notice that these lectures only exoterically lead to those questions which Heidegger at the most outlined at the end of these lectures, questions which he, however, had worked out in notes that to this day unfortunately remain unpublished. The necessity for a turning, if not a conversion of thought, was so great that one believed himself to be able to build a new Heidegger-interpretation on a few ambiguous allusions and relatively arbitrary publications.

Those who studied philosophy in Germany in the years following the Second World War and who considered themselves worth something, went to Freiburg in order to be able to hear Heidegger. Heidegger, however, held at the most one Studium-generale lecture and only a few seminars. It was not this limited teaching load, however, which disappointed those who had gone to Freiburg; rather the style of the later-Heidegger's thought was more and more disappointing. It did not at all correspond to the new, encroaching drive for scholarly method, precision and fine mastery of the problems. Although Heidegger for some time published one book after the other, he remained misunderstood and alone. He had also given up the attempt to relate his thought directly to what was at present being discussed everywhere as scholarship or philosophy. What he wished to accomplish with his publications was the preliminary and only preparatory attempt to pave the way for "a change of the basic mood" (as Heidegger had asserted regarding Nietzsche's publications).[*] The change of the basic mood which actually came about, however, was not the one Heidegger strived for, but was rather a change which more and more closed the ears of the period to Heidegger's word. There may have been earlier a compulsion to want to see in dread the basic mood of existence. Today, there is no longer direct resonance for talk of dread and *Existenz*. And to hope for something ultimate, something which creates a binding obligation, or perhaps something to be called "Being," or to ascribe to thought the necessity of completing a "turn," appeared to the majority as a romantic illusion and an aberration of excessive thought. If one task was to be assigned to thought, it was this: to begin critically and controlled with individual and comprehensible problems, to pay attention to tidiness in the execution of details, but to leave the would-be, great questions of the times alone. There can be no doubt that philosophizing today stands in the wake of a tendency to consider only those questions which allow a succinct answer and thus in one way or another can promote an advance. This tendency led the positive sciences, technology and industry to their unexpected successes, and as a matter of course, these three lend to the contemporary tendency that labor which it needs. Will there ever be a lack of people who can develop a particular type of machine to its final consequences, who can construct a physical apparatus or who can edit

---

[*] Cf. Nietzsche, vol. I., p. 269.

and evaluate historical sources? Will not society make sure that there are always enough people present who are able to control the machinery of the established, positive jurisprudence with virtuosity or to align a traditional religion with the new social and intellectual needs? This tendency to continue what has once been reached, to make applicable what has been handed down, and to control what is to come is spreading over our planet in ever new waves, and no culture today could evade this tendency to care for what every society must care — modern industry, economy, law, even the care for artistic and religious needs. German idealism and also the philosophy which originated in our century under the influence of the World Wars have set this tendency, which was created by the foundations of our modern life, over against another inclination. These philosophies incline to ask whither the tendency toward conserving and applying will lead us and what place these so successful sciences — modern technology, and economics as well as the apparatus of law and the so strangely transformed arts — have in the totality of our life. But even as the German idealism in the 19th Century did not stand under the assault of the positive sciences, so too a philosophy like Heidegger's was unable to convince his contemporaries and those who came after them that the questions of the times are those which are raised and resolved in this philosophy. When today questions are raised in a manner similar to Heidegger's, they are raised all too often in explicit opposition to him. This new mode of questioning does not see the agreement between itself and Heidegger, but sees only an unbridgeable chasm, when, for example, some raise again the notorious antithesis between "existence" ("*Exis-*

tenz") and "the they" in the antithesis between partisan and establishment ("system"),[4] or when the question of the source of that obligation reoccurs in the question of a non-alienated society.

A glance at the history of thought shows that certain thinkers and certain directions of philosophizing do not cease to be discussed simply because their thoughts were refuted or because their presuppositions were proven to be untenable. They lose their relevance because their moving forces were no longer equal to the moving forces of the time. One simply no longer reads their works, but rather dismisseś them as uninteresting before becoming acquainted with them. For many, Heidegger may today already have fallen out of philosophical discussion in this way. (Enclaves, in which Heideggerianism is still dominant or in which dialogue with Heidegger is still usual, as well as an apparent growing interest abroad, do not prove the opposite.) Not without dismay one observes that, for example, literary scholars who once sought in Heidegger's analysis of time the foundation for their scholarship, no longer know what to make of Heidegger's further development of his basic question. That "criticism," however, which erects for itself a whipping boy under the name Heidegger, in order to be able to beat him, is not subsiding. There appears to be a deep need for such an act, but it expresses nothing regarding the task before which Heidegger saw himself.

Nevertheless, the relation of the philosophical present to Heidegger's work ought not to be viewed purely from the negative side. Rather the attempt to take the first steps toward a relevant reception of Heidegger's works stand out more and more clearly, precisely in recent years. This at-

---

[4] An older presentation of the figure of the partisan, "about whom so terribly much is said" (Rolf Schorers, *Der Partisan. Ein Beitrag zur politischen Anthropologie*, Köln and Berlin 1961,7), still points to the connection between the existential protest, the nationalistic or fascist appeal to the home land, and the new protest. One should not allow himself to be deceived—where the effective words are worn out, exchanged and played over against each other, the circumstances only all too often remain unchanged or little changed.

tempt is realized first by the fact that one strives to develop the subject matter with which Heidegger concerns himself in a problem-centered way, both in agreement and disagreement with him — whether the issue be the concept of Being and its specifications or the concept of truth. On the other hand, however, it is important for this attempt that one gets the whole of Heidegger's process in view. Heidegger's works are no longer schematically divided up into early and late works (whether it be for the sake of playing the early works off against the late works, or whether it be for the sake of reconciling the early and the late position with each other). Rather the individual works are being taken as sign posts on the shifting path toward the "determination of the subject matter of thought" (just as Heidegger demanded for those essays which he collected in the volume *Wegmarken*). When in the process that which up to now has been handed on like a myth, (as Heidegger's teaching in Freiburg during the years immediately after the First World War) should now become the object of historical investigation, the limits of such an attempt become clear indeed: the sources are lacking for a developmental-historical presentation of Heidegger's thought. When one, within the given limits, strives to understand Heidegger historically, one cannot avoid asking which historical origin belongs to Heidegger's thought and in which historical context does it stand.

If the works which are representative of Heidegger-interpretation are collected together, then it becomes immediately clear that there has not yet been success at all in determining with any relative uniformity Heidegger's philosophical task. Is Heidegger the thinker who, in a crisis of metaphysics, renews the metaphysical question concerning the guiding meaning of Being?

Scholastic debate over Heidegger tends to this thesis; but even the polemic against Heidegger insinuates that Heidegger is continually oriented toward "Being," the hypothesis of Being found in the surpassed metaphysical tradition. Does Heidegger, in pan-hermeneutical ontological one-sidedness, consider the principle only of historical beings (as Oskar Becker attempted to demonstrate)?[5] Or does Heidegger — as Max Müller stated — no longer have a "thesis about Being" as an answer to the "question of Being"? Does Heidegger introduce historicality into the scholasticly conceived *analogia entis,* so that one can speak with him of "analogy," i.e., of concepts of Being and essence which function historically?[6] Does Heidegger perhaps not even understand himself when he considers the only question of his thought to be in the question of Being? Is the question of the meaning of "is" — as Walter Bröcker emphasizes — answered by the effort of Greek thought, for which the Greek language had paved the way, and does Heidegger's question not at all apply to Being, but rather to the world as the realm of the appearance of entities?[7] Does Eugen Fink rightly demand that the "cosmological" horizon of the question of Being and world be developed distinctly, since Heidegger had first raised this question in *Sein und Zeit* only in a "transcendental-philosophically abstract" arrangement?[8] If Heidegger himself has made clear in the process of his thought that for him the question of Being, i.e., of the manifold meaning of Being, is the question of truth and of the world as the structure of truth, how then can the question of truth be approached as Heidegger's fundamental question? Is one permitted to take art as the guiding thread for unfolding the experience of truth, and at the same time to set truth as an event, which man ultimate-

[5] *Heidegger, op. cit.,* ed. Pöggeler, pp. 261 ff., 321ff.
[6] Cf. Max Müller, *Existenzphilosophie im geistigen Leben der Gegenwart,* Heidelberg, 3rd edition, 1964, pp. 93ff., 251ff., 85ff.
[7] Bröcker, Walter: *Dialektik, Positivismus, Myhologie,* Frankfurt a.M. 1958, pp. 95ff.
[8] Cf. Eugen Fink, *Spiel als Weltsymbol,* Stuttgart 1960, p. 52.

ly cannot prescribe, over against prescriptive "method," as Hans-Georg Gadamer does in the title of his work *Wahrheit und Methode?* Is it precisely the experience of truth, as Heidegger developed it after 1930, which allows Heidegger's thought to be related to the classical tradition of political philosophy, since politics is understood by both as putting truth to work (as Alexander Schwan has shown in one of the few works about Heidegger from which something can be learned[9])? Or is this application of the experience of truth in the later Heidegger materially illegitimate, since in this experience, truth is deprived of its truth-character, taken out of its antithesis to untruth, and no longer referred to demonstration and justification? Is it, however, correct that Heidegger has shown how one can interrogate not only the truth of a statement, but also the truth (disclosedness, clearing[*]) of the horizons of Being-in-the-world (the discovery of what is present-at-hand, dealings with what is ready-to-hand, etc.), but that Heidegger only carried through this "expansion" of the concept of truth at the cost of forfeiting the actual character of truth, and thereby also at the cost of forfeiting the "critical" character of philosophy?[10] Or does Heidegger acquire the possibility for justification and criticism of the horizons of Being-in-the-world precisely by the fact that he attempts to make these horizons, the structure of the world, understandable from the variable happening of truth?

In whatever way Heidegger inquires about Being, truth and world, there can be no doubt that history and historical-ity function as the decisive threads of his inquiry, such that one can also speak of the historicality of the understanding of Being, of the history of Being, of truth and world as event. Thereby, however, it is not yet decided whether Heidegger's philosophy mediates ontology as an unfolding of the question of Being with the experience of history and historicality in such a way that one is ultimately permitted to characterize his thought as historical ontology or ontological historical-philosophy, or whether the guiding thread of the experience of history and historicality on Heidegger's path is itself not rather overcome with questions and abandoned as inadequate. Max Müller attempted to explain historically Heidegger's position by pointing out[11] that Western thought developed at first into a doctrine of the enduring essential orders, that German idealism founded the essences in spirit, and thereby conceived spirit as one which historically comes to itself, which nevertheless ultimately surpasses time, and which is infinitely with itself. Müller asserted that in the catastrophes of our time faith in the infinity of the spirit had suffered an irreparable shipwreck, that historicality had been experienced as finitude. "The new philosophy was, therefore, faced with the problem of seeing historicality and finitude in Being itself. It therefore had to hazard a new model for Being, which no longer sketched 'Being as order' and 'Being as infinity,' but which rather experienced *Being as absolute historicality,* as the whole, the unconditional, the super-individual, and the absolute which historically finitizes itself from

---

[9] Schwan, Alexander: *Politische Philosophie im Denken Heideggers* (Ordo Politicus, vol. 2), Köln and Opladen 1965.

[*] Translator's note—see *Being and Time, Heidegger,* trans. John Macquaine and Edward Robinson, p. 171, note 2.

[10] See Ernest Tugendhat, *Der Wahrheitsbegriff bei Husserl und Heidegger,* Berlin 1967. —In a footnote (p. 358) Tugendhat therefore admits that Gadamer in continuation of Heidegger's point of departure has brought hermeneutics to a new dimension of inquiry; that, however, this gain, in consequence of following Heidegger, was only reached by the forfeiture of the critical concept of truth: "By Gadamer, the large-scale attempt at a hermeneutical theory was unable to orient itself around the concept of truth, precisely because he fundamentally takes over Heidegger's concept of truth."

[11] Müller, Max: *Existenzphilosophie im geistigen Leben der Gegenwart,* p. 37.

itself." It could not fail to appear that talk of the "absolute ahistoricality of truth" was set over against talk of absolute historicality.[11] The question remains, however, whether talk of an absolute historicality is at all tenable. If the absolute is the antithesis to what is relative, while experienced historicality is no longer supposed to be determined by this antithesis, and if, finally, historicality also turns out to be ahistorical, then talk of an absolute historicality becomes questionable. The expression "historicality of truth," as formulated by K.-H. Volkmann-Schluck,[12] seems to be the greatest interrogative of the times, and the expression "absolute historicality" is in itself absurd. Does not talk of the "historicality of truth" itself, however, as much as it imposes itself upon the present, contain aporia which make this talk simply provisional, and does not Heidegger accomplish the self-suspension of the question of the "historicality of truth" when he replaces words like history and historicality with other words?

What actually becomes of the search for truth, of philosophy in Heidegger's thought? When this question is raised, then the question is thereby raised, from which historical origin, from which historical horizons is Heidegger's thought to be understood? Is it permissable to conceive Heidegger's thought, perhaps, as the completion and end of the metaphysical tradition, above all of modern metaphysics? Walter Schulz attempted to show that Heidegger's thought, contrary to Heidegger's own self-understanding, is not *opposed to* modern metaphysics, but is rather to be understood *from* it. Schulz contends that modern metaphysics is not man's revolt in his power and autonomy, as Heidegger assumes along with Hegel and Dilthey. Rather, modern metaphysics sees its basic premise in the fact that finite subjectivity, as it comprehends itself, must experience itself as sustained by the otherness of divine subjectivity, whether this other be the God of Nicolaus of Cusa, the divine nature of Spinoza, the Dionysos of Nietzsche or the Being of Heidegger. The experience of the power and powerlessness of thought, as Schelling construed it in his later philosophy, is supposed to have been already the experience of Nicolaus of Cusa and of Descartes, and is also still supposed to motivate Heidegger's "turn." But in so far as this experience and the philosophical presupposition of a God make the Christian experience of God superfluous, they are supposed to be the "departing stand against the Christian God," and further, in the form of the Heideggerian "turn," they compose the "secularized form of Christian conversion."[14] Overagainst such classifications, however, the question remains whether Heidegger in any way received the decisive impulse for his thought from the classical philosophical tradition. Was not his basic experience the experience of historicality, which was experienced extra-philosophically in the original Christian faith and then once more in the historicism of modern times, but which never was radically sustained by philosophy? The experience of the historicality of all doing

[11] Cf. e.g. Reinhard Lauth, *Die absolute Ungeschichtlichkeit der Wahrheit,* Stuttgart, 1966.

[12] Volkmann-Schluck, Karl-Heinz: *Metaphysik und Geschichte,* Berlin, 1963.

[14] Cf. Walter Schulz, *Der Gott der neuzeitlichen Metaphysik,* Pfullingen 1957, pp. 54f.—Gustav Siewerth, in opposition to Schulz' interpretation, attempted to prove that the rebellion of modern thought into autonomy, which was made possible by the new Christian interpretation of the ancient experience of Being, was not grasped critically enough by Heidegger: *Das Schicksal der Metaphysik von Thomas bis Heidegger,* Einsiedeln 1959.—Overagainst such an interpretation Heinrich Rombach attempted to present the lasting significance of this mode of philosophizing for a phenomenological philosophy in his expansive interpretation of the achievement of the early modern philosophy: *Substanz, System, Struktur. Die Ontologie des Funktionalismus und der philosophische Hintergrund der modernen Wissenschaft,* 2 vol., Freiburg and München 1965/66.

and acting and therewith also the historicality of truth relations, the experience of the multiplicity of perspectives as well as of the untranscendable, perhaps ungraspable restriction to a single perspective, appears to strip truth relations and therewith philosophy of any binding force, and to plunge man into "nihilism." It is still possible for man to see the moment as "eschatological," as a moment which concerns the last of things and involves an "eternal" sense, when that "moment" is recognized as historical? Rudolf Bultmann, in his lectures, *Geschichte und Eschatologie,* attempted to show how the decisive theologians of the Christian faith, Paul and John, historically understood the eschatological understanding of the world which was handed on to them. He attempted to show, further, how, after a long deterioration of historical thought in our time (in the historicism of a Dilthey, Croce, Collingwood, in that "existentielle realism" presented by Erich Auerbach, as well as in the philosophy of existence), the experience of history for the understanding of man and world has again become decisive. Bultmann tightly classifies Heidegger's thought among the explications of this historical experience. Is this classification, however, possible? Is this developed historical understanding in any way appropriate? Is it not also a part of man that he not only has to free himself "eschatologically" from the world, but also must have a home in history (similar to the way a child must grow up in a familiar family or group)? Beginning with this question Wilhelm Kamlah, following Heidegger and Bultmann, developed in a new way the question concerning an adequate explication of our historical understanding in an early work *Christentum und Geschichtlichkeit.* In this work he demanded a positive acceptance and a critical mediation precisely of classical Greek thought, overagainst the radical destruction of traditional philosophy and the juxtaposition of Christian historical experience in opposition to the disposition of Greek thought, which had become common (even cropping up in articles in theological lexicons).

In recent years, the conflict over the theology of Rudolf Bultmann and its relationship to Heidegger's philosophy has been essentially carried on as a debate over the right understanding of history. The objection has been raised against Bultmann that for him the totality of the historical context — the whole of a people, e.g., of the people of Israel, or the totality of world history — becomes completely meaningless in light of the eschatological moment. *Offenbarung als Geschichte* is the title of the book which programmatically developed this objection and which among the theological works of recent years unleashed perhaps the most discussion. The title, "Offenbarung als Geschichte," means that revelation as progressing revelation belongs in the totality of an historical context and not simply in the punctuality of the moment. It means that revelation proceeds with history and does not simply break into it from above as something foreign, as Karl Barth under the influence of Kierkegaard and Rudolf Bultmann in connexion with Heidegger's early work, *Sein und Zeit,* had assumed. It was just the recourse to the historical understanding of the Old Testament — which is itself historically unique — which assisted in clarifying the concept of history. This new attention to the problem of history, arising as a polemic against Bultmann's position and his interpretation of *Sein und Zeit,* again relates to Heidegger, namely to the so called "late work" of Heidegger. The exegete J. M. Robinson attempted to equate directly the "Lichtungsgeschichte" of the "late" Heidegger and the "Heilsgeschichte" of Old Testament prophecy, and could thus write the sentence: "One can therefore assert that in principle (even if not in practice) Heidegger prepared the way, on which Old Testament research, crossing over the borders of its discipline, could acquire a central role

16

in the theological and philosophical discussion of our day." Heinrich Schlier, who was able to make the thought and language of the later Heidegger fruitful for theological exegesis and reflection on theological fundamentals, summarized the much discussed problem of Old Testament hermeneutics in the sentence: "The Old Testament understands the occurrences with and in Israel and the world as 'event' — if, as in Heidegger's understanding, the peculiarity of the event is that 'the legend' resides in it and 'the legend which resides in the event as a sign is the most characteristic mode of happening.' "[15] Are not, however, two heterogeneous elements conceived together in such an identification of *Heilsgeschichte* and *Lichtungsgeschichte?* Is not Heidegger referred to an origin from which he continually attempted to separate himself? Much as event and legend, history and the history of tradition stand in closest connection in the Old Testament, as well as in the hermeneutic of Heidegger (and of Gadamer) — does Heidegger conceive event from the perspective of the Old Testament or does he not rather conceive it from the perspective of an anti-thesis to this tradition? Is not Martin Buber right when he comments that he has nowhere in our times found such an extensive misunderstanding of Old Testament prophecy from a lofty philosophical stance as in Heidegger's sentences on the difference between Hölderlin and the prophets of the Old Testament?[16] This misunderstanding is not at all so surprising when one considers that in German thought, since the works which the young Hegel wrote in proximity to Hölderlin and since Nietzsche's polemic,

it is evidently part of this "lofty philosophical stance" to play off the thought and poetry from the tragic period of the Greeks against the Old Testament. In the meantime, however, we have an attempt to sketch the traditional, philosophical, transcendental, philosophical point of departure from the perspective of the spirit of the Old Testament and to carry through Heidegger's critique of metaphysics from the perspective of the Old Testament, and thereby from the "king's way of ethics": Emanuel Levinas, plugging into the tradition which led from the late Cohen to Franz Rosenzweig, made this attempt in his book *Totalite et Infini.* The critique, however, which is here directed against Heidegger's "aesthetically" oriented thought, appears to remain just as premature as the identification of salvation history and clearing history.[17] It remains confounding that in Heidegger's thought structures of the Old Testament understanding of the world reoccur with great frequency, but that Heidegger speaks on occasion negatively of this understanding of the world, in fact he attempts polemically again and again to remove himself from it.

The question whether it was modern historicism's, or even the New or even the Old Testament's experience of history in which Heidegger's experience of history was preconceived, can not in any case be prematurely answered by a simple identification. Did not Heidegger himself in *Sein und Zeit* criticize that Kierkegaardian view which understands 'moment' as the point of intersection of time and eternity and which then became so significant for dialectical theology? Did he not say

---

[15] Cf. *Offenbarung als Geschichte,* in conjunction with R. Rendtorff, U. Wilckens, T. Rendtorff edited by W. Pannenberg, Göttingen 1961.—J. M. Robinson, "Heilsgeschichte und Lichtungsgeschichte." In: *Evangelische Theologie,* 22, 1962, pp. 113–141.—Heinrich Schlier, *Besinnung auf das Neue Testament,* Freiburg-Basel-Wien 1964, p. 36.—A critique of metaphysics as well as of Heidegger and conjointly of the Old Testament is attempted, e.g., by Walter Strolz, *Menschsein als Gottesfrage,* Pfullingen 1965.

[16] Buber, Martin: *Gottesfinsternis,* Zurich 1953, pp. 87f.

[17] Cf. Emanuel Levinas, *Totalite et Infini,* Den Haag 1961. Cf. hereto R. Boehm, De Kritik van Levinas op Heidegger. In: *Tijdschrift voor Filosofie,* 25 (1963), pp. 585–603.—To this theme cf. Michael Theunissen, *Der Andere. Studien zur Sozialontologie der Gegenwart,* Berlin 1965.

in his Hölderlin lectures of 1942: "Historicality is the distinction of that humanity for whom Sophocles and Hölderlin are poets"? Does not this sentence declare that for Heidegger, in any case for the Heidegger of the Hölderlin lectures, the historicality of distinctively Western man — which is to be thoughtfully developed today—was historically discovered in the mythology and theology of the Greek tragedies and their repetition by Hölderlin. Walter Bröcker also refuted in various works the idea that Heidegger's understanding of historicality was to be interpreted in Bultmann's manner as the eschatological moment in which man was taken out of the world, placed before the claim of the eternal, and then returned to the world (having as if he did not have) as the realm of the verification of an eternal sense. According to Bröcker, the historicality of man is based precisely not on the fact that the final difference between world and self becomes conscious for man in eschatological faith; historicality, rather, is based on the fact that the "world," in which man must be and remain, changes. He contended that this change and transformation of the world, however, is not to be taken as the final loss, but rather as the temporary loss of the world as home, and thus this change and transformation are at the same time to be taken as an awakening to what is new. The distress of being homeless which affects us today is the loss of world, a loss which was already universal in Hellenism. But this loss of world is a definite historical distress, and the Christian faith is incorrect when it interprets this historical necessity eschatologically as final. This necessity is based on the fact that physics and metaphysics had de-divinized the world, which today is effective as nihilism. This nihilism, however, can be overcome and the loss of world and homelessness can be counteracted when man in a legitimate way finds his way back to the mythical interpretation of the world. This return to myth began with Hölderlin, and Heidegger is the

thinker who reflectively attempts to legitimate myth. The eschatology of the Christian faith, Bröcker contends, the doctrine of the resurrection, the kingdom of God, etc., are in truth a mythological indication that in some future time the world can again be home for man. Together with Heinrich Buhr, Walter Bröcker published his theology in a book entitled *Zur Theologie des Geistes*, which appeared in 1960, and which, because of its non-orthodox position, and indeed also because of its crude schematizations, caused some stir. The question, however, was raised whether any orthodox, Christian experience of God was foreseen in Heidegger's obscure and allusive talk of the "more divine God." Obviously, there is not only something like a philosophy in theology, to which reference is made so readily in the discussion between theology and philosophy, but also a theology in philosophy. Given this relation, however, philosophy has the task of inquiring expressly into theology, i.e., into the theological presuppositions in philosophizing, e.g., in the philosophical explication of the concept of history. And it is not only theologically preconceived meaning which can enter into philosophy as a more overt or covert presupposition. Philosophy — in any case a philosophy like that attempted by Heidegger — seeks out the understanding of world in politics, art, language, and technology, and removes itself from it. Thus, a theme like "Heidegger and Hölderlin" or "Heidegger and politics" can be the concern of not only biographers and historians. Rather such themes, if they are only introduced and developed in the right way, also belong in the philosophical debate.

With respect to some other examples, one can show how the interpretation of Heidegger's work brings this work into view from completely different, even mutually exclusive perspectives. The divergence of the perspectives must above all be brought to bear when the question is raised concerning the historical context in which Heidegger's philosophical work stands. Can the chasms be bridged which, over a long period of time, have been built between the great streams of modern philosophical thinking and which have led to to the fact that geographically delimited spheres of influence have actually been formed? In any case the attempt to carry on a dialogue with Heidegger includes the task of actualizing the unity of contemporary philosophical thinking out of substantive themes.[18]

II

If one attempts to obtain results from the debate over Heidegger to date, there remain more questions than answers. Does Heidegger wish to give a final determination for the meaning of Being, or is it just the impossibility of such a determination that he demonstrates? Does he in his later works reach the deciding dimension of the question of truth, or does he lose it? What significance does the experience of history and historicality have for his thought? To what origin does this thought belong? Do theological and political presuppositions play a part in this thought? If the debate with Heidegger does not simply wish to foist upon him would-be questions and answers, it must, as interpretation, set forth from Heidegger's work itself how

Heidegger investigates Being, truth, world and history and how his thought fits into the tradition. This does not mean, however, that the interpretation simply accepts Heidegger's self-understanding as normative. By means of a few comments in what follows I would like at least to point to some undefined questions to which the debate over Heidegger — so it seems to me — must take a stand, if a real interpretation of Heidegger's work is to come about.[19]

1. Heidegger himself has repeatedly alluded to the fact that the question of Being — already developed by Aristotle as the question of the diversity of the meaning of Being — has always been the only question of his thought. In fact, Heidegger, already in his dissertation, designated the ultimate and highest task of philosophy as classifying the "total realm of 'Being' in its various modes of efficacy." What *Sein und Zeit* wishes to accomplish is nothing other than the clarification of the question, "what belongs to the concept of a science *of Being as such,* its possibilities and variations."[20] Clearly, however, Heidegger attempted only relatively late to develop more exactly how the question of Being was variously raised in the individual epochs of Western philosophy, and how on the basis of these historical-philological developments (in the Indo-Germanic language, especially Greek) all philosophical questions could possibly converge in

---

[18] In the works of Oskar Becker the antithesis between the phenomenological and hermeneutical German tradition and Anglo-Saxon pragmatism and positivism was very early bridged by attending to substantive issues. Philosophers who lived in the border areas of these spheres of influence had in any case to take a stand overagainst the antithetical influences, cf. Hermann Lübbe, "Sprachspiele" and "Geschichten." Neopositivismus und Phänomenologie im Spätstadium." In: *Kant-Studien,* vol. 52, Köln 1960/61, pp. 220–243; Karl Otto Apel, "Sprache und Wahrheit in der gegenwartigen Situation der Philosophie." In: *Philosophische Rundschau,* 7th year, Tübingen 1959, pp. 161–184.—Also between Heidegger and Marxism there prevailed not only blind and emotional polemic, but one also attempted to view the point of departure of Heidegger and that of Marxism together, whether it was for the sake of fusing both points of departure together (H. Marcuse), or of criticizing both (J. Hommes). In recent times especially Czechoslovakian and Yugoslavian philosophers have sought a confrontation.

[19] I developed the following thoughts more extensively in a lecture at the University of Heidelberg in the summer semester of 1967.—I have published an exposition of Heidegger's thought, which is limited to the task of introduction, under the title *Der Denkweg Martin Heideggers,* Pfullingen 1963.

[20] *Die Lehre vom Urteil im Psychologismus,* p. 108; *Sein und Zeit,* p. 230.

19

the question of the meaning of that small word "is."[21]

It is, however, paradoxical that philosophy first actually attempted to become a science by classifying the question of Being. One encounters the statement that the word "is" is used equivocally. This determination must actually have devastating consequences: no science can be constructed with ambiguous concepts — i.e., with concepts which have various or even an indeterminate number of meanings. And yet precisely philosophy, as the science of the sciences, is supposed to be founded via a first science, the science of Being, later also called ontology! It should therefore be possible to bring the manifold meanings of "is" into an exactly determined order. Franz Brentano, in his dissertation *Von der mannigfachen Bedeutung des Seienden nach Aristotles* (i.e., in that book which played a decisive role for the young Heidegger), attempted to demonstrate that Aristotle could have a science of Being because he brought the meaning of Being into exact order. Classification with respect to a guiding, normative meaning makes possible an ordering of the meanings of Being and thereby makes possible the science of Being. The question remains, however, wheth-er a simple classification, an alignment with a guiding meaning, makes a consequent, thorough-going order possible. Must not every single meaning be related *in an exactly determined way* to the guiding meaning for such a consequent, thorough-going order? Medieval philosophy provides such a means of alignment; everything that is receives its being according to its determined participation in the most perfect, normative entity; thus it acquires its place in the order of beings. Ontology, the doctrine of Being, is grounded in theology, in the doctrine of a most perfect being.[22]

It is just this consequent thorough-going ordering of the meaning of Being which ended — in the late Medieval and modern philosophy — in the attempt to grasp the concept of Being as a univocal concept, and to limit it to one meaning or perhaps to a few, precisely delimited meanings.[23] Being, whether it is conceived as bare fact or in whatever way, is no longer the source from which a multiplicity of modes of Being arise. The question of the order of the multiplicity of beings and their structures, therefore, can no longer be developed as a question of Being. Philosophical questions can no longer be developed as a question of Being.

---

[21] Compare above all the *Einführung in die Metaphysik* and his works on metaphysics as a history of Being from the second volume of his study of Nietzsche.—Johannes Lohmann attempted to clarify further the relationship between language and thought in various works, especially in his journal, *Lexis* (1948ff.). See also his book *Philosophie und Sprachwissenschaft*, Berlin 1965.

[22] It is still a matter of dispute whether Aristotle already offers a classification of the meanings of Being in the manner just mentioned. Regarding this theme cf. above all Pierre Aubenque, *Ambiguite ou analogie de l'être? (Societes de Philosophie de langue française. Actes du XIII Congres-Geneve* 1966), pp. 11–14; *Le probleme de l'être chez Aristotle*, Paris 1962. —Brentano, like Heidegger, forces from the Aristotelian texts a unified order of the meanings of Being, apparently oriented on the scholastic doctrine of the *analogia entis*. It is imputed right from the start that Aristotle must have sought a normative meaning of Being. Heidegger finds this meaning in his earlier works apparently in *ousia*, later, however, in *energeia* and *entelechia*. Heidegger's student Walter Bröcker, in his book *Aristotles* (Frankfurt, 1935, 3rd ed. 1964) attempts to show that Aristotle conceives Being as motion. Heidegger himself, however, seems to ask: If Aristotle thinks of beings as moved, then how is this motion to be conceived if it is conceived as Being and is thought of in relation to the imperturbability of *ouisa*, and if it is to be conceived together, which is understood as constant presence? Is not Being then to be conceived as motion which moves into the imperturbability of a constant presence, i.e., as the completion of motion in work and reality, as *energeia* and *entelecheia*? Cf. *Nietzsche*, II, pp. 403ff.

[23] From the point of view of linguistic-analytical philosophy, such a limitation is discussed by Ernst Konrad Specht, *Sprache und Sein*, Berlin 1967, Ernst Tegendhat, "Die sprachanalytiseh Kritik der Ontologie." In: *Das Problem der Sprache*. Ed. by H.-G. Gadamer, München, 1967, pp. 483–493.

Philosophical questions can no longer be circumscribed in the question of Being. There is no longer a science of Being as the first science, which delineates the realms for the sciences and the other modes of man's comportment. If "ontology" is still allowed as an option, it is a science among other sciences; the concept of Being also becomes a scientific concept and precisely for that reason can no longer serve to recall the multiplicity of the sciences into a unity. The individual sciences themselves must take care that they base their work on precisely defined concepts and in this way be "sciences." Heidegger, who attempts to retain the question of Being as the basic question of philosophy, contests this development. In this development the concept of Being, so he says in Nietzsche's words, becomes "the last vapour of evaporating reality." No ordered multiplicity can spring from a simple mist. Men no longer know in accord with an organized multiplicity what it means that a mountain chain "is," that a church entrance "is," that a state "is," that a painting "is"; they stagger within this realm of orderless beings, but precisely because of this they are able to make beings the object of caprice machinations. "How," so Heidegger asks in one of his capuchin sermons against the delusion of the times, "would it be, if such a thing were possible, that man, that the peoples procure beings with the greatest of schemes and power and nevertheless have long since fallen out of Being without knowing it, and that this would be the innermost and most potent reason for their downfall?" For Heidegger, that small word "is" is no plain word, its meaning no hazy mist; this word for Heidegger rather contains "the intellectual fate of the Occident."[24]

2. In *Sein und Zeit* Heidegger wishes to explicate the meaning of Being as a multiplicity of meaning and thus present that "science of Being," which first grounds the regional ontologies and the individual sciences and makes possible an ordering of human modes of comportment. The way in which Heidegger unfolds the question of Being as a question of the "meaning" of Being, shows that he does not simply think in an Aristotelian or Scholastic manner. He rather introduces the modern transcendental-philosophical re-inquiry into the knowledge in which "Being" becomes known, i.e., into the question of Being. (In Heidegger's first works the problem of the modes of Being or categories is in an accentuated manner already linked with the problem of judgment and subject, even of language.) The "transcendental ego," however, is conceived by Heidegger as factual existence, and thus the experience of facticity and historicity, as found in the Christian faith, in Kierkegaard's critique of Idealism, and in modern historicism, can be taken up into the initial question. The meaning of Being, which is understood in the ontological understanding (*Seinverstehen*) of factual existence, disseminates in a multiplicity of meanings, corresponding to the possibilities for the modification of ontological understanding (*Seinverstehen*). Heidegger thinks of this dissemination as springing from a source, which is from the guiding meaning of Being. In the many scattered "methodological" comments which are inserted in *Sein und Zeit,* Heidegger speaks of a modification of this guiding meaning, of a derivation in deficient, originating modes, even of privation, which deprives something from the source and thus allows the extraction to spring up, of a "geneology" of the modes of Being. The meaning of Being is conceived as the "whereupon" of that projection, in which Being is understood in different ways as Being, and thereby also as the "ground" for the multiple meanings of Being. The meaning of Being is thought of as a ground from which the understanding

---

[24] *Einführung in die Metaphysik,* pp. 28f.

21

of the individual meanings "nourishes" itself, but which as ground is not at all like a "background." What these paraphrases for the springing up of the multiple meanings from the guiding meaning is supposed to say can only be clarified when one observes what Heidegger really *does* in his development of a science of Being.

Our work with *Sein und Zeit* must first learn in all those analyses which have so strongly touched upon the thought of contemporaries to perceive a way of working out the question of Being, without, however, allowing the question of Being as a question to perish in an empty formalism of distinctions between various modes of Being. —Such analyses include that of dread as the basic disposition, the differentiation of self and "the they," death, the summons to the authenticity of wanting to have a conscience, exhibiting historicality. When Heidegger in the first section of *Sein und Zeit* designates in a preparatory way the being of *Dasein* (thus of man, insofar as he is an understanding of Being) as "care," this designation has its point: A being can only show itself in Being, because there is a being which relates itself to itself and to things, and by means of this reflexive relation allows a clearance to become open in which then a being can show itself in Being, in which, therefore, man can say "is" to things, as well as also to himself. The clearance of this openness is not simply given, but rather is left to "care." Heidegger uses the term "care" because he wishes to avoid a term like reflexive relation or praxis, and he wishes to choose a designation which lies beyond the traditional differentiation between theory and practice. In just this way he moves against the prejudice of traditional ontology that things show themselves as they are in themselves when we bring them before us in an indifferent viewing, in pure theory. Heidegger seeks to resolve into a new point of inquiry this ontological way of distinguishing 'theory' as well as the traditional antithesis of theory and practice by distinguishing in an exemplary fashion between 'present-at-hand' and 'ready-to-hand' as modes of how something is given to us.

Thus he asks, how is a hammer authentically accessible to us in its being? Do we experience what a hammer is when we only stare at it as something 'present-at-hand'? We never experience what a hammer is when we take it to be something isolated and 'present-at-hand.' A hammer is not 'present-at-hand,' but rather 'ready-to-hand' and is only occasionally simply 'present at hand.' It is present for the sake of hammering and as 'ready to hand' it is not an imaginary thing, but rather a serviceable implement, a tool. The implement is serviceable for something; by means of its serviceableness, it points to other things (to the leather which is hammered, to the shoe which is supposed to be made, etc.). One implement refers to another and thus stands in the totality of a referential context. Within this referential context there is a certain involvement with the implement, and thus the implement has a certain significance. The significatory context within which things confront us in daily life is ultimately the world as the world around us. It has its center in that "for-the-sake-of" in which Being is a question for *Dasein* and in which *Dasein* as actual existence relates itself to things, to itself and to other *Dasein,* and thus is "care."

"Practical" dealings with the hammer as something 'ready to hand' is not "atheoretical." This practice rather has its own mode of view, or "theory": circumspection. To be sure, this circumspection can modify itself to a simple observation. We look very carefully at the hammer when our hammering goes awry. Even then we still investigate the hammer according to those considerations which are suggested to us by the implemental-context of the world around us. We must conduct ourselves very abstractly if we no longer take the hammer to be 'ready to hand,' but rather consider it disinterestedly, e.g., when we want to inquire of the composition of the metal from which the hammer-head is made —even such inquiry is usually still motivated in the interest of acquiring a good, hard-hitting hammer. Nevertheless, simple observation can be highly stylized into pure theory which has largely separated itself from guiding practical interests. Even this pure theory, however, which according to its simple 'presence at hand' perceives something in indifferent observation, is still to be comprehended as a certain modification of care. This kind of observing involves above all the prejudice: only disinterested, indifferent observation is able to discover a being in its own being, to revise in accord with the experiment, and to say under which conditions a being confronts us as something 'ready to hand' (or perhaps as "nature" which encompasses us), and in what situations a being shows itself in a simple 'presence at hand.'

The modes of a being's givenness— e.g., 'presence at hand' and 'readiness to hand,' which are simply two modes among others—should be made clear in their difference. Heidegger finds the principle of distinction in care, which is disclosed in the second section of *Sein und Zeit* as the temporality of *Dasein*. What, however, is temporality and time? In order to be able to develop this question, Heidegger proceeds from the traditional Aristotelian concept of time: time is what is counted in motion. I look at the sun, pay attention to its motion, see that it has passed its highest elevation, distinguish between what is earlier and later. I thus reckon time and say: it is afternoon. Or I look at the clock, pay attention to the motion of the hand, calculate what is earlier and later and thus reckon time. In order for there to be time, must there not always be someone who counts? In fact, the philosophical tradition ascribes to time an es-

sential relationship to the "soul." But how, asks Heidegger, is this relation of time to the "soul" or to *Dasein* to be conceived? I do not look at the clock in order to ascertain with complete disinterest and indifference an absolute time. I rather look at the clock in order to ascertain that there is still time to do this or that. Time is thus "time in order to . . ." It is the right time or wrong time. Significance belongs to time. This significance leaves its mark as well in the attempts at dating, which reckons according to the way time is significant for us in hours or in years or in milleniums which proceed from the birth of Christ, the founding of the city of Rome, or the respective present. Time, however, is not only "time in order to . . ."; it ultimately turns out to be the time of *Dasein,* which is mortal, which can allow itself to be called forth by its conscience into this mortality, which always is already standing in a situation, and which itself is only historical.

Dasein is in time in such a way that it must expressly temporalize time. Its temporality is historicality (the temporalization of time which one expressly takes over) as well as being within the demands of time (*Innerzeitigkeit*) (finding oneself within erected temporal limits). The temporality of *Dasein* is modifiable — there is a difference whether I myself am young with an open future, I am old with a rich past and near death, I must take leave of some beloved one who has died, or whether others declare: he is still young, he is old, he has lost a friend. In the first instance it is a matter of enduring a fate in hope, dread, pain, and joy; in the second, it is a matter of ascertaining something within the limits of time. Historicality, however, is not without the inner limits of time and being within the limits of time is not free of historicality. Even the scientists in their highly stylized theoretical attitude could never say that the world exists for so many billion years, that man appeared so many hundred-thousand years ago, that there were civilized cultures for so many thousand years, and that man, insofar as he does not destroy the planet, has the expectation of moving about this earth for still a long time — the scientists could never say these things if they themselves were not mortal and historic and if they did not allow time to arrive as time in their mortality and historicality, in the uniqueness of their here and now.

Dasein is temporal by virtue of temporalizing time in the mode of historicality as well as being within the demands of time, and by these modes of temporality it is in various ways transported into the dimensions of time — into the future, present, and past. These transportations, the "ecstases" of *Dasein,* these modes of standing out into the horizons of time, are, in the mode of historicality, which is the authentic mode of temporalizing time, the "anticipation" of future possibilities (above all, of the most extreme possibility, death), the momentariness of its time, and the "repetition" of the past or of what has been. When *Dasein* temporalizes time in the inauthentic mode of simply being within the element of time (thus forgetting that temporal limits are not simply given, but rather must first be erected in the actual temporalization of time), then *Dasein* is not transported into its future in such a way that it anticipates its possibilities as its own possibilities; it rather "awaits" what is future as what will one day be given. In this modification of its temporality it does not have the character of momentariness of its time, taking over the present as situation, but rather presupposes situation and "makes" beings "present" in it. It does not repeat what has been as a possibility of its own *Dasein,* but "forgets" this repetition and thus on the basis of *such* forgetfulness can retain or forget what is past like something which is given. Schemata, which state the whither of these transportations, correspond to the (authentic as well as inauthentic) transportations into the dimensions of time: the "anticipation" of possibilities and awaiting are transported to a "for-the-sake-of," from which a "toward-which" or an "alongside-of-which" of involvement can arise. The "momentariness" in a situation and "making present" are transported to an "in-order-to," which includes in the situation what is present as what is present, or presents it also as something 'present at hand.' "Repetition" and "forgetting" are transported by the "that-in-the-face-of-which" or the "where-at" of facticity, from which what is retained can arise in the "by which" of an involvement.[25]

Can the way that a being is given to us (as the present-at-hand of pure theory, as the ready-to-hand of active practice, etc.) thus be made understandable at any given time from the

[25] Cf. *Sein und Zeit,* pp. 325ff., 336ff., 365, 353, 360.—The analysis of ecstatic temporality and its schemata do not appear to have been finally clarified in the published section of *Sein und Zeit.* Precisely this part of *Sein und Zeit* is characterized by a formalism which is able only forcibly to include the earlier analyses devoted to the subject matter. This is illustrated, for example, by the fact that the modification of authentic *Dasein* to inauthentic *Dasein,* decay, is added abruptly as a fourth classification to the three classifications of care (Understanding, State-of-mind, Discourse), or even supplant the third element (Discourse) (pp. 346, 231). The analysis of time is in general totally questionable. Heidegger says, for example, instead of "past" (*Vergangenheit*), "the state of having been" (*Gewesenheit*). This manner of speech includes the thesis that the past must be viewed above all from the aspect of repeatability (or non-repeatability). The state of having been is supposed to be more profound than 'past.' The question remains, however, whether the opposite is not true, whether departed withdrawal and self-refusal in relation to the present, i.e., the past in an emphatical sense, does not influence the experience of time more decisively than "the state of having been." Another question within the same problem complex is the one frequently raised, whether Heidegger does not unjustly shove aside the death of the other, as distinct from one's own death, i.e., whether he does not in general insufficiently take the experience of the "thou" into consideration.

modifiable temporality of *Dasein*, from ecstases and the schemata of these ecstases? A hammer is ready-to-hand in that there is an involvement *with it*. It is there *in order to* hammer shoes. There can only be an involvement with it because *Dasein* exists from a "for-the-sake-of" and the "*for*-which" arises from this "for-the-sake-of," to which making shoes is oriented. *Dasein* actualizes the hammer in an "in-order-to" in that it expects a "for-which" and at the same time retains the hammer in that "with-which" of its involvement in which it is given. The temporality, in which I have to do with what is ready-to-hand, is thus expectancy-actualization-preservation. Temporality is within the demand of time as inauthentic temporality, and thereby includes forgetfulness of historicality as the authentic temporalization of time. In fact, manual activity forgets itself and is lost to its activity. The self-forgetful occupation with the ready-to-hand is directed to the "in-order-to"; nevertheless, the expectancy of the "for-which" is still in play. This future is largely excluded when the use of what is ready-to-hand is shifted to the simple discovery of what is present-at-hand. This shift, however, cannot simply be negatively understood as a "privation," as the repression of the schema of future ecstasy (*ekstase*), for the schema of present ecstasy acquires at the same time a greater and different significance: the actualization is accentuated, a simple theoretical ("apophantical") "as" arises from the "in-order-to" of the present ecstasy— something is taken to be something else without practical intent. This actualization can then also make use of expectancy for itself; theory can have its own practice — which applies even to the highly stylized theory of academics, say for the construction of a technical apparatus in physical experiments, for biological observation or for archaeological "spade-research."

Dealing with what is ready-to-hand and discovering what is present-at-hand are both grounded in the inauthentic temporalization of time. This statement provokes the question: is there not also a relation to beings which is grounded in the authentic temporalization of time? Heidegger makes at least allusion to such a relation: the ring which someone wears on his finger — in remembrance of someone else or as a sign of fidelity — is not something present-at-hand that will be discovered by its characteristics; it is also not something ready-to-hand with which one busily deals. This ring does not at all belong to self-forgetful dealings with what is ready-to-hand. It is supposed precisely to alleviate self-forgetfulness and to keep alert essential relations of *Dasein* — remembrance of someone deceased or fidelity to one's partner. Thus wearing a ring could by all means be grounded in an authentic mode of time's temporalization. Heidegger, however, only touches this question in *Sein und Zeit* without going into detail. What Heidegger worked out as the authentic temporalization of time — the existing of factical existence, its anticipation of death and its "desiring-to-have-a-conscience" — is, then, also characterized by a peculiar "worldlessness." [26]

Dasein, according to its various possibilities of temporalizing time, can take beings as something present-at-hand or as something ready-to-hand or even as

---

[26] Rudolf Bultmann characterized precisely this authentic existing (as the Christian faith is supposed to make possible) as "de-secularization" *(Entweltlichung).* This contradicts not only Heidegger's terminology (Heidegger used this terminus for that flattening out of the Being-in-the-world, which occurs in the simple discovery of what is present-at-hand, cf. *Sein und Zeit*, pp. 65, 112), but also the basic tendency of his thought (which later comes more strongly to the fore). Hans Jonas, who with Heidegger and Bultmann offered an existential interpretation of *Gnosis,* attempts in later works conversely to demonstrate a "gnostic" tendency in *Sein und Zeit:* "Gnosis, Existentialismus und Nihilismus." In: *Zwischen Nichts und Ewigkeit,* Göttingen, 1963.

a "ring"; it is able itself to exist as factical existence. When, however, *Dasein* takes a being to be something present-at-hand, something ready-to-hand or a ring, or even when it is well versed in existing, does it not already have to be familiar with the being of what is present-at-hand, the being of what is ready-to-hand, the being of a ring, the being of existence? How is time, which is temporalized by *Dasein* in modifiable ways, to be conceived? Must we not understand on the basis of this time and the various ways that it can be temporalized that *Dasein* can allow beings to come forth in the being of what is present-at-hand, ready-to-hand, the ring, or in the existentiality of existence? Must not, then, the meaning of Being and the possible significances of Being be explicable from time? In that third unpublished section of *Sein und Zeit,* which we must always have in mind when we wish to make the direction of inquiry in *Sein und Zeit* clear, *Time and Being,* was supposed to become clear as the transcendental horizon of the question of Being. The transcendental horizon is that horizon in which one is transcended, in which a being is surpassed in that one comes back to it from surpassing it in its Being and thus takes it as the being it is — as something present-at-hand, something ready-to-hand or as existence. The possible meanings of Being reveal themselves in this horizon, and in it the meaning of Being is formed. Time is that transcendental horizon because it contains in itself various possibilities of being temporalized and thus by the diverse interplay of its ecstases and the schemata of these ecstases it allows a being to be determined in various modes of Being.

Heidegger calls time "temporality" insofar as it is conceived as this transcendental horizon for the structuring of the meaning of Being. He calls this time (in order to differentiate it from that which one usually calls time) with a name which does not deny its Latin origin. Heidegger obviously wanted correspondingly to call the dimensions of time also with names which stem from Latin, e.g., the present (*Gegenwart*) with the word "Presence" ("*Präsenz*"). If I take a being to be something ready-to-hand or not ready-to-hand, as something present-at-hand or not present-at-hand, then I take it to be something in the present or not in the present and am thus very well carried into the dimension of the present. Time temporalizes itself under the pre-eminence of the present and the Being of beings reveals itself in the horizon of presence (*Präsenz*), in a 'presencial' sense. The other ecstases of time are also involved, but the ecstase of the present and with that the 'presencial' sense of Being, predominate. Just as the change over from dealings with what is ready-to-hand to the simple presentation of what is present-at-hand is to be made clear from a diverse interplay of time's ecstases, so correspondingly the meaning of Being and the multiple significances of Being must be rendered intelligible from this interplay.

Time, which is temporalized in various ways, discloses a multiple historical interlacing of horizons, in which Being can be understood again in multifarious ways. The predominance of the present, e.g., conditions a predominance of the 'presencial' meaning and thus makes possible an understanding of Being as the being of what is ready-to-hand or of what is present-at-hand. But a being is not only present-at-hand or ready-to-hand; it confronts man, e.g., also as embracing nature or as a ring. How is the being of nature or the being of a ring to be made intelligible? Man confronts not only a being which is a thing, but he encounters also himself. A being which is a thing, so stipulates Heidegger, is comprehended in its being by categories, man by existentials. How is this distinction between categories and existentials to be more precisely determined? Heidegger would have developed this question in the third section of *Sein und Zeit,* and he would then also needed to have shown how the content of the categories can be developed even to the extent of all its filiations. That is to say that Heidegger would have had to demonstrate the possibility of a "science of Being"; he would have had to develop how the significations of Being arise from the meaning of Being and how modifiable time functions as the principle for the formation of the meaning of Being. An interpretation of the published section of *Sein und Zeit* such that it is concretely referred to this task has up to the present time not been successfully accomplished in the many works on Heidegger.

3. Why is it precisely time as the principle of differentiation regarding the significations of Being which Heidegger reckons in his account? In his preview of the unpublished second section of *Sein und Zeit*, as it is given in the introductory § 6 of his work, Heidegger attempts to expound briefly the "prejudice" of all previous interpretations of Being: Being is interpreted along the lines of *legein* taken as *noein*, as *ousia* or *parousia*, as the continual presence or presence-at-hand of what is present-at-hand, thereby, however, with regard to the present. Heidegger then asks: if Being is interpreted with regard to the present, though the present is only *one* of the dimensions of time, must not then Being be interpreted in light of full and primordial time, if the full and primordial sense of Being is to reveal itself? On the basis of this supposition, the mode of Being which corresponds to historicality as the authentic temporalization of time — thus something like "Being-historically-factical" — becomes for Heidegger the guiding sense of Being, the "ground" for the multifarious significances of Being, even, as Heidegger imputes with reference to Plato, the *agathon* as the last 'for-the-sake-of,' thus the Idea of ideas, the "Being" of being. Is this ground, then, that Principle of principles which permits us not only to develop sciences or individual philosophical disciplines, but also to test by a first science these sciences as well as other human modes of comportment with respect to their legitimacy and to place them into an ordered context? Does Heidegger wish — as appears to be the case in the program of a fundamental ontology or even a metaphysic of metaphysics — to give the final foundation for every "ontological construction," or is this, his fundamental ontology, also — as is expressly developed in the cited § 6 of *Sein und Zeit* — historical, "historiographical" in itself (since indeed nothing happens other than this, that the prejudice of the previous ontological construction is broken and what is forgotten in the previous experience of Being is brought into language)? If *Sein und Zeit* stands in a hermeneutical circle and this circle is later articulated as turning, then this turning does not simply come into play between the 2nd and 3rd sections of the 1st part of *Sein und Zeit*, as was supposed, following ambiguous statements by Heidegger, but rather primarily between the first and second parts of *Sein und Zeit*.

The investigation of the meaning of Being, with its differentiation of phenomenological construction as the first part and phenomenological destruction as the second part, fell into an aporia because it did not keep the circle in which it stands constantly in the present: if temporality and time are a derivable principle for the differentiation of *Dasein's* modes of comportment and characteristics of Being, then temporality and historicality, i.e., historicity can no longer be later reckoned to this principle. And conversely: if this investigation is itself inherently historical, then temporality or historicality and historiological-factical-Being cannot function as the final, founding principle, as the foundation of all ontologies. The use of the word "historicality" in *Sein und Zeit* remains ambiguous, both meanings of which conceptually are not sufficiently brought together. The one meaning rather destroys the other, so that an exit from the hermeneutical circle cannot come about. Heidegger dispenses with this ambiguity, which turns against him, by attempting to show in the works which follow the published part of *Sein und Zeit* that the guiding meaning of Being as the "ground" from which all understanding of Being is "nourished," is itself abysmal and groundless. The modes of Being are not derivatively extracted from it in such a way that privation deprives it of its abundance; "privation" in another sense belongs to it itself as abysmal self-withdrawal and groundless self-dissimulation. If this ground is the source from which all modes of Being arise, then it is not as a final principle, but rather as a source which is in itself historical and therefore never to be finally apprehended. Thus with that everything which arises from this source, the modes of Being and the order of these modes of Being, bears historicality in itself. System and history, phenomenological construction and destruction are no longer in any case to be separated. Heidegger now speaks less of the meaning of Being, and more of the truth of Being, whereby truth is conceived as non-concealment (aletheia), as the abysmal-groundless ground of non-concealment, which only discloses itself by also concealing itself and dissembling itself. In its first programmatic statements, such a lecture as "Vom Wesen der Wahrheit" itself, however, gives rise to the impression that there is *the* nature of truth, the one and, in its uniformity, encompassing truth.

What thought, which wishes to contemplate itself as Being's coming-into-language, must denounce is the "onto-theoretical" character of hitherto existing "metaphysical" thought: the orientation toward a guiding meaning of Being, which is acquired from the being of a representative entity, of the

"god of the philosophers," even if this god (the axis on which the doctrine of Being hangs) is also the "god" of the atheists, i.e., the conclusively determined mortality and "historicality" of man. The "recollection into metaphysics" or the "ontological-historical consideration," which Heidegger developed after the revision of *Sein und Zeit*'s approach and to which a new line of research soon attached itself, is supposed to show precisely that the task given to our thought is the "overcoming" of the onto-theological character of thought. Thought which is penetrated by ontological-historical consideration, pays attention to the fact that it does not give "the" Being or "the" difference, but rather transcendental characters like Being, truth, identity, difference, and ground are only given respectively in epoch-making coinages. Heidegger does not bring out this insight from the perspective of *Being and Time* without polemicizing against his own contemplative attempts.[27]

When *Sein und Zeit* distinguishes or claims to distinguish existentials as the characteristics of the being of *Dasein* from categories as the characteristics of the being of entities inappropriate to *Dasein*, it nevertheless remains undeveloped in what manner a presence-at-hand, a readiness-to-hand, an historicality and, correspondingly, a being-present-at-hand, being-ready-to-hand and being-historical is mentioned at all. Is there any sense at all in speaking of "the" readiness-to-hand? Is there such a thing as "the" readiness-to-hand, which is the same in the ancient agrarian cultures, in the association between farmers and aristocracy, in the civic city culture and in the now encroaching age of industry? Is the weapon, which was decorated with symbols and consecrated, ready-to-hand for the man of ancient cultures in the

---

[27] Cf. *Der Satz vom Grund*, pp. 48, 85, 176; *Identität und Differenz*, pp. 63ff.—We must not forget that the lectures here adduced and the addresses here quoted present a theme in a pedagogically adapted and popularized form, which in its original was attained by Heidegger by his work in the Thirties, but which in this form was not yet published.

same way that a Starfighter is ready-to-hand or suddenly no longer ready-to-hand for a contemporary pilot? And is there something like "the" historicality, which in the same way characterizes the man of pre-history and the man of civilized cultures as well as ultimately the man to come? For which man is the analysis of the understanding of Being, of the *"Dasein"* in man, as developed in *Sein und Zeit* appropriate? In § 11 of this book Heidegger takes precautions against prematurely connecting the analysis of everyday *Dasein* with the analysis of the world of primitive peoples, and on p. 82 (English, p. 113) he even says:

> Perhaps even readiness-to-hand and equipment have nothing to contribute as ontological clues in Interpreting the primitive world; and certainly the ontology of Thinghood does even, less. (*Being* and *Time*)

Heidegger then means, however, that what the world is in any case must be understood in the formal way if the world of primitive man is to be interpreted. What, however, does "formal" mean here? Does it mean a structure which belongs in the same way to man as such, to the man of ancient cultures as well as to the man of the age of industry, or does it mean something like an epoch-making structure which changes and in so doing also endures?[28]

Philosophy, which attempts in itself to overcome the antithesis of system and history, cannot neglect the fact that it stands in proximity to other attempts to withstand history. In the Thirties, therefore, Heidegger's thought displays a — perhaps strange — new character: exactly in the year 1933, this thought becomes involved with politics. In the winter semester of 1934/35, the then Freiburg professor of philosophy did not lecture on logic or metaphysics, nor on Aristotle or Kant, but rather on a poet, on Hölderlin, but not even on Hölderlin's relationship to German Idealism, but rather on his late Hymns. Soon thereafter followed lectures on the origin of a work of art. If in the Twenties, under the convulsions of the times and under the impulse of critical spirits like Dostoevski and Kierkegaard, Heidegger in the solitude of reflection had prescribed for himself the destruction of the tradition and the radicalness of a new beginning, he now confronted his thought with the powers who made history. To be sure, *Sein und Zeit* (pp. 9f.) already relates the question of Being to the whole breadth of scientific work: it was precisely the "crisis in the basic fundamentals," into which mathematics, physics, biology, the humanities and theology had fallen, which was supposed to lead to a joining of scientific and philosophical inquiry. When Heidegger, however, in *Sein und Zeit* reflects on theory and practice, he did so not with a view to modern mass research, the connection of science, technology, industry and politics, but rather with a view to a realm which had just begun to disappear or at least to sink into obscurity: mechanical practice was illustrated by the occupation of the shoemaker, which at that time was still found everywhere; the appearance of directional signals on automobiles was analyzed with visible wonder at this new invention. To such a shoemaker-perspective was appended the solitude of existence prepared for death, which attempted to make significant again the *individual's* "desire-to-have-a-conscience." Thus Heidegger quoted Count Paul Yorck of Wartenburg (p. 403 — *Sein und Zeit,* English trans. p. 455), "To dissolve elemental public

---

[28] If Heidegger's thought is to be made philosophically fruitful, then it must be related to the abundant results of the work of philosophical anthropology as well; at the same time the accusation of an "ontologizing" of anthropological research, as was raised against *Sein und Zeit,* can today be revised from the perspective of Heidegger's later thought. Cf. regarding this, O. Pöggeler, "Existenziale Anthropologie." In: *Die Frage nach dem Menschen.* Festschrift für M. Müller. Ed. by Heinrich Rombach, Freiburg und München 1966, pp. 443–460.

opinion, and, as far as possible, to make possible the moulding of individuality in seeing and looking, would be a pedagogical task for the state." In the Thirties, work, the community which bears it, and the great creative geniuses come into view: work as a political institution, as the Greek temple in which everything comes together, as the mythology and theology of a Sophoclean tragedy and a Hölderlin Hymn.

It appears that philosophy as a universal theory can make everything and anything its object, e.g., art, poetry, politics. It can also give a theory of art, poetry and politics. Because it is able to give a theory of practice, it can be practical philosophy. Is practical philosophy, however, in truth, simply a theory of practice and in itself not "practical"? Is it practical in the sense that it not only makes practice the object of its theory, but as theory attempts an introduction to practice, without, however, wanting to make a decision about the concrete goals of practice? Philosophy knows that I cannot prescribe for practice what it has to do. It knows that practical endeavor gives an insight the likes of which philosophy can perhaps not attain. It also knows that philosophy as the universal self-reflection of man nevertheless opens up certain paths for practice, by means of the acuity of its inquiry, even though advances remain the task of practice itself. In any case, for Heidegger art, poetry and politics are rather ways that man as one who understands Being, as *"Dasein,"* helps to open certain courses and paths so that an entity can reveal itself in a being, and thus truth takes place: truth as truth of Being, i.e., truth as the realm in which Being reveals itself as Being, divides itself in various modes of Being (being-present-at-hand, being-ready-to-hand, Being as 'being constant' vis à vis technical supplies, Being as the being of work relative to a work of art, a political institution, etc.).

Philosophy then asks how art, poetry, and politics are related to truth when 'truth' means the truth of Being. Thus it inquires into the essence of art, poetry, and politics. At the same time, however, philosophy is certainly prepared to concede that, as philosophy, it can not fully overlook that truth which art, poetry or politics allow to take place. Thought does not claim to be able to translate fully into concepts the truth as, for example, disclosed by poetry, or to be able theoretically-conceptually as well to promote the openness of a being as practice produces it apart from the deployment of practice. Philosophy inquires into the essence of art, poetry and politics by attempting in general to determine that 'How' characteristic of the relation to the truth of Being, which is at any given time fundamental for art, poetry and politics. Philosophy, however, can only so inquire by being clear that it itself lives from such a relation to the truth of Being, that it itself has a very specific relation to the truth of Being. Its inquiry into the essence of art, poetry, and politics is thus its distinguishing its relation to the truth from other possible, competing relations to the truth. This inquiry does not delve into the being of an object (the object politics, poetry, art), which philosophy "theoretically" brings under its observation, but this inquiry is right from the start a philosophical self-characterization over against other competing relations to truth. Thought is a way of allowing the truth of Being to take place. As such it distinguishes itself from art, poetry and politics as other possible modes. Yet, thought also refers precisely to these other modes and, given its character, is not permitted to presuppose ever again that there is "the" essence of art, poetry, politics. It is certainly possible that art and politics undergo a transformation in their essence when they enter into our epoch. When Heidegger inquires into the essence of poetry and wants this essence to be disclosed by Hölderlin, he is not inquiring into some super-temporal essence, but into the essence which is supposed to be essential for man in the future. He is inquiring into the epochal essence of poetry, that essence which poetry is supposed to acquire or could acquire in a certain epoch and for a certain historical community of men.

Thought, poeticizing, art and political action are understood from the perspective of a common task: in them, as developed by Heidegger, it is a matter of putting "truth" into practice, of allowing that event to take place in which the paths stand out on which what is confronts us as what is, on which what is confronts us in its Being. Truth, which is set free from the one-sided relation to theory and science, is at the same time conceived as historical, as the truth of an epochal community of men, of a "people." When *Sein und Zeit* for the most part brackets out the problematic of an "objective spirit," or in any event refers to this problematic by the *coup de main* of introducing the term "people" (*Volk*) (p. 384), then the thematization of this problematic takes place in conformity with Herder's Hölderlin's and Hegel's concept of People (*Volksbegriff*). But it does not take place without risky references to contemporary parallels. The truth, which is truth for a people and which is to be founded by creative people in contemplative-work, poetry- and art-work, and state-work, and which is to be preserved by those so inclined, is characterized as an event and as history by its reference to a specific historical situation, the hour of common fate. The present hour, however, according to Heidegger's interpretation, is determined by Nietzsche's talk of the death of God, by Hölderlin's articulation of the flight of the "gods" and of their new, self-preparing arrival. Thus the great creative geniuses are cast into the "breech" between the gods and men; they are themselves "demigods" in Hölderlin's words. They first have to experience anew the way and proper setting of the new paths on which what is finds its way into its Being, and thus

they have to experience anew the truth of Being.

When Heidegger attempted in his lecture from the winter semester of 1934/35 to make Hölderlin's work visible as an "advancement in the *Dasein* of our people which is in itself solidified," and as a "veiled poetical foundation of our being," the question for him was not simply one of Hölderlin's poetry or poetry in general. Rather, the character of his philosophizing was for him then altered, because his philosophizing was from then on determined as thought only by reference to other modes of truth's occurrence (poetry, art, politics, then also technology) and by differentiation from these modes. "Because our *Dasein*," so Heidegger asserted in this lecture, "is a knowing *Dasein*, which can not be taken as synonymous with intellective calculation, there is, therefore, for us no longer a *pure poetical* genesis of *Dasein*, just as little as there is a *pure contemplative* genesis; however, there is just as little a genesis from *simple activity*. We are under the demand not only to arrange appropriate and continual settlements between the poetical, contemplative and acting powers, but to take seriously their hidden, summit-like isolation, therein to experience the secret of their primordial correlation, and primordially to form it to a new, up to now unprecedented articulation of Being."

4. In that transition which Heidegger's thought experienced a few years after the publication of *Sein und Zeit,* the transcendental horizon, in which the meaning of Being was unfolded in a multiplicity of significations, became the world as the structural nexus of the truth of Being. (Since the essence of world was first read off in a one-sided way from the openness of the horizon or "heaven," the structural nexus of truth was for some time conceived as the reverse of "world" in the narrower sense of the word and as the "earth" which closes off itself.) World is a multi-layered nexus which is construct-

ed according to the various ways that time is temporalized. Since time's mode of temporalization is not viewed as something supertemporal, but rather as itself historical, the layering of this nexus is also historical and at any given time may make yet another epoch.

In that Heidegger attempts to unfold an experience of this nexus, his thought once more changes fundamentally. First, during the Thirties, Heidegger seeks truth as the truth for an historical community, a "people." With Hölderlin he calls the great creative geniuses who help to elicit this truth, "demigods," and he demands the self-adaptation of truth in "work." Heidegger, however, (decisive to the political realm) had to allow himself to be instructed that one still can only speak of a "people" in the sense in which German Idealism spoke of it — with a view to the great period of the Greek Polis — when one does not see the way things are today. What today comes to the fore is totalitarianism, whether it is in the Fascist form of re-activating outlived contents of a tradition, the liberal form of agreement and compromise between ostensible representatives of the plurality of societal groups, or the perversion of Socialism to unadulterated imperialism. The age of the great totalitarianisms is for Heidegger, however, nothing other than the end age of "metaphysics." Metaphysics, the classical form of Western thought, reveals itself in this age, in light of all its consequences, as the attempt of man to put at his disposal the totality of what is by means of grasping its ground, and further to dispose of himself as the "lord of the Earth." Metaphysics in this last form becomes a technologically and ideologically supported "world-view" which attempts to create for itself an image of the world as a whole and to obligate itself by means of a building, cultivating formation according to this image. A world-view, however, exists only in the plural of world-views, and thus world-views and ideologies must be elaborated in a totalitarian way and assert themselves with force if they wish to remain existent. The fact that scholarly work does not remain unaffected by this event, should have become clear. We cannot forget (what Heidegger had already attacked in his Hölderlin-lecture of 1934/35), that before 1933, the so-called free sciences, which were only obligated to the truth, spoke, e.g., of psychoanalytically comprehensible grounds for literature, and after 1933 of blood and earth. We cannot forget that in the spring of 1945 the ideological construct of National Socialism disappeared like a nightmare in the morning, and no one wanted to have been the one who had said and done all the things which had been said and done. Nor can we forget that the decades which followed the Second World War stepped on reason and freedom no less than Fascism had done and made it in fact into *an* example of totalitarianism. It is precisely because world-views can be undermined, dissembled, and exchanged over night, because Nihilism constantly eats away at its highest values, that these creations attempt to assert themselves with every means possible. Because Heidegger interprets their battle as a consequence of the conceptual point of departure of metaphysics, he can also on the other hand explain metaphysics from the slogans of the various forms of this "battle over the rulership of the earth," e.g., Nietzsche's concept of truth from the modern propaganda war.[29]

It is not a people, but totalitarianisms, not the great creative geniuses, but functionaries of totalitarianism, not a work, but mechanization, which are characteristic of our time. The dispositional force of modern technology, which had climbed to monstrous proportions, increases on its side the

---

[29] Cf. *Nietzsche,* II, p. 298; cf. also *Vortrage und Aufsatze,* pp. 93ff.

dangers of totalitarianism to monstrous proportions, and thus Heidegger's vigilance in his later works was directed above all to this technology. If one inquires, however, as to which positive possibilities for political action in the age of technology Heidegger exhibits, one receives no answer. Negative-critical tendencies dominate his comments concerning politics, and the assertion seems unavoidable that because of illusory hopes Heidegger was plunged into despair, a despair which on its side could be blind for possibilities which nevertheless exist. Already in the Thirties, Heidegger evaded the analysis of the work of politics by analysing the work of art. Even if one today grants that Heidegger's early comments concerning the work of politics can not be passed off as his political philosophy, one is inclined nevertheless to construct a philosophy of art from his essay on art-work from 1935/36. But when one makes that move, he ignores the further path of inquiry along which Heidegger has proceeded, and his earlier starting point of inquiry, which is passed around as a questionable romanticism, is forced into illusory and peripheral realms. If one takes the whole of Heidegger's way of contemplation into consideration, his inquiry into the possibilities of present and future art can only be developed

as the question of the possibilities of art in the age of technology.[30]

But why is it precisely art which is the guide line for a question which inquires into the event of truth? Art, namely, as that event of truth which in temples, tragedies and hymns binds together the divinities and mortals, the openness of horizons or heavens, and the self-closure of the earth vis à vis the world as a "four-fold polyvalance"? Why is the vision of a continually isomorphic "nature" (as asserted by O. Becker), or the "Kingsway of ethics" (E. Levinas), or history and in it especially work as the self-production of man, not the guide line? The event of the truth of art, as Heidegger attempts to make clear, shows us a feature of truth which is decisive for our experience of truth: every significant work of art shows itself to be inexhaustible and allows truth to be seen as an event which always withdraws into its inexhaustibility. Art, however, exists today only as art in the age of technology; the world as a "four-fold polyvalance" shows itself only together with the world as "framework," the totality of scientific-technological presentation and conveyance. The identification of this constellation of four-fold polyvalence and framework is still an elaboration of what *Sein und Zeit* wanted to make perceptible as the

---

[30] Heidegger therefore wanted to present an analysis of contemporary art and art interpretation in a pendant to his essay on the origin of a work of art. Cf. also his comments from *Der Satz vom Grund*, pp. 41, 66, as well as the following review of expositions which Heidegger delivered in Bühler Höhe many years ago: "In conclusion Martin Heidegger conducted the theme into a new realm. In making a negative reply to the question whether modern art still has something to do with art in the old sense, Heidegger made clear that with respect to the disputed "objectlessness" it was not a question of an historical novelty, but it was rather a question of something essentially different in the fulfillment of Western destiny. Due to the fact that this new phenomenon—from which we still know absolutely nothing as to what it is and what it makes present—still has no place at all, but rather must allow itself to be presented without belonging anywhere in museums and exhibits, we may see with terrible clarity how inadequate to date all attempts have remained to get a hold on this new phenomenon by means of a "title" or even to classify it somewhere prematurely. This view, which Heidegger demonstrates, reached its peak when he pointed to the relationship in which objectless "art" is obviously related to the essence of technology (in relation to which it is decisive to conceive the word "essence" not substantively, but verbally!). Such a relationship, however, has no portraying character: wheels and pistons, for example, would have to appear here like they would appear by Leger or as mirror images would appear in physic's experiments. The essence of objectless pictures, which is still little experienced and unreflected, concerns us much more directly than every re-presentation ever could." (Heinrich W. Petzet, "Preetorius and Heidegger über abstrakte Kunst," *Universitas*, 8. Jg., Stuttgart 1953, pp. 444–445.).

transcendental horizon for the unfolding of the meaning of Being in the
multiplicity of its significations. But
this constellation is, other than the
constellation of presence-at-hand and
readiness-to-hand or being-present-at-
hand and being-ready-to-hand found
in *Sein und Zeit,* experienced as something which was historically developed
in a concrete way and which is in this
way delivered to us.

When Heidegger inquires into the
truth of Being in a developed sense,
one no longer asks whether a certain
physical theory is verifiable or under
which claims a certain work of art
places us. One asks, rather, what it
means in any case for the totality of
our life and Being-in-the-world, that a
being encounters us within physical research or also in a work of art. By developing this mode of inquiry, Heidegger's thought converges with the burn-
ing questions of our time. That and
how there are such things as the complex of atomic research, economy of the
atom, and atomic armament, cannot
simply be accepted by us as something
given. Care therefore applies not only
to the verifiability of physical theories,
the effectiveness of the economy of the
atom, and the hyper-effectiveness of
atomic armament. Rather the question
arises as to the way contemporary and
future humanity can be responsible for
this complex in the totality of its Being-in-the-world. The question of responsibility remains acute, although it
is senseless simply to make the physi-
cists responsible for this complex or the
military men who expected something
from atomic research, or the politicians
who encouraged this research by their
incalculable decisions. Biological research and technology (with their in-
trusions into the most private spheres)
already inspire the mind today, when
only their presumably initial beginnings stand out. Without man's being
able to perceive the consequences of
his action, he is today continually
forced to make and accept decisions
which alter the nexus of his world —

decisions, e.g., as to whether his wealth
is to be used primarily for economic
aid or new forms of armament or
space projects, for the development of
new forms of food-production or for
the biological-medical manipulation of
life, etc. Creators as well as receivers
of art are undergoing a change in the
role of art in life without being able
to know already what is actually happening. Humanity is in general inexperienced in the thinking which is being demanded of it.

The issue before us involves one's
not simply accepting blindly those ways
in which beings confronts us (in a being-present-at-hand, a being-ready-to-
hand, the being of work, the being-a-
product-of-technology), i.e., the guiding
paths in the nexus of "truth," and not
relinquishing them to irrational decision. When Heidegger considers how
a picture by Klee, an entity in a physical experiment, a poem by Trakl, and
a product of technology are given, he
attempts to retract the different modes
of the sway of Being, truth and world
into a unified and ordered experience.
Hegel, embracing the history of Western thought, unfolded such an experience by referring it to a "speculative
principle." This principle was formulated by Hegel at the beginning of his
thought process as the identity of
identity and non-identity. He then developed in his speculative philosophy
the dispositions of consciousness and
with that the modes of the understanding of what is (*Ist-Verstehens*) (in the
Phänomologie des Geistes), as well as
(in the *Wissenschaft der Logik*) the
possible ongoing determination of "is"
as the "methodical" justification of the
speculative principle. Today one is
inclined to understand Heidegger's talk
of "event" as the pan-hermeneutical
dissolution of every systematic into an
uncontrollable 'coming to pass" and
'taking place.' One would do better,
however, to ask whether Heidegger
does not also formulate a speculative
principle when he, with a direct, verbatim translation of the Hegelian for-

mula, speaks of the "harmony" between "event" (co-adaptation, sameness of thinking and Being) and "settlement" (difference, differentiation of Being and beings).[31] In his discussion of the essence of "ground," Heidegger nevertheless expresses to what extent the "speculative principle" is no longer a principle for him: event is no longer an expoundable and then fixed principle — as temporality in *Sein und Zeit* could still be understood — from which the differentiation of all characteristics of Being and *Dasein* becomes possible by a "science of Being." Event is rather the same historical mode as that of time, comprehended traditionally only in its derivative form with the guide line of thought and representation) and Being (interpreted traditionally in the direction of presence and Present) when they belong together and are thus in harmony with that settlement of the differentiation of beings and Being, a settlement which first encounters a being as a being and allows it to arrive in the multiplicity of "is."

The "geneology" of Being as conceived by Heidegger provides neither an unhistorical ordering of substances and essence nor (in the unfolding of a transcendental subject) a "transcendental history" that is itself more than historical. It also does not plunge speculative thought, dissolving it, into the abyss of "actual history," which should simply be accepted or be mastered by the proclamation of a "bearer" and "lord" of history (the nation, culture, class or race). In this sense, the occurrence of truth does not have a bearer, in a transcendental or in an actual ego, such that it could be tied down to him — although this event always needs men, "bearers" for itself. Thus one may comprehend this event from "work," to which men lay claim, and it remains itself only in ever

new historical efficacy. The modes of such a Being-at-Work must expressly be layed out — e.g., language as the element in which thinking and poetic composition particularly take place, also technical conveyance (and further, work and control, the forms of which curiously receive little attention by Heidegger). Truth's Being-at-Work is task, and it can not be related to a fixed, constant measure. Indeed, to present the world as "four-fold polyvalence," which is understood as the final measure of every event of truth, would be a romantic regression which must invert to totalitarianism in the same way as the attempts to establish the utopia of absolute "socialistic" practice or the postulate of the harmony of all emancipated spheres of life as trans-historical goals. Even though the event of truth knows no final fixed standard to which it were to be subordinated, there nevertheless are at any given time standards, and with regard to the eliciting and admission of truth as the truth of Being this rule applies: truth is to be elicited in such a way that the total nexus of truth does not collapse (as would take place, according to Heidegger's exposition, by means of absolutely fixed technology).

One cannot finally expect from the "geneology" of Being an a priori framework which would simply need to be filled out by empirical methods. Rather, one may approach a speculative middle, which is itself historical and always evades grasp, in the "geneology of Being" from the periphery of the empirical only by changing the guide lines in various ways at any given time. In that way, however, is this field of truth, with its speculative middle, "historical"? Is this talk of the historical oriented to that history in which a general conquers today and tomorrow is executed, in which social tendencies persist over the centuries? Is it orient-

[31] Cf. the publication *Identität und Differenz* as well as the lecture *Zeit und Sein* (in: *L'endurance de la pensée. Pour saluer Jean Beaufret*, Paris 1968, pp. 12–71) held in 1962 and published in 1968.

ed to that history in which, in a dark corner of the Roman Empire, a "Messiah-Pretender" becomes God's message to men? Is it oriented to that history in which the sciences find a new foundation through "Copernican revolutions"? Is it perhaps even oriented to that history under which the evolution of life will also be subsumed? Or are we to speak in still another way of history — "history of Being"? In those years in which Heidegger attempted to retrieve metaphysics into a history of Being, he called truth a "becoming" and a "coming to pass" and thus "history." If truth is called a becoming and a coming to pass, however, is it not again conceived from a metaphysical system of reference, namely anti-metaphysically from the antithesis to Being which is posited as constant presence? If truth is called history, is it not then likewise conceived metaphysically from the antithesis to immutable eternity on the one hand, and to nature conceived at all events within set distinctions on the other? Nevertheless, Heidegger does not conceive history as the history of Being in this way, and therefore he has to dispense with such ambiguous titles as "historicality" and "history." What, for example, history is, in distinction to nature, is supposed to be made comprehensible primarily from the experience of the event of truth. This event, therefore, cannot be conceived on the basis of that derivative which can first be made comprehensi-

ble from it, and thus it cannot be conceived as "history." Talk of the history of Being or of the historicality of thought and truth, therefore, remain provisional and misleading. Heideger, overcoming his own position with question, thus introduces new words like fate, destiny and event. Instead of simply taking over such words and manners of speech, or instead of simply rejecting them as mere linguistic spinning and playing, the interpretation of Heidegger's work should attempt to develop the problem, which lies hidden behind the fact of his grappling with the matter of thought, that in his late work, e.g., he avoids a word like "historicality" which in large part came into circulation because of him.

The question with which Heidegger's thought is concerned is none other than the question of how philosophy is at all possible today and how philosophy belongs in the life of those men who are irresistably forced into a new, technical, but not simply technical age. If this present collection of interpretations of Heidegger's work* is able to make this state of affairs visible and thereby contribute in its way to the fact that the reception of Heidegger reaches beyond the simple paraphrasing of Heideggerian expositions, premature identification with his isolated tendencies, and blind polemics, then it will have fulfilled its task.

---

* Note: ref. to *Heidegger: Perspektiven zur Deutung seines Werks*, op. cit.

THE NATURE OF MAN AND THE WORLD OF NATURE FOR HEIDEGGER'S 80TH BIRTHDAY*

KARL LÖWITH

Emeritus Professor, *University of Heidelberg*

On this unique occasion I should first like to express my personal thanks for being allowed to take part, although I do not belong to those students who have developed philosophically the direction which you began. If I nevertheless feel like one of your students, the reason does not lie in my positive acceptance of your inquiry into Being. It lies, rather, in the fact that you were the only teacher who permitted me to experience what a philosophical lecture can offer in forcefulness and concentration, and that during the confusion following the First World War, you gave me decisive incentives for self-reflection, made stiff demands, set standards, and opened up perspectives. Or, expressed with one of your succinct words, you demonstrated 'differences' — the difference between what and who something is, and that whereby there is nothing. I would like to take the liberty of allowing you personally to speak with some passages from letters which you wrote to me between 1919 and 1929. They belong to my most valuable possessions which I have from my university days, and today I would like to thank you expressly for your having honored that twenty-two year old with your friendship. In 1925 you wrote to me: "One must be glad today when one stands outside of what attracts and does not attract. Where things age so quickly there must be a lack of soil . . . And since smartness and penmanship have become most unusual . . . one will only with difficulty be able to demonstrate the other 'nice' differences." (June 30, 1925). Concerning the evaluation of your work and the possibility of its be-

ing carried on further by pupils, however, I have relied on what you wrote to me personally in 1924: "What is accursed in my obligatory work is that it has to operate in the realm of ancient philosophy and theology, and I have to do it critically, with a view to inconsequential matters like "categories." It seems as if something's *having a corresponding content* is supposed to be contrasted by critique with what is negated. And as if my work were something for a school, a particular persuasion, continuation, supplementation! My work is unique in a limited way and can only be done by me—on account of the uniqueness of this constellation of conditions" (March 26, 1924). This individual uniqueness and solitude, from which your later great effectiveness could not mislead me, was, I felt, your essential distinction from Husserl. He, in accord with his idea of philosophy as strict science, wanted and was able to work so as to create a school, whereas, by contrast, you always persisted in the development of individual autonomy and even expected no immediate results from *Sein und Zeit*. "Whether one goes along with *Sein und Zeit* is a matter of complete indifference to me. I have never, even for one moment, expected that my work would directly and over night engender a real impetus. I would understand myself badly regarding what I wish to accomplish if I did not know that everything to begin with and over an

Karl Löwith is Professor Emeritus of Philosophy at the University of Heidelberg. His books include: From Hegel to Nietzsche, Martin Heidegger: Denker in durftiger Zeit, *and* Nature, History and Existentialism.

* Delivered in June, 1969, in Heidelberg, Germany, at a colloquium honoring Heidegger's 80th birthday. Subsequently published in *Die Frage Martin Heideggers, op. cit.* Translated by R. Phillip O'Hara.

extended period of time must go through the phase of idle talk. That out of this would come a new fashion, however, and that even the apparently well-intended professorial chit-chat aimed toward understanding would turn out to be so extremely superficial . . . , I would not even have dreamed of such a thing. I am thankful to destiny that I . . . am still made out of a wood which cannot be worn away by this murmuring and whining. If I had to base my own work on this business, I would rather decide on complete silence in spite of the inner necessities for creating." (September 3, 1929).

In the same letter you wrote me that the youth "do not want to know anything about making sects, and that they are thankful when they . . . are guided beyond all school quarrels and scholarly futility." With regard to your judgment of sects, the creating of schools and discipleship, I believe that it was not without your agreement that I quoted from Nietzsche (in the Foreword to my critical-polemical publication [1]): "One poorly repays a teacher when one always remains simply his pupil. And why do you not want to pull at my garland?" To be sure, the circle of your significant effectiveness certainly has not been diminished by the fact that I have pulled at it! The impetus which I received from you in my early years remained nevertheless—or precisely for that reason—continually effective. And I indeed did not first pull at your garland after my return from emigration, but in my inaugural dissertation.[2] Following your call to Marburg, you not only permitted, but incisively recommended that I go away and take advantage of an opportunity to earn my living in a bookstore in Rome, instead of sitting out the preparatory period for my anticipated inauguration into an academic career near you. "The opportunity in Rome comes just at the right moment. You would not be the first to prepare yourself in Italy for your inauguration into an academic career. Whether you work in a bookstore or collate manuscripts on the side . . . seems to make no difference to me. I would definitely take advantage of this opportunity. To sit here is an agonizing thing. In one way or another one tunes into and is interested in the respective business. If there were something which drove me to go to Japan — which is quite definitely out of the question — it would be the aspiration to withdraw from my "students," since it does not enter into their own minds to study somewhere else. Everything here is all clogged up anyway." (Aug. 21, 1924). When I then gave you my dissertation in 1927, you responded to me generously: "Whether or not you materially agree with me is for me no reason for acceptance of rejection; whether or not you have understood my work in all its elemental tasks is also no reason for acceptance or rejection. In your own interest I have occasionally made marginal comments that you here and there took the easy way out in your critique and underestimated the difficulties of the problems and their presuppositions. The indirect attacks and considered innuendoes are part of the atmosphere in which one publishes his first pieces. Such gestures calm down after a decade" (Aug. 20. 1927) — a far too optimistic prognosis! Since then four decades have passed without my desisting from such gestures. And two years later when I once was afraid that you had taken offence at my divergence, you wrote me: "How could I take offence with you over such matters as these! In that case I could have most comfortably and without much difficulty thwarted your inauguration into an academic career. Try to find one among the governing bigwigs who has inaugurated one of his students into an academic career, who wrote such an antithetical dissertation! I do

---

[1] *Heidegger, Denker in durftiger Zeit,* 1964. Regarding the question of nature, see pp. 61ff.
[2] *Das Individuum in der Rolle des Mitmenschen,* 1928, preliminary remark note 1.

not reckon that to my merit, but I am surprised . . . how little you . . . understand me in my conduct, when you suspect an irritation such as your comments suggest." (Feb. 3, 1929).

Why these personal reminiscences? Because my relationship to your philosophical life's work cannot well be mentioned without also including our personal relationship. If philosophy is a matter concerning the whole man, his "existence," then person and subject matter cannot be separated. During my first semesters in Freiburg I also wrote to you concerning this, because I could not, without further ado, combine your emphasis upon scientific-conceptual intention with the *existentielle* pathos as it was familiar to me from Nietzsche and Kierkegaard. "Initially the discussion is thwarted by the basic mistake that you and Becker evaluate me (hypothetically or not) by standards like Nietzsche, Kierkegaard . . . and some creative philosophers. That is not to be prevented—but one then must say that I am no philosopher, and I do not presume for myself that I am doing anything even comparable —I do not at all have this intention . . . Thus it cannot at all be settled which of the two of you correctly understands me — whose side I belong to and what I say is not supposed to be any idle meditation — to the contrary: you and Becker are equally distant from me — simply in different directions . . . I can emphasize research — but in a fundamentally different direction of concern from Becker — I consider the person decisively important —but only in those possibilities of fulfillment which I, to be honest, have at my disposal — without the intention of being creative — thus in danger — compared with the greats, of threshing empty straw — if from *my* own position I really do nothing more than thresh" (Aug. 19, 1921).

And now to the actual matter which concerns me in my relationship to your work. I studied philosophy and biology together and had already had inspiring instruction in biology at secondary school. Here, by the microscopic investigations of the flux of protoplasm in the filament of a blossom and of the motion of one-celled algae and infusoria, it occured to me for the first time what a marvel of organization the liveliness of an organism is. Accordingly, what I missed by the existential-ontological mode of inquiry was *nature* —which is all about us and in our own selves. When nature is lacking, however, a being or a realm of being among others is not lacking, but the totality of a being in its character as a being is mistaken, and it cannot be brought in supplementarily afterwards. For what is nature supposed to be if it is not the one nature of all beings, whose power of generation permits everything which in any way is — thus even man — to proceed from it and to pass away again? In *Sein und Zeit* nature seems to me to disappear in the existential understanding of facticity and throwness. To these observations — my earliest hesitation and opposition — you responded: "The 'nature' of man is not something for itself and pasted onto 'spirit.' The question is: is there a possibility of acquiring such a basic and guiding clue for the *conceptual* interpretation of *Dasein* from *nature* or from 'spirit' —or from neither of them? Or can we gain our clues primordially from the totality of the constitution of Being, in which one intentionally gives the *existentiale* priority in determining the possibility of ontology in general? For the anthropological interpretation, when taken ontologically, can be carried out only on the basis of a clarified ontological problematic in general" (Aug. 20, 1927). But when I confront the ontological question, irrespective of your emphasis on conceptual interpretation, I ask: what *is* this nature, which I presuppose as first and last? And I can only respond with the same answer which you once offered in reference to "Being": nature is "itself"— absolutely autonomous (*id quod substat*)[3]—it exists out of itself and is

---

[3] Regarding this see: *Das Individuum in der Rolle des Mitmenschen,* Reprint 1962, pp. 44f.

constantly moved. But as to the uncertain nature and non-nature of man,
I helped myself out of this dilemma
by attempting to comprehend existence,
as transcending and standing out from
nature, in terms of ontological ambiguity[4]: as a thinking nature man
can live personally only insofar as he
himself takes charge of his *Dasein*. But
he is able to take charge of himself
only because he is by nature already
there and lives, has a relationship to
himself and thinks. The traditional
designation of man as an *animal ra-
tionale* consequently returns, i.e., the
one which you all along the line oppose
and which you attribute to metaphysics'
forgetfulness of Being. It has the advantage that it does not unequivocally,
uniformly and unilaterally determine
man by soul and spirit or consciousness
and existence or as the "there" ("*Da*")
of Being (*Sein*), but as personal conflict of animality and rationality. The
most extreme mode of this conflict is
attested in the possibility of self-destruction: man is the only creature
which has the drive toward self-preservation, but also the "freedom towards
death." The decisive difference in the
point of departure and goal confronted me in this central part of the analysis of *Dasein*. For I was never satisfied
that the "Being towards death," which
was existentially-ontologically understood, could be isolated from the natural phenomenon of becoming decrepit
and dying. I did not think that in general an understanding of life should
be possible only by a private reduction
of the existential constitution of Being.[5]

Death in *Sein und Zeit* is *Dasein*'s
end which is to be brought into existence as part of each one's own Being-
in-the-world and 'Being-towards-death'
such that it is a possibility of authentic
existence. 'Freedom towards death,'
which is mentioned with double spac-
ing (§53) in reference to one's own
'potentiality for being a whole,' is based

precisely on the fact that no human
Dasein ever freely decided whether or
not it wanted to come into *Dasein*
(§44c). Man is cast into his there
(*Da*) and must therefore "take over"
himself with his perishable end in order
to be able to exist freely and to project
himself upon his possibilities. Freedom
towards death is the "highest instance"
of our Being-in-the-world (§63). But
this ultimate instance of existing freely is in no way to be understood as
the freedom to destroy oneself. To the
contrary: it throws man back upon his
momentary existence in order to permit
the imminence of death to become effective in this instance. On the other
hand, self-destruction would remove
from *Dasein* the basis for an existential
'Being towards death.'

In spite of this existential concept of
death, the possible reality of self-destruction is also considered. We can
see that it was on Heidegger's mind by
the allusion (§44c) to the "skeptic"
who in the "despair of suicide" brings
his life to an end and thereby also ex-
tinguishes his relation to the imminence
of death. Death interpreted existentially is and remains, however, a possibility of being which each *Dasein* itself ʹhas to take over. It is the utmost, most authentic and most individual possibility of being, which is unrelated to others and to other things
and is unsurpassable (§50). Death understood existentially is no perishing,
becoming decrepit and dying, but
rather dying is grounded existentially
in 'Being-towards-death'! The experience of death by others who have
died before us, thus the only experience
of death which we in fact have, has
as little interest from this perspective
as does the physiological process of dying. What concerns the existential
analysis of death is exclusively the possibility of relating oneself to it.

At this central part of the analysis
of *Dasein* I was unable to follow your

---

[4] *Ibid.*, pp. 22f.; cf. *Gesammelte Abhandlungen*, 1960, pp. 179ff. and 205ff.
[5] *Sein und Zeit*, 10; cf. regarding this E. Straus, "Philosophische Grundfragen der Psychiatrie
II, Psychiatrie und Philosophie" in: *Psychiatrie der Gegenwart*, 1963, pp. 928ff.

train of thought. When *Dasein* takes over itself, it is just not possible for it to take over its end in the same way, because the real end is not one's most individual possibility. It is rather a natural necessity which is before all of us, which we have in common with every man. Death equalizes and makes us equal. It is first death which teaches us in an irrefutable way that one man is like another. Death is not at all to be separated from the general phenomenon of life and decay. The birth and death, the beginning and end of every existence, whose natural presupposition is the process of procreation, are existentially not comprehensible, because they do not rest on a self-conscious and self-willed relation. They simply take place independently of our possibilities or our potentiality for being. And how could one ever acquire the idea of death as a being towards the imminence of one's own death if one had not seen others die? To be sure no one will deny that the experience of death which we have vis à vis others is something penetrating enough to allow us to perceive our general human perishableness. Such an experience of death is also something profoundly satisfying, because the deceased enters the fulfilled peace and quiet of a totally completed life. *Requiescat in pace* is and remains the most appropriate epitaph. More cannot be said about death. It is not a key to the understanding of our *Dasein,* but it belongs indeed to the nature of man in so far as he is an earthly creature. What can be frightening about death during life is not death itself, but rather the imaginary notion that one experiences it and the death-throes of the dying. "Death speaks to us with a deep voice in order to say nothing." [6]

One could add that sleep speaks to us with an inaudible voice in order to say that an analysis of man which is oriented around an awake *Dasein* suppresses half of human existence. As-

sume that we would one day fall asleep without waking up again and without our being able to relate to ourselves or to the world — then we would be dead. This shows that sleep is the other side of our total living existence. It is just as little to be separated from its life as each one's most individual being towards death is to be separated from the mortality of the creature.

The nature of man is revealed not only in his total corporeality, with its world-disclosing senses and sexual drive, but above all in the inconspicuous phenomenon that we sleep away one third of our existence and live without consciousness. Let us say that one does not presuppose the traditional ontology of a self-conscious being. He does not think of a self-conscious being as a being-for-oneself and as an existence which relates to itself, i.e., one does not think that man is as he knows himself to be and as he is in his conscious relations. Rather, when one makes clear to himself that he is also a man when he is not there for himself and when he does not relate to himself and to the world, namely when he is asleep, then the direction of his gaze is changed as to what and how man is in the totality of what naturally is.

In connection with a descriptive analysis of being awake by E. Straus [7] I would like to attempt to concretize my thesis on the nature of man. Every thought about oneself and the world and the relationship of one to the other presupposes that one is really awake and is not asleep and dreaming. These alternating conditions of the human *Dasein,* relative to which one is really "there" only while awake, goes hand in hand with a variety of bodily postures. For sleeping one lies down. Being awake begins with waking up and getting up and is itself a matter of being up. The organic functions continue unconsciously during sleep just as they

---

[6] E. Valéry, *Mauvaises Penseés,* ed. Pleiade II, p. 842.
[7] E. Straus, *Vom Sinn der Sinne,* 2nd Ed. 1956, pp. 279ff.

do while one is awake, but the total sensibility and motor functions, and with that the openness for the world around us, is reduced in the state of sleep. Man in sleep is withdrawn to himself, he lives in a dream world until in waking up again he returns to the daylight world which he shares with others. We are hardly awake before we connect up to the time before we fell asleep, as if nothing at all had happened in the intervening eight hours. We do not continue the life of our sleep, but deal with sleep simply as an interruption of our wakeful daytime life, which we take up again at the point where it was interrupted when we fell asleep. Thus we do not live simply continuously, but in a volatile continuation of an awake *Dasein* with its recollecting and anticipating passage of time. Birth, issuing forth into the light of the world, is the first elementary waking up which the new born child experiences in a presumably shocking way, but of which we have no personal consciousness and which we are unable to recall. We are not even able to recall the first four or five years which are so decisive for all further human development. But even after birth the new born child spends most of his time sleeping. This periodic change from being asleep to being awake is not pronounced among the lower animals. They are neither awake nor asleep. A regulated change according to the time of day is first established by an adult human. Civilized man can transgress and penetrate this natural determination. He can limit the time for sleeping to a few hours and can make the night into day, but in fact no man can live without sleep. In waking up man awakens to self-reliance and self-consciousness. It is first by means of this relation to ourselves that everything else is set off over against ourselves as something else. The self finds itself confronted. When by awakening I come to the consciousness of myself, I have already had the other experience that there is

something other than myself. Being awake is the establishment of the habitual distinction between self and other, a distinction which is again suspended in sleep. Falling asleep, the transition from being awake to sleeping, however, does not mean that sleeping is simply a reduced level of being awake. Falling asleep can require a longer or shorter period of time. But the transition as such takes place abruptly by means of a sudden and no longer conscious break in the continuity of awake life. All at once one is no longer there for oneself, but gone and present only for others who are awake. One is even present for them differently than before. Waking up takes place just as abruptly as falling asleep, even if a partial consciousness preceeds it before one opens his eyes and gets up. In order to fall asleep one closes his eyes, i.e., one closes oneself off from the sensual impression of the world around him. What one experiences while sleeping in dreams, is, even if it is dreamed in a lively manner, nevertheless always a dream world in which the laws of waking life do not apply. In a dream everything can be transformed into each other. Persons, events, things shift, superimpose, and compress themselves. A person can look like A, act, however, like B, and be transformed into a third person. Everything can merge without any resistance. What is forgotten in waking life, what is suppressed and repressed, can reappear in a dream. Something which has long been forgotten can be recollected just as, vice versa, something in the future is sometimes sensed before hand. In a dream one is immediately with oneself, but not, as in waking life, with oneself by *being something else,* because the life of a dream does not know the act of self-differentiation. One has attempted again and again to ascertain an objective criterion for differentiating being awake from dreaming, with the negative result that there is no such a thing. This is explained by the fact that the distinction between being awake and dreaming results just in the act of self-differentiation, and self-differentiation is the sudden awakening from one's dreams. Even when one dreams that one is dreaming, one is not therefore awake, and the doubt whether something was simply dreamed or actually happened may not be theoretically eliminated.

In Rosenkranz's anthropology, which is oriented on Hegel's *Phänomenologie des Geistes*,[8] sleep and its dream world are rightly interpreted from awake life and in the direction of awake life insofar as sleep and its dreams are a privation of awake and conscious life and insofar as they are unable to understand and interpret themselves. Everything which is unconscious is interpreted as something not conscious from the perspective of consciousness, and when one wants to know what sleep and dreams and the unconscious are, one is not permitted to sleep and dream and unconsciously live on. In spite of this methodological priority of consciousness and self-conscious spirit for understanding those processes which, in accord with their essence, take place without consciousness, we can see nonetheless that the 'primordial' condition of man before birth, in the literal sense of the word, is that of unconscious sleep. We daily return to this primordial condition because even the awake adult cannot live purely as conscious being. If he were able to do this, he would not be an embodied human being, but a natureless spirit or a ghost.

The presupposition of the ontology of consciousness from Descartes to Hegel and continuing to the philosophy of existence is that being which is conscious of itself and has a relation to itself is decisive even for an understanding of being which is unconsciously alive. But that is a presupposition which is only half the truth. If it were taken for the whole truth,

it would be false, for a mode of human *Dasein,* not determined by awake consciousness, precedes self-conscious being. The circumstance that consciousness is decisive for *understanding* the unconscious does not mean that it is also decisive for what something alive *is,* namely something that is other and more than a simple lack of self-consciousness. Even if one assumed that all pre-conscious, subconscious, and unconscious being were oriented towards becoming conscious, the other half of the whole truth would then still be no less true, namely, that even during our conscious and awake living and existing most things take place without consciousness, and in general we do not know how sleep and to what extent the *physis* of a living person reaches into his conscious existence. The total vegetative and organic processes take place even in man during his whole life unconsciously and therefore with great certainty. We could not even think and speak if our brain were not constantly saturated with blood. One can also not think simply because one consciously wishes to think. Something must involuntarily occur to one's mind, thoughts must come to and befall someone and connect themselves to each other. But they also do not come to someone from a lifeless and natureless being, which intends itself for us and addresses itself to us.

Corresponding to the nature of *man,* I also attempted to proceed from nature with respect to *world.* For our corporeal senses, the world is a world of nature, because our senses, with which we perceive the things of the world, are themselves a product of nature. We may assume right from the start, that they correspond respectively to that which is perceived. The eye develops with and in light for light. The world of nature, formally defined, is the unity and totality of everything which exists from nature. The context, which uniformly holds together everything individual and divergent as

---

[8] K. Rosenkranz, *Psychologie, Wissenschaft vom subjectiven Geist,* 1837.

a totality, can only be an order in which everything is co-ordinated with something else. Although man may very much stand out from nature, ex-ist, transcend and reflect, he nevertheless is not precluded from belonging to and being co-ordinated with the totality of the natural world, even if he is not directly aware of it. This co-ordination, e.g., of our corporeal movement and orientation towards the magnetic field of the earth via a certain organ in the inner ear, takes place just as unconsciously as the orientation of birds of passage according to the rotating position of the sun. This order, which harmonizes the multitude into a unity of the whole, is not to be taken as ordering at one time thus and at another time some other way. To be an order, it must always be just as it is. That, however, which is always just as it is and which can not be something else, is called necessary. If the world were not a dependable world order in the totality of its movement, then it would be no world. And if it is assumed that its realms are more or less complete, then its co-ordination would at the same time be an order of precedence and one could not avoid the question: What level does man assume in the totality of natural beings? Measured on the totality of the physical world, it is presumably a very subordinate one. For this world can be conceived without an essential relationship to man's *Dasein,* but no man is conceivable without the world.[9] We enter into the world, and we depart from it. It does not belong to us, but we belong to it. This world of nature is always itself, and it does not change according to the measure of our capricious world-interpretation. It was the same in Aristotle's time as in Newton's and Einstein's. The world of

nature never permits itself to be sufficiently determined relative to our conduct and understanding. Elemental nature reveals itself to us in an especially obtrusive way in relation to an environment cultivated by man, but the elements themselves, say the power of fire and water, cannot be appropriately understood when one takes a flood control project or a heating-installation as the point of departure. What one discovers in this way is always simply what you called the "environmental world" of our most proximate world. Only this most proximate world can be presented in a convincing way as a "totality of involvement" of referential connections. These connections all refer to a 'for-the-sake-of," from which everything in the environment is structured in the sense of an "in-order-to" and a "towards-this," an "upon-which," a "with-which" and a "for-which." But let one leave his four walls and his home town, the historical land and people to which one accidently belongs, let him step out of civilization—then the elemental force and monotonous magnitude of *the* world, which is not ours and which does not refer to us as its "for-the-sake-of," but refers only to itself, *that* world will possibly be manifest to the contemporary cave-dwellers of the historical world of man.

Since *Sein und Zeit* one indeed often speaks of *Dasein* as Being-in-the-world, but the world of *Dasein* is not the ordered comos. It is our most proximate and more distant world of human involvement (*Mitwelt*) and our environment (*Umwelt*). We need not deny that this world, understood in this way, is our most intimate and daily world, but the question must indeed be raised whether from this daily

---

[9] In opposition to this, Heidegger expresses in "Was ist Metaphysik?" (5th ed., p. 13) "the all-sustaining conjecture" that human nature is essential for Being itself and that Being needs nature. Cf. regarding this point *Einführung in die Metaphysik,* pp. 124 and 156; *Holzwege,* pp. 337ff.; *Vorträge und Aufsätze,* pp. 41 and 99; *Was heisst Denken,* pp. 114ff; *Identität und Differenz,* pp. 23ff.; *Satz vom Grund,* pp. 146 and 157; *Gelassenheit,* pp. 64ff.; *Unterwegs zur Sprache,* pp. 30, 155, 197, 254, 260f.

THE NATURE OF MAN AND THE WORLD OF NATURE

world the world itself *in toto* becomes accessible. In the end the world first begins to appear where it no longer runs along at *Dasein*'s leash, but where it revolves about itself. The uttermost extremity of the world which appears in the existential perspective is that the world-building *Dasein* is at the same time also thoroughly determined and ruled by that which it surpasses, and that it is fascinated and captivated by beings *in toto,* in the midst of which *Dasein* is. The converse correspondence of comporting oneself towards and finding oneself in, of projection and throwness, of surpassing and captivation, in general, of power and powerlessness, simply illustrates once again that your interpretation of "Being-in" as well as of "being-in-the-midst-of" results from a *Dasein* which is concerned primarily, not with the totality of the world, but for its ownmost potentiality-for-being-a-whole. In the essay "Vom Wesen des Grundes," in which the world-analysis of *Sein und Zeit* is continued, a positive stance is taken towards the anthropological world concept. The discussion proceeds from the fact that "comos" does not so much designate the totality of what is, as it designates a mode of being. The totality of beings can be composed in a cosmic way or chaotically. Instead of concluding, however, that the world, understood in a Greek manner, is primarily a world-order,[10] it is asserted that it was not first the world understood in a Christian manner that is relative to the human *Dasein,* but rather that it is the Greek cosmos, which is relative to the human *Dasein,* although the cosmos encompasses *Dasein* at the same time. In this view, Christianity simply sharpened and clarified the essential relation of the world to man. To substantiate this relativity of the world to *Dasein* you appeal to the eighty-ninth Fragment of Heraclitus, where it says that those who are awake live in a common

world, but that those who sleep live in their own individual worlds. But does this distinction imply that the world of those who are awake, just as the world of those who are asleep, "belongs" to man's *Dasein* and is thus relative to us and is nothing in itself? Or does this sentence of Heraclitus not rather imply the reverse, that the cosmos—"which is that same for everything and everybody" — only appears real to those who are awake, namely in its super-human self-constancy? The Greek cosmos has a relation to man only insofar as the just order of man's world also refers to the ideal world order *in toto.* A being which is disordered with himself, which essentially "exists"—in "border situations" or as a "thrown facticity" or even as an "opening" in the totality of beings in themselves, and which exists "for itself"— cannot discover the cosmos-character of the world and the naturalness of nature. Nature cannot disclose itself to any supersensual, incorporeal *Dasein. Sein und Zeit* speaks of nature only insofar as it is an inner-worldly being among other beings and a "limiting-case," because it neither ex-ists like man, nor is it "ready-to-hand" like equipment, nor is "present-at-hand" like a stone. That there is a different involvement with living nature than with inner-worldly being and with the world as the "for-the-sake-of-which," is mentioned, albeit in a footnote,[11] but without questioning the existential starting point of the world analysis. Even the experience of nature is supposed to be based on care. A reversal of the direction of inquiry first occurs in the essay "Vom Ursprung des Kunstwerks" and regarding "Das Ding," where heaven and earth are first mentioned.

With that I would like to conclude my attempt to vindicate the world of nature which in itself is beyond all question and is speechless overagainst

[10] Cf. regarding this the *Gesammelte Abhandlungen,* 1960, pp. 238ff., by the author.
[11] *Vom Wesen des Grundes,* 1929, p. 95, note 2.

the question of Being. In one point, however, I think I am at one with you, in spite of all inadequate critique and deficient explication: that what is essential is something simple — for me, perhaps, something all too simple.

HEIDEGGER'S QUESTION: AN EXPOSITION

ALEXANDER VON SCHOENBORN

The University of Texas at Austin

The first task in seeking to understand Heidegger's work is, as Poeggeler has reminded us, "... first to hear the one question meditated on by Heidegger."[1] This question is the question of being (*die Seinsfrage*). I shall here attempt an exposition of this question as construed by Heidegger at and around the time of the publication of *Sein und Zeit*.

Such an exposition calls for laying out the question of being in the manner it happens to have been formulated by Heidegger. But such a laying out does not suffice. For, as Heidegger notes, "the question of being does not attain its true concretion until we have carried out the process of destroying the ontological tradition" in terms of which this question is formulated.[2] In other words, the question of being becomes genuinely askable and appropriate in form only when that which it seeks and the manner in which it happens to be formulated can be exhibited as an authentic appropriation of the pertinent tradition and thus as required. I will therefore first lay out Heidegger's question as he happened to formulate it at the time specified, and then sketch those historical reasons which led him to the view that this formulation is the one the question of being must take.

Only in the circumscription of the locus of this question in the tradition does the specific direction of Heidegger's path of inquiry become clear.[3] This clarification in turn both permits and requires greater focus on the roadsigns involved, especially on that matter for thought labeled "being and time" which Heidegger emphasizes as "the roadsign" of his *Denkweg*.[4]

An initial and deceptively simple characterization is provided by Heidegger himself in commenting on the classical metaphysical question about the *on hēi on*.

In the question what a being is as such, we wish to know what determines a being as a being [*was ueberhaupt das Seiende zum Seienden bestimmt*]. We call it the being of beings [*das Sein des Seienden*] and the question which is concerned with it the question of being. This question investigates that which determines a being as such. This determinant is to be recognized in the how of its determining and to be interpreted as such and such, i.e., it is to be conceptually grasped. In order, however, to be able to conceive the essential determination of beings through being, the determinant must itself be sufficiently graspable. It is necessary first to comprehend *being as such* and this comprehension must precede that of that-which-is [*das Seiende*] as such. Thus the question *ti to on* (what is that-which-is) implies a more original question: What does the being already pre-

Alexander von Schoenborn is presently Assistant Professor of Philosophy at The University of Texas at Austin. He received his Ph.D. from Tulane University in 1971 and has several previous publications dealing with Heidegger's work.

1 Otto Poeggeler, *Der Denkweg Martin Heideggers* (Pfullingen: Guenther Neske Verlag, 1963), p. 14.
2 Martin Heidegger, *Sein und Zeit* (Tuebingen: Max Niemeyer Verlag, 1957), p. 26.
3 Martin Heidegger, *Ueber den Humanismus* (Frankfurt am Main: Vittorio Klostermann Verlag, 1947), p. 47.
4 Martin Heidegger, *Holzwege* (Frankfurt am Main: Vittorio Klostermann Verlag, 1957), p. 195.

understood in that question signify?[5]

Yet, even in this "more original question," what is asked about exhibits a structural diversity which requires that Heidegger's question be specified further.

One of the aspects included in Heidegger's question are the various possible regional ontologies. Thus, in understanding something *as* something there is involved a prior implicit understanding of the latter's essential what-being, which in turn implies some understanding of the what-content of a being-domain, of a region of beings. Heidegger considers the elucidation of such a regional *a priori* and of the interconnection of various such regions a legitimate ontological task.[6] But he not only does not engage in this task;[7] he claims that it cannot fruitfully be engaged in until his own question has received a sufficiently determinate answer as "an *a priori* condition of the possibility" of such regional ontologies.[8] Thus regional ontologies are but one aspect, methodologically posterior, of the ontological problem as envisioned by Heidegger.

A second aspect presents itself when we turn from being as what-being or essence to that-and-how-being. Heidegger distinguishes multiple modes of existence—using "existence" here in its classical sense rather than in its Heideggerian usage where it is applied only to the being of man or Dasein—and much of *Sein und Zeit*, among other works, is taken up by an analysis of such modes as readiness-to-hand

(*Zuhandenheit*), presence-at-hand (*Vorhandenheit*), existence etc. But all such analyses "are to be evaluated *only* in terms of making possible the question of being"[9] and Heidegger cautions throughout *Sein und Zeit* that adequate explication, in contrast to preliminary characterization, will have to be consequent upon an answer to his question.

Heidegger's comments and attitudes are the same when we turn to those further aspects classically termed the categories and the transcendentals, to some of which, notably being-true, he devotes extensive attention. Thus he writes:

All ontology, no matter how rich and firmly compacted a system of categories it has at its disposal, remains blind and perverted from its ownmost aim, if it has not first adequately clarified the meaning of being, and conceived this clarification as its fundamental task.[10]

In short, Heidegger's question includes all of these aspects and their structural interrelations as what is asked about (*das Gefragte*). But they are not as yet what is to be found out by the asking (*das Erfragte*).[11] What then has been neglected? What has been neglected thus far is what, in the quotation immediately above, is referred to as "the meaning of being."

Heidegger's conception of meaning is both complex and difficult. For the present purpose, it must suffice to note that, according to Heidegger, all understanding exhibits a fore-structure of possibilities in terms of which what is

[5] Martin Heidegger, *Kant und das Problem der Metaphysik* (Frankfurt am Main: Vittorio Klostermann Verlag, 1959), p. 201.
[6] Heidegger, *Sein und Zeit*, p. 241.
[7] Brock's and Langan's suggestions to the contrary, i.e., that *Sein und Zeit* is the mapping of one such region, are simply mistaken. Cf. Werner Brock, 'An Account of *Being and Time*' in Martin Heidegger *Existence and Being* (Chicago: Henry Regnery Co., 1949, p. 33. Cf. also Thomas Langan, *The Meaning of Heidegger* (New York: Columbia University Press, 1961), p. 56.
[8] Heidegger, *Sein und Zeit*, p. 11.
[9] Martin Heidegger, *Vom Wesen des Grundes* (Frankfurt am Main: Vittorio Klostermann Verlag, 1955), n. 59, p. 42.
[10] Heidegger, *Sein und Zeit*, p. 11.
[11] *Ibid.*, pp. 5–6.

to be understood is understood and interpreted as what it is and how it is. This fore-structure, in terms of which or whence something becomes intelligible, Heidegger terms "meaning."[12] The latter must be made explicit if the understanding of something is to become conceptual knowledge. In reference to the problematic of being as developed thus far, this means the following:

The question of "first philosophy" namely, "What is a being [*das Seinde*] as such?" must force us back beyond the question "What is being [*das Sein*] as such?" to the still more fundamental question: Whence are we to comprehend a notion such as that of being, with the many articulations and relations it includes?[13]

That "whence" is the meaning of being sought by Heidegger.

How is the search for this "whence" to proceed? It is to proceed by making explicit, and thus bringing to conceptual articulation, what is already implicit. By this, Heidegger means that "the question of being as the question about the possibility of the concept of being arises from the pre-conceptual understanding of being."[14] This understanding of being is not a mode of knowledge, hence called "preontological" by Heidegger,[15] but it is constitutive of the being of Dasein. "But then the question of being is nothing other than the radicalization of an essential tendency-of-being which belongs to Dasein itself—the pre-ontological understanding of being."[16] This recognition in turn modifies the

question of being, for that question "as the question about the possibility of being" must now become the question about "the nature of the understanding of being in general."[17] Thus the task is to illuminate the inner possibility of the latter. Since this understanding is, as mentioned, constitutive of the being of Dasein, the first step in this illuminating must be "the unveiling of the being-constitution [*Seinsverfassung*] of Dasein.[18] This "unveiling" does not seek to proffer a complete ontology of Dasein. Rather, its limits are set by "the guiding task of working out the question of being."[19] Methodologically, it takes the form of a phenomenological hermeneutic of the existentiality of existence.[20]

Now the actual analyses seeking to implement the above program of an analytic of Dasein bring to light temporality "as the meaning of the being of the entity we call Dasein."[21] This result does not constitute an answer to the question of being, but it does, according to Heidegger, provide the basis for that answer.

We have already intimated that Dasein has pre-ontological being as its ontically constitutive state. Dasein *is* in such a way entitatively as to understand something like being. Keeping this interconnection firmly in mind, we shall show that whence Dasein implicitly understands and interprets something like being is time. Time must be brought to light and genuinely conceived as the horizon for all understanding of being and for every interpretation

12 *Ibid.*, pp. 151–152.
13 Heidegger, *Kant und das Problem der Metaphysik*, p. 203.
14 *Ibid.*, p. 204.
15 Martin Heidegger, *Vom Wesen des Grundes* (Frankfurt am Main: Vittorio Klostermann Verlag, 1955, p. 14. Cf. Heidegger, *Sein und Zeit*, p. 12.
16 Heidegger, *Sein und Zeit*, p. 15. Cf. Heidegger, *Vom Wesen des Grundes*, p. 14.
17 Heidegger, *Kant und das Problem der Metaphysik*, p. 204.
18 *Ibid.*, p. 209. Cf. Heidegger, *Sein und Zeit*, p. 16.
19 Heidegger, *Sein und Zeit*, p. 17. Cf. Martin Heidegger, *Was ist Metaphysik?* (Frankfurt am Main: Vittorio Klostermann Verlag, 1960), p. 16.
20 Heidegger, *Sein und Zeit*, p. 38.
21 *Ibid.*, p. 17.

of it. For this to become visible, there is required an original explication of time as the horizon for the understanding of being, and in terms of temporality as the being of Dasein, which understands being.[22]

If, moreover, time serves as horizon for any understanding of being, it follows that being itself exhibits "Temporal" character. Hence, the question of being culminates in "working out the Temporality of being."[23]

The preceding is, at least in programmatic outline, what Heidegger construes as his task and the way he seeks to carry out that task. But, as indicated earlier, any such outline must remain incomplete and abstract as long as it does not adduce those historical reasons which dictate the specific formulation Heidegger gives to the question of being. I thus now turn to this latter requirement.

I noted earlier that the first step in illuminating the inner possibility of "the nature of the understanding of being in general" must be the unveiling of the being-constitution of Dasein. In taking the first step, Heidegger unveils the essential historicity of Dasein, and hence asking about being is itself subject to this characterization. The question of being, as thus an historical inquiry, intrinsically demands inquiry into the history of that inquiry. Questioning, must therefore, take a form

> in which by taking the *question of being as our clue*, we are to *destroy* the traditional content of ... ontology until we arrive at those primordial experiences in which we achieved our first ways of determining the

nature of being—the ways which have guided us ever since.[24]

The "primordial experiences" here mentioned include that which was ingredient in these experiences without attaining to articulation. The "destruction"—whose intent is positive and not, as so frequently alleged, destructive—is therefore not only an appropriation but also a transformation of the tradition.

The heeding hearing, for which the "destruction" makes us free and which in turn makes adequate destruction possible, Heidegger terms "repetition." Repetition is that modality of Dasein's being in which Dasein relates authentically and explicitly to the tradition in which it stands and which, in some sense, it itself is.[25] Hence, Heidegger can say that

> to ask "How does the matter stand with being?" entails no less than to repeat [*wieder-holen*] the beginning of our historico-spiritual Dasein in order to transform it into another beginning.... But a beginning is not repeated by worming oneself back to it as something past and now known and merely to be imitated. Instead, the beginning must again be begun, but more originally [*urspruenglicher*] and this, of course, with all the strangeness, darkness and insecurity that a true beginning carries with it.[26]

Since *Sein und Zeit* is such a repetition,[27] it is hardly surprising that the first section of the first chapter of that work is entitled "The Necessity of Explicitly Repeating the Question of Being."[28]

Though the above sufficiently es-

[22] *Ibid.*
[23] *Ibid.*, p. 19: 'temporal' and 'Temporalitaet' are translated by 'Temporal' and 'Temporality.' The use of capitals is to distinguish these terms from 'temporal' and 'temporality' as translations of 'zeitlich' and 'Zeitlichkeit.' Cf. Martin Heidegger, *Being and Time* translated by John Macquarrie and Edward Robinson (New York: Harper and Row, 1962), n. 3, p. 38.
[24] Heidegger, *Sein und Zeit*, p. 22.
[25] *Ibid.*, p. 385.
[26] Martin Heidegger, *Einfuehrung in die Metaphysik* (Tuebingen: Max Niemeyer Verlag, 1958), pp. 29–30. Cf. p. 146.
[27] Heidegger, *Kant und das Problem der Metaphysik*, p. 216. Cf. p. 218.
[28] Heidegger, *Sein und Zeit*, p. 2.

tablishes the intrinsic unity of the question of being, as I unfolded it earlier, and the destructive repetition just discussed, we still lack a bill of particulars. The destruction is, after all, not only to indicate the necessity of posing the question of being, but also to provide clues as to how this question needs to be posed. This was to be the function of the second part of *Sein und Zeit*.[29] But this part, together with the third division of the first part, was never published. In commenting on this fact in his Preface to the seventh German edition, Heidegger refers the reader to another work, namely his *Introduction to Metaphysics*.[30] It is to this work, "a meditation on the origin of our *hidden history*,"[31] that we must turn for the requisite bill of particulars.

The largest part of this work consists of an analysis of the initial delimitation of being through the Greeks' differentiation between being and becoming, being and appearance, being and thought, and being and the ought. It is not readily possible nor, for my present purpose, necessary to summarize Heidegger's detailed exegeses of the various Greek poets and thinkers, notably Parmenides and Heraclitus, or his explanation of the genesis of these four differentiations in terms of the interpretation of the nature of truth. Instead, I will focus on those ensuing conclusions which deal with the repetition I am trying to explicate.

"In the differentiations presented, being is delimited against an other and thus, *in* this de-limiting posing of boundaries, already has a determination."[32] This delimitation occurs in four respects which are mutually and necessarily interrelated. Among these four, the differentiation between being and thought has a unique and preeminent role. Why? We saw earlier, in specific reference to the question of being, that being is always already somehow understood. "All understanding, however, must, as a fundamental mode of revealing [*Eroeffnung*], move within a specific view-path [*Blickbahn*]."[33] This view-path, here called "the 'perspective',"" we encountered earlier as the "whence" and as horizon. Now it is Heidegger's contention that the initial pre-Socratic belonging-together of being and thought increasingly gave way to a separating out of *logos* from *physis* and that this separated *logos*, due to changes in the understanding and interpretation of truth, became qua assertion (*Aussage*), "the controlling view-path for the interpretation of being."[34] This contention might be given the primarily methodological sense illustrated, for example, in the fifth book of the *Metaphysics*, a book of definitions, where Aristotle, in dealing with "being as such," refers us to the schemata of the categories, or to the multiple ways we speak about being, instead of proffering the expected definition.[35] But this methodological sense is only a consequence. The point of Heidegger's contention is that, given this particular view-path, being cannot manifest itself as itself, i.e., in its truth, and that thought consequently attains to "dominance over being"[36] by becoming its "carrying and determining ground."[37] This dominance, which might be granted readily enough in such cases as the

---

[29] *Ibid.*, p. 39.
[30] *Ibid.*, p. V.
[31] Heidegger, *Einfuehrung in die Metaphysik*, p. 70.
[32] *Ibid.*, p. 152, Cf. p. 72.
[33] *Ibid.*, p. 89.
[34] *Ibid.*, p. 144. Cf. Martin Heidegger, *Die Frage nach dem Ding* (Tuebingen: Max Niemeyer Verlag, 1962), p. 49.
[35] Aristotle, *Metaphysics* 5. 7. 1017a 22–25.
[36] Heidegger, *Einfuehrung in die Metaphysik*, p. 94.
[37] *Ibid.*, p. 149.

work of Descartes or of Kant, is seen by Heidegger as not only becoming explicit already in Plato but as the fundamental trait of the course of the history of philosophy and thus of the Western tradition up to and including the present.[38] Finally, Heidegger also concludes that the significance (*Bedeutung*) of "being" as differentiated in this four-fold manner is, in each case, that of "constant presence."[39]

Granted these conclusions, it becomes readily feasible to ascertain some of the "moves" required if the question of being is to be raised as a repetition of that tradition. And the requiredness of these "moves" is their historical justification.

Heidegger points out that these "powers" standing opposed to being—becoming, illusion, thought, and the ought—themselves are. In fact, they "are more so [*seiender*] than what is taken as being [*seiend*] in accordance with the de-limited essential determination of being [*Sein*]." But if we go on to ask in terms of what meaning of being these powers might be said to be, it becomes clear that this cannot be that meaning against which they are differentiated, i.e., the meaning that is and has been current throughout the tradition.[40]

Thus the [following] insight arises out of the original questioning through the four separations [*Scheidungen*]: being, which is delimited [*eingekreist*] by them, must itself be transformed into the encompassing circle and the ground of all that is. *The* original separation, the closeness and original moving-out-of-itself [*Auseinandertreten*] which

carries history, is the differentiation of being and beings [*Unterscheidung von Sein und Seienden*].[41] This differentiation, termed "the ontological difference" by the early Heidegger[42] and simply "the difference" by the later,[43] is the theme of his lifelong quest.

What is thus required, then, is a thinking of the ontological difference. How is this requirement to be met? Here too the tradition in which we stand provides the requisite clue. As I noted above, the separation of being and thought serves as the ground for the determination of being in and as that tradition.

The thinking guided by the *logos* as assertion gives and receives the view-path within which being is sighted.

If, consequently, being itself is to be opened up and grounded in *its* original differentiation from that which is, then there is required the opening up of an original view-path.[44]

This requires and presupposes the overcoming of the extant view-path. The latter can be overcome only *originally*, that is, in such a way that its initial truth is placed into its own limits and thereby newly grounded.[45]

These limits consist, at least in part, of the requirement that emerges from our discussion of the ontological difference: thinking must allow for and be exhibited as belonging to being. Whatever the precise character of thought, it is constitutive of human being. Hence, a new determination of thought entails a new determination of human nature as related to being. The

[38] Perhaps the clearest exposition of this his thesis can be found in Martin Heidegger, *Kants These ueber das Sein* (Frankfurt am Main: Vittorio Klostermann Verlag, 1963), pp. 29–36 *passim*.

[39] *Ibid.*, p. 154.

[40] *Ibid.*, p. 155.

[41] *Ibid.*, p. 156.

[42] Heidegger, *Vom Wesen des Grundes*, p. 15.

[43] Martin Heidegger, *Identitaet und Differenz* (Pfullingen: Guenther Neske Verlag, 1957), p. 46.

[44] Heidegger, *Einfuehrung in die Metaphysik*, p. 156.

[45] *Ibid.*, p. 89.

question of being is thus intrinsically connected with the question as to who man is. But the latter question is, as we saw earlier, determined in its scope and direction by the question of being.

Within the question of being, the nature of man is to be conceived and grounded, in accordance with the hidden indication of the beginning, as *the locus* (*die Staette*) which being requires for its revelation. Man is the in itself open there, into which beings stand.... We say, consequently, that the being of man is, in the strict sense of the word, the 'there-being' [*Da-sein*[. In the nature of Dasein as such locus of the revelation of being must be originally grounded the view-path for the revealing of being.[46]

This passage contains, in germ, a number of key Heideggerian doctrines. But more important for my present purpose, we now have the requisite key for making sense of Heidegger's claim that *Sein und Zeit*, though consisting, as published, of an hermeneutic interpretation of being-in-the-world and its meaning, is a repetition of the question of being. For Heidegger claims that

if the distinction of Dasein lies in that, understanding being, it comports itself towards beings, then that power to differentiate, in which the ontological difference becomes factical, must have taken the root of its own possibility in the ground of the nature of Dasein. This ground of the ontological difference we term anticipatorily the "transcendence" of Dasein.[47]

Dasein understands beings in the light of an antecedent understanding of their being. This latter understanding is a peculiar passing over and beyond beings to their being, a transcending of beings towards their being. But this transcending is not exhausted by an understanding of the being-constitution of a region of beings or even of several such regions; transcending also involves, as prior condition, the understanding of the inner unity and organization of such ontological regions in their totality. This prior understanding Heidegger terms "passing over to world"[48] or, more frequently, "being-in-the-world." Being-in-the-world is thus a structural determination of transcendence.[49]

Though this explains how the published content of *Sein und Zeit* can be designated a "repetition," it does not yet explain why that repetition should bear the title it does. In short, what does time have to do with the question of being and with the interconnected question about transcendence and its meaning? To answer this question, we only need to see the connection between the last of the conclusions drawn by Heidegger from his analysis of the Greek beginning and the as yet unfulfilled requirement of an adequate view-path or horizon, grounded in the nature of Dasein, for the question of being. The conclusion in question is that being as first delimited in the Greek beginning signifies constant presence (*staendige Anwesenheit*). But if this is so, "what then underlies, ununveiled [*unenthuellt*], the nature of constancy and the nature of presence other than time?" This means that "time is the *view-path guiding* the revealing of being in the beginning of Western philosophy, but in such a way that this view-path remained, and had to remain, hidden *as such*."[50] This view-path must be appropriated and made explicit as the horizon of all understanding of being. If "being" is

---

[46] *Ibid.*, p. 156.
[47] Heidegger, *Vom Wesen des Grundes*, pp. 15–16.
[48] *Ibid.*, p. 37.
[49] *Ibid.*, p. 20.
[50] Heidegger, *Einfuehrung in die Metaphysik*, p. 157.

here taken to refer not only to the beingness of beings, but to the full ontological difference, then this understanding is transcendence as the being of Dasein. Hence this explication must occur in terms of the being of Dasein. As Heidegger puts it programmatically in a passage already cited in my elaboration of the question of being:

> There is required an original explication of time as the horizon for the understanding of being, and in terms of temporality as the being of Dasein, which understands being.[51]

But whereas my earlier reference to this text sought to indicate how the phrase "being and time" describes the way Heidegger happens to formulate the question of being, we should now understand how that same phrase designates the matter for thought imposed on us as task (*das Aufgegebene*) by the tradition in which we stand and how consequently it designates the formulation which the question of being must take.[52]

I began this paper by laying out Heidegger's formulation of the question of being. I did so by tracing his progressive radicalization of the classical question about the *on hēi on*. In then showing how that which the *Seinsfrage* seeks and the manner in which this question is formulated are dictated by the tradition in and from which this question arises, I have now completed this brief exposition.

---

[51] Heidegger, *Sein und Zeit*, p. 17.
[52] Heidegger, *Einfuehrung in die Metaphysik*, p. 157.

HEIDEGGER ON TIME AND BEING

JOSEPH J. KOCKELMANS
Pennsylvania State University

Introduction

On January 31, 1962, Heidegger gave a lecture at the University of Freiburg in a Studium Generale directed by Eugen Fink. The title of the lecture, *Zeit und Sein,*[1] is a reference to the third section of the first part of *Being and Time,* which was originally announced under that title in 1927, but not published at the time. The first part of *Being and Time* was devoted to an interpretation of *Dasein* in terms of temporality, and to an explanation of time as the transcendental horizon for the question concerning the meaning of Being.[2] In 1927, however, Heidegger felt he was not able to deal adequately with the theme indicated by the title of the third section of Part I of the book and decided therefore to publish his work in incomplete form. In 1962 Heidegger stated explicitly that the lecture, *Zeit und Sein,* represented an attempt to solve the question which had been left unanswered in *Being and Time*; what he said in his lecture on the issue, however, is substantially different from what he would have said about it, had the essay been written in 1927. "That which is contained in the text of this lecture, written 35 years later, can no longer be linked up with the text of *Sein und Zeit*," Heidegger wrote. "And yet the leading question has remained the same; however, this simply means that the question has become still more questionable and still more alien to the spirit of the time."[4]

A first reading of the text shows that in 1962 Heidegger continued to subcribe to the *basic* ideas developed in *Being and Time.* Therefore, however new this essay may be in many aspects, one must read it so that its interpretation will remain in harmony with the basic conception of his original view.[5] On the other hand it is clear, also, that the text of the lecture contains many elements which transcend the general perspective of *Being and Time.* This is due mainly to the fact that Heidegger's investigations from 1927 to 1962 on the meaning of Being (*Sein*) opened up new insights which could not have been expected on the basis of *Being and Time* in 1927. One sees in the Time-lecture, too, that whereas Heidegger's view on the meaning of Being and the aboriginal Event (*Ereignis*) is the same as that found in the main works written from 1935 to 1962, the conception of time defended in it is relatively new, and the explanation of the relationship between time and Being and their mutual relationship to the aboriginal Event (which constitute the main themes of the lecture), again move along lines which are new and partly even surprising.

Joseph J. Kockelmans, born in the Netherlands, is currently professor of philosophy at Pennsylvania State University. He has studied mathematics, physics, and philosophy. Among his publications are: three anthologies, six books pertaining to the realm of philosophy of science, two books on Husserl's phenomenology, and two books on Heidegger. He has taught at the New School for Social Research and at the University of Pittsburgh.

[1] Heidegger, Martin: "Zeit und Sein," in *L'endurance de la pensée. Pour saluer Jean Beaufret,* ed. René Char (Paris: Plon, 1968), pp. 13–71; also in: *Zur Sache des Denkens* (Tübingen: Niemeyer, 1969), pp. 1–25.
[2] Heidegger, Martin: *Being and Time,* trans. John Macquarrie and Edward Robinson (New York: Harper and Row, 1962), p. 63.
[3] *Zur Sache,* p. 91.
[4] *Ibid.*
[5] "Protokoll zu einem Seminar über den Vortrag 'Zeit und Sein,'" in *Zur Sache,* pp. 27–60, pp. 29–35, 46–48. (These 'minutes' were written by Alfredo Guzzoni and later corrected and completed by Heidegger himself.)

The questions I wish to deal with in this essay are the following: 1) Precisely what does the Time-lecture say about 'time'? 2) How does Heidegger conceive of the relationship between 'time' and Being? 3) What does he say about the relationship between 'time' and Being on the one hand and the ab-original Event on the other? But in order to be able to compare the later view with the view found in *Being and Time,* I wish first to add a few reflections on Heidegger's original conception of time and attempt to present an idea of what Heidegger might have said in the section "Time and Being," if it had been published in 1927. It seems to me that this way of approaching the Time-lecture is the one which will best enable us to appreciate the new ideas suggested here.

I am well aware of the fact that all of these questions are difficult as well as of far-reaching importance for a genuine understanding of Heidegger's thought. Obviously, I shall not be able to deal exhaustively with them within the space limitations set for this essay. But I hope, nonetheless, to be able to bring to light the elements which are vital for a *preliminary* understanding of the contributions Heidegger wished to make in his 1961 essay.

1. *Heidegger's Original Conception of Time* (1927)

As the title of the book would suggest, the concept of time occupies a privileged position in *Being and Time.* Already in the book's brief preface Heidegger presents his view on how Being and time are to be related. "Our aim in the following treatise is to work out the question concerning the meaning of Being . . . Our provisional aim is the interpretation of time as the possible horizon for any understanding whatsoever of Being." [6] In the title of the first Part of the book Heidegger returns to this rela-

tionship: the interpretation of *Dasein* in terms of temporality (*Zeitlichkeit*), and the explication of time as transcendental horizon for the question concerning the meaning of Being. [7]

The first Part of the Book consists of two major divisions: A preparatory analysis of *Dasein* and a second division on the relationship between *Dasein* and temporality (*Zeitlichkeit*). In the first division Heidegger takes as his guiding clue the fact that the essence of man consists in his ek-sistence, that toward which man stands out is 'the world,' and thus that for this reason man can be described as 'Being-in-the-world.' The main task of the first division is to unveil the precise meaning of this compound expression; but in so doing the final goal remains the preparation of an answer for the question concerning the meaning of Being. Heidegger justifies this approach to the Being-question by pointing out that man taken as Being-in-the-world, is the only being who can make himself transparent in his own mode of Being. The very asking of this question is one of this entity's modes of Being, and as such it receives its essential character from what is inquired about, namely Being. "This entity which each of us is himself and which includes inquiring as one of the possibilities of its Being, we shall denote by the term '*Dasein*'." [8]

A preparatory analysis of *Dasein's* Being can only serve to *describe* the Being of this being; it cannot interpret its meaning. As a preparatory procedure it merely tries to lay bare the horizon for the most primordial way of interpreting Being. Once this horizon has been reached, the preparatory analytic of *Dasein* is to be repeated on a higher, genuinely ontological level. Heidegger repeats here that this horizon is to be found in temporality, taken as the *meaning* of the Being of *Dasein.* That is why on a second level all

---

[6] Heidegger, Martin: *Being and Time,* p. 19.
[7] *Ibid.,* p. 67.
[8] *Ibid.,* p. 27.

structures of *Dasein,* exhibited provisionally in the first division, must be re-interpreted as modes of temporality. But in thus interpreting *Dasein* as temporality, the question concerning the meaning of Being is not yet answered; only the ground is prepared here for later obtaining such an answer.[9]

If it is true that *Dasein* has a pre-ontologic understanding of Being and if it is true that temporality is the meaning of the Being of *Dasein,* then one can show that whenever *Dasein* tacitly understands and interprets Being, it does so with time as its standpoint. Thus time must be brought to light as the horizon for all understanding of Being and this horizon itself is to be shown in terms of temporality, taken as the Being of *Dasein* which understands Being. It is obvious that in this context our pre-philosophical conception of time is of no help and the same thing is true for the conception of time which has persisted in philosophy from Aristotle to Bergson. This traditional conception of time and the ordinary way of understanding time have sprung from temporality taken as the meaning of the Being of *Dasein.*[10]

Normally we conceive of time as an endless succession of 'nows,' whereby the 'not-yet-now' (future) passes by the 'present now' to become immediately a 'no-longer-now.' The future thus consists of the 'nows' that have not yet come, whereas the past consists of the 'nows' that once were but no longer are; the present is the 'now' which at the moment is. On the basis of this conception we can make a distinction between temporal and non-temporal entities; 'temporal' then means 'being in time.' Thus time, in the sense of 'being in time,' functions as a criterion for distinguishing realms of Being. No one has ever asked the question of how time can have this distinctive ontological function; nor has anyone asked whether the authentic ontological relevance which is possible for time, is expressed when time is used in such a naively ontological manner. These questions must be asked here and it will be clear that if Being is to be understood in terms of time and if its various derivatives are to become intelligible in their respective derivations by taking time into consideration, then Being itself must be made visible in its 'temporal' character; but in this case 'temporal' no longer means 'being in time.' From this perspective even the non-temporal and supra-temporal are 'temporal' with regard to their Being, and this not only privatively but also positively. It is this temporality of Being which must be worked out in the fundamental ontology whose task it is to interpret Being as such.[11]

Temporality is furthermore the condition which makes historicity possible as a temporal kind of Being which Dasein itself possesses. Historicity stands here for the state of Being which is constitutive for Dasein's coming-to-pass *(geschehen)* as such. *Dasein* is as it already was and it is what it already was. It is its past, not only in the sense that its past is, as it were, pushing itself along 'behind' it, and which Dasein thus possesses as a kind of property which is still present-at-hand; *Dasein* is its past in the way of its own Being which, to put it roughly, 'comes-to-pass' out of its future on each occasion. *Dasein* has grown up in a traditional way of understanding itself interpretatively. Its own past, which includes the past of its generation, is not something which just follows along after *Dasein,* but something which already goes ahead of it. But if *Dasein* itself as well as its own understanding are intrinsically historical, then the inquiry into Being itself is to be characterized by historicity as well.

[9] *Ibid.,* p. 38
[10] *Ibid.,* p. 39.
[11] *Ibid.,* pp. 39–40.

57

Thus by carrying through the question of the meaning of Being and by explicating *Dasein* in its temporality and historicity, the question itself will bring itself to the point where it understands itself as historical (*historisch*).[12]

After making these preliminary remarks which merely describe what is to be accomplished by the analytic of man's Being, Heidegger does not return to the question of temporality and time until the last chapter of the first division which is devoted to care (*Sorge*) as the genuine Being of *Dasein*. In trying to explain just what is meant by the compound expression 'Being-in-the-world' Heidegger first focusses on the ontological structure of the world,[13] then he tries to answer the question of who it is that *Dasein* is in its everydayness,[14] and finally proceeds to explain what is meant by "Being-in-as-such."[15] In the introduction to this last issue Heidegger explicitly repeats that that being which is essentially constituted by its Being-in-the-world, is itself in every case its own 'there' (*Da*). When one speaks of the *lumen naturale* in man, one refers to this existential-ontological structure of man that he *is* in such a way that he is his own 'there.' This means among other things that *Dasein* carries in its ownmost Being the character of not being closed off; *Dasein* because of this 'there' is to be characterized by its disclosedness. By reason of this fundamental disclosedness *Dasein*, together with the Being-there (*Da-sein*) of the world, is 'there' for itself. In the existential constitution of *Dasein's* disclosedness three equally constitutive components are to be distinguished, namely original understanding, original mood, and *logos* (*Rede*).[16]

After explaining the meaning of the compound expression "being-in-the-

world" along these lines by describing its basic constitutive elements, Heidegger sets out to account for the unity of *Dasein's* Being: How are the unity and totality of that structural whole which we have pointed out, to be defined in an existential-ontological manner?[17] Heidegger tries to answer this question by pointing out first that care (*Sorge*) is the unifying factor which integrates into a unity the multiple elements of the Being of that being whose Being is precisely such that it is concerned about its own Being. By taking his point of departure in a descriptive interpretation of anxiety (*Angst*) Heidegger is able to show that *Dasein* is a being who has the inexhaustible potentiality of transcending beings into Being; but, if *Dasein* has the ek-static nature of ek-sistence, it is always ahead of itself. *Dasein's* ek-sistence, however, is essentially co-determined by thrownness; *Dasein* is like a process which is not its own source; it always is already begun and yet it is still to be achieved. Finally, *Dasein* in its essential dependence upon world is fallen to the 'world,' to the intramundane things of its everyday concern and thus caught by the way things are publicly interpreted by the 'they.' Ek-sistentiality taken together with thrownness and fallenness explains why the very Being of *Dasein* is to be understood as care.[18]

In order to be able to show *Dasein's* Being in its totality Heidegger turns to *Dasein's* final term, death. He describes death as a genuine, but also as the ultimate possibility of man's Being. It is that possibility in which man's own Being-in-the-world as such is at stake. Death reveals to man the possibility of his further impossibility. In other words, death is that possibility which makes the potentiality which *Dasein* is,

---

[12] *Ibid.*, pp. 41–42.
[13] *Ibid.*, pp. 91–148.
[14] *Ibid.*, pp. 149–168.
[15] *Ibid.*, pp. 169–224.
[16] *Ibid.*, pp. 171–172.
[17] *Ibid.*, p. 225.
[18] *Ibid.*, pp. 228–241.

limited through and through. Man is thoroughly and irretrievably finite because his own death is that fundamental possibility which from the very beginning leaves its mark upon man's life and, thus, is a manner of Being which *Dasein* must assume as soon as it begins to ek-sist.[19]

In his fallen condition *Dasein* tries to forget the authentic meaning of death so that the question now becomes one of how one is to come to an authentic interpretation of the meaning of death, and thus to genuine authenticity. In Heidegger's view this can be shown by interpreting the basic constituents of care (ek-sistence, facticity = thrownness, and fallenness) in terms of an existential-ontological conception of death.

Dasein which has come to authentic Being knows that death is constitutive for all of its possibilities and that the ultimate possibility of its own ek-sistence is to give itself up.[20] If *Dasein* genuinely realizes this then it no longer flees from the definitiveness of its end and accepts it as constitutive of its finitude and thus makes itself free for it.[21] Now at the moment that *Dasein* understands death as its ultimate possibility, as that possibility which makes its own Being impossible, and at the moment that it accepts this final possibility as its very own by listening to the voice of conscience,[22] *Dasein* begins to become transparent to itself as that which it is in itself, in its own Self. For death does not just appear to *Dasein* in an impersonal way; it lays claim to it as this individual *Dasein*. By listening to the voice of conscience, by really understanding the genuine meaning of death in 'guilt,' and by accepting it as its own

death, *Dasein* breaks away from inauthenticity in resolve.[23]

Now it will be obvious that if all of this is to be true, then man's Being must be intrinsically temporal and temporality, in the final analysis, must constitute the primordial ontological basis of Dasein's ek-sistentiality.[24] For what does the authentic man do? He realizes his radical finitude by anticipating death, by including it in advance in every project. By anticipating death in all its projects *Dasein* receives its Being precisely as its own, as its ownmost 'personal' ek-sistence so that it really comes to itself.[25] But this coming-to-itself is what is meant by 'future,' if the term is taken in its primordial sense: This letting itself come towards itself in that distinctive possibility which *Dasein* has to put up with, is the primordial phenomenon of *Zu-kunft,* coming-towards, future.[26]

But Dasein's temporality extends not only to the future; it has also the character of a 'having been.' *Dasein* can project itself towards its own death only insofar as it already is. In order to realize its ownmost Being, *Dasein* has to accept, together with its own death, also its thrownness, its facticity, that which it is already. Death cannot be *its* death if it has no relation to what *Dasein* already is. Authentically futural, *Dasein* is equally authentically 'having been' (*Gewesen*). To anticipate one's ultimate and ownmost possibility is to come back understandingly to one's ownmost 'having-been.'[27]

Thus far we have seen that *Dasein's* coming is a coming to a Self that already is as having-been; on the other hand, *Dasein is* what it has been only as long as the future continues to come.

---

[19] *Ibid.,* pp. 279–290.
[20] *Ibid.,* p. 308.
[21] *Ibid.,* pp. 308–309.
[22] *Ibid.,* pp. 315–335.
[23] *Ibid.,* pp. 341–348.
[24] *Ibid.,* pp. 349–364.
[25] *Ibid.,* pp. 364–370.
[26] *Ibid.,* p. 372.
[27] *Ibid.,* p. 373.

We must now turn to temporal nearness, the present. According to Heidegger, the genuine meaning of the present consists in a 'making present' (*Gegenwärtigen*). *Dasein*, as temporalizing, makes things present; this is the essential meaning of the present as it primordially appears to *Dasein*. Anticipating resolve discloses the actual situation of the *Da* in such a way that ek-sistence, in its action, can be circumspectively concerned with what is factually ready-to-hand in the actual situation, that is letting that which has environmental presence be encountered, is possible only by *making* such a being *present.*[28]

The 'making present' of what has presence presupposes, on the one hand, the future as anticipation of *Dasein's* possibilities and, on the other, the return to what has-been. By virtue of Dasein's understanding of its own Being, thus, *Dasein* is able to understand the human situation as a whole; at the same time intramundane beings can manifest themselves to it in their belonging to a world. Thus, what Heidegger calls 'making-present' presupposes the 'having been' and the 'future.' The present is as the resultant of the two other ek-stases of time. 'Having been' arises from the 'future' in such a way that the future which has already been releases the present from itself. What is meant by temporality is precisely the unity of this structural whole; the future which makes present in the process of having been. Only insofar as *Dasein* is characterized by temporality can it realize its authentic Being. Thus temporality reveals itself here as the meaning of authentic care.[29]

From all of this, it becomes clear that *Dasein* can realize its total unity only by temporalizing itself. This 'becoming temporal' includes at the same time future, having-been, and present. These three 'phases' of time imply one another and nonetheless are mutually exclusive. For this reason Heidegger calls them the 'ek-stases' of primordial time. We must now examine the nature of the relations which connect these ek-stases of time with the structural elements of care. According to Heidegger, care must be characterized by ek-sistence (having to be ahead of itself), facticity of thrownness (already being in the world), and fallenness (being absorbed in intramundane things). As basically Being-able-to-be (*Seinkönnen*), *Dasein* is always ahead of itself, ahead of what it actually is. That is why its understanding has the character of a project. It is precisely because *Dasein* possesses the ontological structure of projecting (*Verstehen*) that it can always be ahead of its actual being. However, being ahead-of-itself, *Dasein always* is already in a world and is of necessity involved in it. Thus, *Dasein* cannot go beyond itself without being 'thrown' into the world. This means that ek-sistence as Being-ahead-of-itself always includes facticity. Finally, *Dasein*, which is in a world into which it has been thrown, always discovers itself there as absorbed by that which immediately manifests itself there and with which it deals concernfully (fallenness). But now the relationship between *Dasein's* essential temporality and care will be clear at once. Heidegger expresses it as follows: "The 'ahead-of-itself' (ek-sistentiality) is grounded in the future. The 'being-already-in' (facticity) makes known the 'having been.' 'Being-at' (fallenness) becomes possible in 'making-present'."[30]

After showing that the very Being of *Dasein* consists in care whereas care, in turn, is understood in terms of temporality, Heidegger tries to explain how man's temporality in its modifiability is the principle for the distinction of his possible modes of Being. *Dasein* is essentially temporal; it tem-

---

[28] *Ibid.*, pp. 373–374.
[29] *Ibid.*, p. 374.
[30] *Ibid.*, p. 375.

poralizes time. If it takes the temporalization of time upon itself, it *is* in an authentic way; however, if it takes itself as a temporal thing which finds itself in a temporal horizon, it is in an inauthentic manner. One has to realize, however, that *Dasein* would not be able to temporalize time authentically, if man did not always find himself already in a temporal openness, somehow connected with his own 'inner-temporality.' In other words, man can ek-sist authentically only if in his historicity he expressly endures his destiny of having to temporalize time as finite, that is as a mortal being. But this means that 'inner-temporality' and historicity are inseparable. When man turns toward historicity, he is able to ek-sist authentically; however, if he turns to his own 'inner-temporality' he forgets himself in his concern for what is ready-to-hand or in his presentation of what is present-at-hand.[31]

Ek-sistence, Being-present-at-hand, and Being-ready-to-hand, thus, are intrinsically connected with man's temporality. But this means that the temporality of *Dasein* is not only the principle for the division of *Dasein's* modes of Being, but the time which is temporalized by *Dasein* is also the principle of the division of the meaning of Being into possible significations of Being (namely Being as ek-sistence, as present-at-hand, as ready-to-hand, etc.). But this means, in turn, that a description of the various interplayings of the three dimensions of temporality can give us a guiding-clue for the division of the significations of Being.[32]

We have defined *Dasein's* Being as care and found that the ontological meaning of care is temporality. We have seen, also, that temporality constitutes the disclosedness of *Dasein's* there. Now in the disclosedness of this 'there,' the world is disclosed along with it. But this means that world, taken as Total-meaningfulness, must likewise be grounded in temporality. The existential-temporal condition for the possibility of the world lies in the fact that temporality, taken as ek-static unity, has something like a horizon within it. For ek-stases are not simple 'raptures' in which one gets carried away; rather, there belongs to each ek-stasis a kind of 'whither' to which one is carried away. Let us call this whither of the ek-stases the 'horizonal schema.' The schema then in which *Dasein* comes toward itself futurally is the 'for the sake of which;' the schema in which *Dasein* is disclosed to itself in its thrownness is to be taken as that 'in the face of which' it has been thrown and that 'to which' it has been abandoned; this characterizes the horizonal schema of what has been. Finally the horizonal schema for the present is defined by the 'in order to.'

The unity of the horizonal schemata of future, present, and having been, is grounded in the ek-static unity of temporality. The horizon of temporality as a whole determines that whereupon each ek-sisting being factically is disclosed. With its factical Being-there, a Being-able-to-be is projected in the horizon of the future, its being-already is disclosed in the horizon of having-been, and that with which *Dasein* concerns itself in each case is discovered in the horizon of the present. The horizonal unity of the schemata of these ek-stases connects in a primordial way the relationships of the 'in order to' with the 'for the sake of which' so that on the basis of the horizonal constitution of the ek-static unity of temporality, there belongs to *Dasein* in each case something like a world that has been disclosed. Just as the present (*Gegenwart*) arises in the unity of the tem-

[31] *Ibid.*, pp. 383–401.
[32] *Ibid.*, pp. 401–418. See for the foregoing passage also: Otto Pöggeler, "Heideggers Topologie des Seins," in *Man and World*, 2 (1969), pp. 331–357, pp. 337–345, and William J. Richardson, *Heidegger. Through Phenomenology to Thought* (The Hague: Nijhoff, 1963), pp. 71–93.

poralizing of temporality out of the future and the having-been, so in the same way the *horizon* of a present temporalizes itself equiprimordially with *those* of the future and the having been. Thus, insofar as *Dasein* temporalizes itself, a world *is*. In temporalizing itself in regard to its own Being, Dasein as temporality is essentially in a world because of the ek-statico-horizonal constitution of his temporality. The world, therefore, is not ready-to-hand as a piece of equipment, nor present-at-hand as a thing, but it temporalizes itself in temporality. It is there with the outside-of-itself typical for the ek-stases. If no *Dasein* ek-sists, then no world is 'there' either.

In all forms of concern and in all objectification the world is always already presupposed; for all of these forms are possible only as ways of Being-in-the-world. Having its ground in the horizonal unity of ek-static temporality, the world is transcendent. It is already ek-statically disclosed before any entities-within-the-world can be encountered. Temporality maintains itself ek-statically within the horizons of its own ek-stases and in temporalizing itself it comes back from these ek-stases to those entities which are encountered in the 'there.' Thus the Total-meaningfulness which determines the structure of the world is not a network of forms which a worldless subject lays over some kind of material; *Dasein,* understanding itself and its world ek-statically in the unity of the 'there,' rather comes back from these horizons to the entities encountered within them. Coming back to these entities in understanding is the existential meaning of letting them be encountered by making them present.[33]

There is finally a relationship between *Dasein's* spatiality and its temporality. *Dasein* must be considered as temporal and 'also' as spatial coordinately. In clarifying this relationship, Heidegger says, it cannot be our intention to explain Dasein's 'spatiotemporal' character by pointing out that *Dasein* is an entity which is 'in space as well as in time.' Furthermore, since temporality is the very meaning of the Being of care, it will be impossible to 'reduce' temporality to spatiality. On the other hand, to demonstrate that spatiality is existentially possible only through temporality is not tantamount to deducing space from time. What we must aim at is the uncovering of the temporal conditions for the possibility of the spatiality which is characteristic of *Dasein* — a spatiality upon which the uncovering of space within the world is to be founded. When we say that *Dasein* is spatial, we do not mean to say that as a thing *Dasein* is present-at-hand in space. *Dasein* as such does not fill up space, but it rather takes space in, this to be understood in the literal sense. In ek-sisting *Dasein* has already made free for itself a leeway (*Spielraum*). It determines its own position or location by coming back from the space it has made free to the place which it occupies.

When *Dasein* makes room for itself it does so by means of directionality and de-severance (by making distances disappear). How is this possible on the basis of *Dasein's* temporality? Let us give an example of our everyday concern with things. When *Dasein* makes room for itself and the things with which it is concerned, it has first to discover a region in which it can assign places to the things in question. In so doing it must bring these things close, and situate them in regard to one another and in regard to itself. *Dasein* thus has the character of directionality and de-severance. All of this, however, presupposes the horizon of a world which has already been disclosed. But if this is so, and if it is essential for *Dasein* to be in a mode of fallenness, then it is clear also that only on the basis of its ek-statico-horizonal tem-

---

[33] *Being and Time,* pp. 415–418.

porality is it possible for *Dasein* to break into space. For the world is not present-at-hand in space and yet only within a world does space let itself be discovered.[34]

It seems to me that this brief resumé of some of the basic ideas of Heidegger's original conception of time should suffice to explain what Heidegger intends to say in his 1962 lecture. But before turning to the lecture itself I wish first to reflect for a moment upon the intrinsic limitations of his original view of time, particularly with respect to the problem concerning the meaning of Being.

II. From *Being and Time* to *Time and Being*[35]

In Heidegger's view *Being and Time* (1927) was meant to be a 'fundamental ontology' which was to prepare the way for a 'genuine ontology' whose main task it would be to focus on the question concerning the meaning of Being. Fundamental ontology consists substantially in an analytic of *Dasein's* Being as Being-in-the-world, to be developed by means of a hermeneutic phenomenology. In the first part of the book Heidegger conceives of *Dasein* in terms of care, whereas in the second part care is understood as temporality: The meaning of the Being of *Dasein* is temporality. All of this was to prepare the answer for a more basic question concerning the temporal character (*Zeithaftigkeit*) of the meaning of Being itself. "In our considerations hitherto, our task has been to interpret the primordial whole of factical *Dasein* with regard to its possibilities of authentic and inauthentic Being, and to do so in an existential-ontological manner in terms of its very basis. Temporality has manifested itself as this basis and accordingly as the meaning of the Being of care . . . Nev-

ertheless, our way of exhibiting the constitution of *Dasein's* Being is only one way which we may take. Our aim is to work out the question of Being in general.''[36] In other words, once temporality is laid bare as the meaning of *Dasein's* Being, the decisive step is still to be taken: The step namely which leads from this kind of temporality to the temporality characteristic of the meaning of Being. This last step is not taken in *Being and Time*. Heidegger published the book in an incomplete form and in the last sentences of it pointed to the work that in his view remains to be done: "The existential-ontological constitution of *Dasein's* totality is grounded in temporality. Hence the ek-static projection of Being must be made possible by some primordial way in which ek-static temporality temporalizes. How is this mode of temporalizing temporality to be interpreted? Is there a way which leads from primordial time to the meaning of Being? Does time itself manifest itself as the horizon of Being?''[37]

By publishing the book in an incomplete form in 1927 Heidegger admitted that he had not completely succeeded in the task he had set for himself. The basic question he encountered was the following: Once the temporality of *Dasein* is grasped in the unity of its three ek-stases, how can this temporality of *Dasein* be interpreted as the temporality of the understanding of Being and how is the latter, in turn, related to the meaning of Being? Originally Heidegger thought he had found a way to answer this question, but it appeared almost immediately that that way led away from what he really wished to accomplish, namely to show that time is the transcendental horizon of the question of Being.[38] For on the basis of the analyses as they are actually found in *Being and Time*

---

[34] *Ibid.*, pp. 419–421.
[35] See for what follows: Otto Pöggeler, *Der Denkweg Martin Heideggers* (Pfullingen: Neske, 1963), pp. 63–66.
[36] *Being and Time*, pp. 486–487.
[37] *Ibid.*, p. 483.
[38] *Ibid.*, p. 63.

it is still not yet clear precisely what is to be understood by 'transcendence' taken as the overcoming of beings in the direction of Being. In addition there is the question of the exact relationship between *Dasein's* temporality and time as the transcendental horizon for the question concerning the meaning of Being. Exactly what is meant here by 'transcendental'? This much is clear: The term 'transcendental' does not mean the objectivity of an object of experience as constituted by consciousness (Kant, Husserl), but rather refers to the project-domain for the determination of Being as seen from the viewpoint of *Dasein's there.*[39] But even in this supposition it is still not yet clear what the precise relationship is between the temporality of *Dasein* and time as the transcendental horizon for the question of Being, because it is not clear how *Dasein's* understanding of Being is to be related to the meaning of Being. Heidegger says that meaning is that in which the intelligibility of something maintains itself.[40] The meaning of Being then is that in which the intelligibility of Being maintains itself. But what is the precise relationship between Being's intelligibility and *Dasein's* understanding of Being? In the introduction to the second part of the book Heidegger argues that "to lay bare the horizon within which something like Being in general becomes intelligible, is tantamount to clarifying the possibility of having any understanding of Being at all — an understanding which itself belongs to the constitution of the being called *Dasein.*"[41] But precisely what is meant by 'being tantamount to'? If one takes this statement literally, it means that *Dasein* has an absolute priority over the meaning of Being and then relativism seems to be the final outcome of the investigation. Heidegger saw this dan-

ger and it took him a number of years to find a way to avoid it without being forced into a position of having to appeal to a 'God of the philosophers,' regardless of the concrete form in which this 'God' might be proposed.

There are a number of other issues which did not receive *final* answers in *Being and Time,* problems such as the idea of phenomenology, the relationship between ontology and science, the relationship between time and space, a further determination of *logos,* the relationship between language and Being, the relationship between Being and truth, etc.[42] But rather than focussing on any one of these, let us turn our attention again to the problem concerning the relationship between *Dasein's* temporality and time as the transcendental horizon for the question of Being, and this time from a slightly different point of view.

In *Being and Time* Heidegger was guided by the idea that in the ontological tradition Being was understood mainly as presence-at-hand[43] as continuous presence, and thus from one of the dimensions of time, namely the present. Heidegger wished to bring the onesidedly accentuated 'continuous presence' back into the full, pluridimensional time, in order then to try to understand the meaning of Being from the originally experienced time, namely temporality. In his attempt to materialize this goal he was guided by a second basic idea, namely that each being can become manifest with regard to its Being in many ways, so that one has to ask the questions of just what is the pervasive, simple, unified determination of Being that permeates all of its multiple meanings. But this question raises others: What, then, does Being mean? To what extent

[39] *Zur Sache,* p. 29.
[40] *Being and Time,* p. 193.
[41] *Ibid.,* p. 274.
[42] *Ibid.,* pp. 133–134, 203, 273, 382, 400, 402–403, 408–409, 411–412, 420, 423, 458, 487.
[43] *Ibid.,* pp. 41–49, 244–256.

(why and how) does the Being of beings unfold in various modes? How can these various modes be brought into a comprehensible harmony? Whence does Being as such (not merely being as being) receive its ultimate determination? "

Heidegger had studied some of these modes of Being in the interpretative analyses of *Being and Time* and thus, at the very end of the book, found himself led to consider the question of whether or not there is a basic meaning of Being from which all other meanings can be derived *by taking time* (understood as temporality) *as a guiding clue.* In view of the fact that man's understanding is intrinsically historical, the further question must be asked of whether man's understanding of Being's meaning is intrinsically historical, also, or whether the understanding of Being can perhaps in some sense have a 'supra-temporal' character. In *Being and Time* Heidegger was unable to answer the first question adequately because he had not been able to find a satisfactory solution for the second. For upon closer consideration his conception of historicity as found in *Being and Time* seems to be ambiguous. Historicity is described in the book first as the genuine temporalization of time and the principle of the distinction between *Dasein's* modes of Being, and then later it is said that historicity is the medium in which all ontological understanding must maintain itself." It does not seem to be possible to defend both theses simultaneously; and even if there should be a position from which one could defend both, even then it would still not be clear in what sense the meaning of Being itself is affected by historicity.

In the decade following the publication of *Being and Time* Heidegger eliminated part of the initial ambiguity by first examining more carefully how different significations of Being become differentiated in the fundamental meaning of Being and how temporality, indeed, is the principle of these distinctions. In so doing, he could maintain his original view that the meaning of Being is the 'Ground' in which all significations of Being are to be grounded and from which all understanding of Being nourishes itself. On the other hand, however, the meaning of Being cannot be understood in terms of an eternal standard being ('the God of the philosophers'); rather it must be conceived of as an abysmal, groundless 'ground.' For the *fact* that Being comes-to-pass in the way it does, and for the *fact* that an understanding of Being emerges in the way we actually find it, no one can indicate a ground, because each process of grounding already presupposes the meaning of Being. When the meaning of Being lets a determinate signification of Being become the standard signification, then it 'groundlessly' bars other significations and even itself *as* the ground of the manifold possible other significations. It is in this sense that Being shows and hides itself at the same time and why the meaning of Being is to be called 'truth,' unconcealment, whose coming-to-pass is and remains a mystery and whose 'happening' is historical in a sense which cannot be understood on the basis of what we usually call history.

Furthermore, the world taken as the building-structure of the truth of Being is that organized structure which is stratified in many ways and is constructed according to the manner in which time temporalizes itself. This temporalization of time itself is historical and thus the stratification of the organized structure of Being's truth is historical, too; as such it can be distinguished in various epochs. In each epoch we find in the world as the building-structure of the truth of Being manifold organized and systematized 'layers' of meaning all of which refer to basic forms of 'experience' between which there is a tension, and concern-

---

" Heidegger in a letter to William J. Richardson, in Richardson, *op. cit.*, p. *x.*
" *Being and Time*, pp. 41–62, 424ff.

ing which it is difficult to see how they can all belong together. Heidegger's main concern is to explain how in a certain epoch (particularly our own) all these 'layers' can belong together in a whole, the world, and how in this world as the building-structure of Being's truth for this particular era the 'courses of Being are already traced out' and how therefore Being can encounter us in these particular, different ways, and not in others; thus how in this world Being itself shows and hides itself at the same time.[46]

But between 1927 and 1962 Heidegger never explicitly returned to the main question underlying the basic idea which directed all of these investigations: The nature of time. It is obvious that the conception of time as temporality, found in *Being and Time,* is not adequate to account for all of this. Whereas in *Being and Time,* where Being and time are concerned, the priority is attributed to man, in the later works the privileged position is given to Being. If the original relationship between Being and time is to be maintained, then it would seem logical to attribute a privileged position to time in the coming-to-pass of truth, also. But if both Being as well as time do not depend upon man in the final analysis, do they then perhaps refer to 'something' else which precedes them in some sense? This is indeed the main theme of the Time-lecture which we shall now consider.

III. *Time and Being* (1962)

The *Zeit und Sein* lecture begins with a short preface in which Heidegger explains that he intends to say something about the attempt "which thinks Being without any reference to a foundation of Being from the side of beings."[47] In other words, in this lecture there will be no reference to a

summum ens taken as *causa sui* which could be conceived of as the foundation of all that is; nor is Being to be understood here within the perspective of the metaphysical interpretation of the ontological difference, according to which Being is thought of merely for the sake of beings.[48] Heidegger believed such an attempt to be necessary for at least two reasons. First of all, without such an attempt it will be impossible to bring to light in a genuine way the Being of all that which we today encounter in the world as beings and which are fundamentally determined by the essence of technique (*Ge-stell*).[49] Secondly such an attempt is necessary if one is adequately to determine the relationship between man and that which until now has been called 'Being.'[50]

Many people believe that philosophy should be oriented toward 'world-wisdom.' According to Heidegger, philosophy today finds itself in a position in which it must stay away from useful 'life-wisdom,' and must abandon immediate understanding, because a form of thought has become necessary from which everything that makes up the world in which we live receives its determination (works of art, complicated physical theories, technical instruments, computors, etc.)[51]

What is contained in the lecture to follow, Heidegger says, is no more than an attempt and a venture. The venture consists in the fact that the essay is formulated in propositions whereas its theme is such that this way of 'saying' is incongruous. What is important in the essay, therefore, is not so much the propositions of which it consists, but rather that to which the questions and answers by means of which Heidegger tried to approach that theme, point (*zeigen*). These questions and answers presuppose an ex-

[46] Pöggeler, Otto: "Heideggers Topologie des Seins," pp. 337–345.
[47] *Zur Sache des Denkens,* p. 2.
[48] *Ibid.,* p. 36.
[49] *Ibid.,* p. 35.
[50] *Ibid.,* pp. 1–2.
[51] *Ibid.,* p. 1.

perience of 'the thing itself,' and it is for this experience on the part of the reader that Heidegger's essay tries to prepare.[52]

1. *Being and Time*

The first part of the essay deals with the relationship between Being and time. These two themes are mentioned together here because from the very origin of Western thought Being has been interpreted as Being-present (*Anwesen*), while Being-present and Presence (*Anwesenheit*) refer to the present (*Gegenwart*) which, in turn, together with the past and the future constitute what is characteristic of time. Thus as Being-present Being is determined by time. But in how far is Being determined by time? Why, in what way, and from what is it that time re-sounds in Being? It is obvious that any attempt to think about this relationship with the help of our everyday conceptions of Being and time is doomed to failure.

In our everyday life we say that things are in time; or also that they have their time. This way of speaking, however, does not apply to Being, for Being is not a thing. And since Being is not a thing it is not in time either. And yet Being is determined by time. On the other hand, what is in time we call the temporal. The temporal refers to what elapses with time. Thus time itself elapses; but while elapsing continuously, time nevertheless remains as time. Now 'to remain' means 'not to perish,' and thus 'Being-present.' But this means that time is determined by a kind of Being. But how then can Being be determined by time? We must, therefore, come to the conclusion that Being is not a thing and thus not something temporal, although as Being-present it is determined by time. And on the other hand, time is not a thing and thus not something-which-is, and

yet in elapsing it permanently remains, without it itself being something temporal. Therefore, Being and time determine one another in such a way that Being is not something temporal and time is not something-which-is.

By adopting Hegel's dialectic approach one could try to overcome these contradicting statements by transcending Being and time toward a higher and more encompassing unity. But such an approach would certainly lead away from the 'things themselves' and their mutual relations; for such a procedure would certainly no longer deal with time as such nor with Being as such, nor with their mutual relationship. The genuine problem with which we are confronted here seems precisely to consist in the question of whether the relationship between Being and time is a relationship which results from a certain combination of Being and time, or whether perhaps this relationship itself is primary, so that Being and time result from it. In order to find an answer for this question we must try to think circumspectly about these 'things themselves,' that is about Being and time, which are perhaps the two main themes of thought. The labels 'Being and Time' and 'Time and Being' refer to the relationship between these two themes, to that which keeps these two themes together. To reflect circumspectly upon this relationship is *the* theme of thought.[53]

Being is a theme of thought, but it is not a thing; time is also a theme of thought, but it is nothing temporal. Of a thing we say: It is. With respect to Being and time we are more careful; here we say: There is Being, and there is time.[54] 'There is,' this English expression stands for the German '*Es gibt.*' This can be understood to mean: 'It gives' in the sense of 'there is something which grants.'[55] If we follow this suggestion then the question is one of

[52] *Ibid.*, pp. 2, 27–28.
[53] *Ibid.*, pp. 2–4.
[54] *Ibid.*, pp. 4–5.
[55] *Ibid.*, pp. 41–43.

what this 'It' is which grants Being and time. And also: What is Being which is granted here? What is time which is given here? Let us first try to think about Being in order to grasp it in what is characteristic of it.

Being which marks each being as such means Being-present (*Anwesen*). In regard to that which is present, Being-present can be conceived of as letting-something-be-present. It is on this letting-be-present that we must focus our attention here. It is characteristic for this letting-be-present that it brings something into unconcealment. Letting-be-present means to unveil, to bring into the open. In the process of unveilment there is a kind of granting at work which grants Being-present, while it lets-be-present that which is present, namely beings. In this process we come again upon a granting, and thus upon an 'It' which grants.[56] We do not yet know precisely what this granting means, nor do we know what this 'It' refers to. One thing is clear, however. If one wishes to think about what is characteristic of Being as such, he must abandon the attempt to understand Being from the viewpoint of beings, to conceive of Being as the ground of beings. On the contrary, he must focus his attention on this typical granting and that mysterious 'It' which grants. Being somehow belongs to this granting; it is the gift of the 'It' which grants. Being is not something which is found outside the granting, as is the case with a common gift. In the granting Being as Being-present becomes changed. As letting-be-present it belongs to the unveilment itself, and as gift it remains contained in the granting. For Being is not. Being as the unveilment of Being-present is granted by a mysterious 'It.'[57]

Heidegger is of the opinion that the meaning of this 'It grants Being' can be explained in a clearer way by means of a careful reflection on the various changes which have taken place in what has been called 'Being.' As we have mentioned, since the origin of Western thought in Greece, Being has been referred to as Being-present. And even today, in the era of modern technique, Being is still pointed to as Being-present, namely as Being-present in its availability on which one can continuously count (*Ge-stell*). The fact that Being must be referred to as Being-present manifests itself in an analysis of what is ready-to-hand and present-at-hand. We find the same thing back when we reflect on the meaning of *Hen, Logos, Idea, ousia, energeia, substantia, actualitas, perceptio, monad,* objectivity, Reason, Love, Spirit, Power, Will-to-will in the eternal return of the same.

The unfolding of the fullness which shows itself in these changes manifests itself at first sight as a history of Being. However, Being has no history in the way a city or a nation has its history. The history-like character of the history of Being is determined only and exclusively from the way Being comes-to-pass, that is from the way in which 'It' grants Being.[58]
Now from the very beginning people have reflected on Being, but no one has ever thought about the 'It' which grants Being. This 'It grants' withdraws in favor of that which it grants, namely Being. And Being itself, in turn, was almost immediately thought of in terms of beings, that is in its relationship to beings.

According to Heidegger, the kind of granting which grants only its gift but which itself withdraws should be called 'sending' (*Schicken*). This becomes immediately clear when one compares the case in which someone *gives* someone else a present with the case in which he *sends* it to him. Viewing it

[56] *Ibid.*, pp. 5, 39–41.
[57] *Ibid.*, pp. 5–6.
[58] *Ibid.*, pp. 6–8.

from this perspective, one may say that Being which is granted is that which has been sent and which (as sent) remains in each one of the modifications which we find in history. Thus, the historical character of the history of Being must be determined from that which is characteristic of this sending, and not from an undetermined coming-to-pass.

History of Being, therefore, means mittence of Being. And in the various ways of sending, the sending itself as well as that mysterious 'It' which sends, hold themselves back in the various manifestations in which Being shows itself. To hold oneself back means in Greek *epoche.* That is why we speak of epochs of Being's mittence. Epoch does not mean, therefore, a certain period of time in the happening, but the basic characteristic of the sending itself, that is to say this holding-itself-back in favor of the various manifestations of the gift, namely Being with respect to the discovery of beings. The sequence of the epochs in Being's sending is neither arbitrary nor can it be predicted with necessity. And yet what is co-mitted manifests itself in the mittence also, just as well as that-which-belongs-to manifests itself in the belonging-together of the epochs. These epochs overlap in their sequence so that the original mittence of Being as Presence is more and more concealed in the various modifications of the unveilment. Only the 'demolition' of these concealments (destruction) will grant to thought a provisional insight into what then manifests itself as the mittence of Being.

When Plato represents Being as *Idea,* when Aristotle represents it as *energeia,* Kant as positing, Hegel as absolute Concept, and Nietzsche as Will to power, then these are doctrines which are not just accidentally brought forth. They are rather the 'words' of Being itself as answers to an address which speaks in the sending but which hides

itself therein, that is to say in that mysterious 'It grants Being.' Each time contained in a mittence which withdraws itself, Being is unconcealed for thought in its epochal variational fullness. Thought remains bound to the tradition of these epochs of Being's mittence. This is true also, and particularly so, when thought reflects upon the question of how and from what Being itself receives the determinations which each time are characteristic of it, namely from this mysterious 'It grants Being.' For this granting manifests itself as mittence.

But how are we to conceive of this 'It' which grants Being? From the preceding pages as well as from the title of this essay, Heidegger says, one might expect that this is to be found in time.[50]

Briefly summarizing this part of the lecture, we may say that Heidegger for the greater part repeats his view of Being as contained in *Letter on Humanism* (1947) and later works. Just as in *Letter on Humanism,* Heidegger states here that the basic conception of *Being and Time* is to be maintained in this new perspective, although he warns explicitly that we should not confuse *Dasein's* historicity with the 'historicity' of Being itself. Finally, in this part of the lecture many references are made to the aboriginal Event (*Ereignis*) under the guise of that mysterious 'It' which grants. Heidegger is to return to this in the last part of the lecture. But let us first look at his view on time.

We all know what time is and just as was the case with Being we have a common sense conception of it. It will be clear once again that this common sense conception is of no help here. We do not yet know what is characteristic of time as such. We have just seen that what characterizes Being, that is to say that to which it belongs and in which it remains contained, manifests itself in that myster-

---

[50] *Ibid.,* pp. 8–10.

ious 'It grants.' That which is characteristic of Being is not something being-like (*Seinsartiges*). Trying to understand what Being us, we are led away from Being toward the mittence which grants Being as a gift. We may expect that the same thing will be true for time and that is why our common sense conception will be of no avail here, either. And yet the titles 'Being and Time' and 'Time and Being' suggest that we try to understand what is characteristic of time, the moment we try to understand what is characteristic of Being. For, as we have seen, Being means Being-present, letting-something-be present, Presence.

Presence is not the present, although the former almost immediately leads to the latter. Present (*Gegenwart*) suggests past and future, the earlier and the later in regard to the 'now.' Usually time is described in terms of the 'now,' assuming that time itself is the 'sum' of present, past, and future. We seldom think of time in terms of Presence. The conception of time in terms of the 'now,' as a series of 'nows' which succeed one another, of a one-dimensional continuum, was suggested by Aristotle and has since been defended by many thinkers. It is this time which we refer to when we measure time, when a 'temporal interval' is to be measured.[60]

But obviously all of this does not answer the question of precisely what time is. Is time and does time have a place? Time is obviously not *nothing*. If we wish to express ourselves more carefully, we should say here again: There is time (*Es gibt Zeit*). Time must be understood from the 'present' and this must not be taken as 'now' but as Presence.

But what is to be understood by Presence (*Anwesenheit*)? Presence is that which determines Being as letting-be-present and revealing. But what kind of thing is this? In *Anwesen* (Being-present) we find *wesen* and *wesen* means *währen* (to last, to continue). But by realizing this we much too often jump immediately from *währen* to *dauern* (to last, to endure); this duration, in turn, conceived of in the light of our common sense conception of time, is mostly understood as an interval between one 'now' and another one. However, our speaking about *An-wesen* demands that we become aware of a staying and lingering (*weilen*) and dwelling (*verweilen*) in this *währen* as *Anwähren* (continuous lasting). This *An-wesen* concerns us men. But who are we? In trying to answer the question we must again proceed carefully; for it could very well be the case that man is to be defined in terms of what we are trying to reflect on; man himself is affected by the Presence while this 'goes on' and it is because of this that he himself can be present to all that is present and absent. Man stands in that which thus goes on (*Angang*) and in which Presence takes place; it is man who receives the Presence which that mysterious 'It' grants as a gift, while he learns what appears in the letting-be-present. If this were not so, man would not be man.[61]

It seems that by talking about man, we have lost the way, Heidegger says; for we are trying to determine what is characteristic of time. In some sense this may be true, and yet we are closer to what we are looking for than it may seem at first sight. Presence means: The continuous lingering-dwelling (*verweilen*) which concerns man, reaches him, and is granted to him. But from where does this granting reaching come? We must realize here, Heidegger continues: 1) that man is always concerned with the presence of something which is present, and that he never immediately heeds the Presence itself; 2) that which is no longer present still concerns man and as such it is still present to him; in what has been,

[60] *Ibid.*, pp. 10–11.
[61] *Ibid.*, pp. 12–13.

Presence is still granted in some sense; 3) that which is not yet presented is present in the sense that it approaches man; in that which approaches man, Presence is already granted to him. From this it follows that Presence does not always have the character of the present.

But how are we to determine this granting of the Presence in the present, past, and future? Does this granting consist in the fact that it reaches us, or does it reach us because it is in itself a granting? There is no doubt that the future grants and adduces the past, whereas the past grants the future. And this mutual granting gives the present at the same time. In this way we attribute a temporal character to this mutual granting. And thus it is not right to call the unity of this mutual granting time, for time is not something temporal; nor can we say that present, past, and future are there 'at the same time.' And yet their mutual granting of one another to each other belongs together in a unity. This unity which unites them must be determined from what is characteristic of them, namely from the fact that they grant one another to each other. But what is it that they grant to each other? Themselves, that is to say the Presence which is granted in them. That which comes to light in the mutual granting of one another to each other of present, past, and future is the Open, or also the time-space. This time-space precedes what we commonly call space and time. It is a three-dimensional Open in that it comes to light by means of a three-fold granting of present, past, and future.[62]

But from what are we to determine the unity of the three dimensions of this time-space? We know already that a Presence is at work in the coming of what is not-yet-present as well as in the having-been of what is no-longer-present, and in what we usually call the present. This Presence does not belong to one of these three dimensions to the exclusion of the others. While the three dimensions give themselves over to one another and precisely in this passing of the one to the other (*Zuspiel*) still another granting manifests itself which opens up a fourth dimension. It is this latter granting which is characteristic of time itself and which brings about the Presence which is typical in each case for the coming, the having-been, and the present. It keeps these latter dimensions separated, and nevertheless it keeps them in each other's proximity, also, so that these three dimensions can remain close to one another. This is why one can call the primordial granting in which literally everything begins (*anfängt*) and in which the unity of genuine time precisely consists, a proximity which brings near (*nahernde Nähe*). It brings close to one another the coming, the having-been, and the present by keeping them apart. For it keeps open the having-been by denying it its coming as present, just as it keeps open the coming by withholding the present in this coming, that is by denying it its being present. Thus the proximity which brings near has the character of a denial and withholding.[63]

Time *is* not. 'It' gives time. The granting which gives time is to be determined from the proximity which denies and withholds. 'It' grants the Open of time-space and guards that which is denied in the having-been and that which is withheld in the coming. This granting thus is revealing and concealing at the same time; while granting the Open of time-space it hides itself as granting.

But where now is this mysterious 'It' which grants time and time-space? Obviously this question is not correctly formulated, for time has no place, no 'where.' Time is that pre-spatial 'place' which makes each 'where' precisely pos-

[62] *Ibid.*, pp. 13–15.
[63] *Ibid.*, pp. 15–16

sible. Since the beginning of Western thought, people have asked this question and many of them have said with Aristotle and Augustine that 'time is in the soul.' Thus, time cannot be without man. The question, however, is one of whether or not it is man who gives time, or whether it is man to whom time is granted. In the latter case the question still remains of who or what 'It' is which gives time. One thing is clear, however, man is what he is only and exclusively because he stands within the three-fold granting and 'endures' the proximity which denies and withholds, and determines this granting. Man does not make time, and time does not make man. Expressions such as 'making,' 'producing,' and 'creating' do not make sense here.[64]

Notwithstanding the great differences, the preceding passage on time undeniably is strongly reminiscent of what was said in *Being and Time* about the 'horizonal schemata' and spatio-temporality. It seems to me that the last paragraph of the Time-lecture which we have just considered refers to these sections of *Being and Time* and reminds us that the perspective of *Being and Time* is and remains pre-understood in the current reflections on time. *Dasein* plays an essential part in the coming-to-pass of Being as well as in the coming-to-pass of time as the transcendental horizon of Being. It is clear by now, however, that in this complex process *Dasein* is not the one who grants, but rather the one to whom all of this is given. But this still entails that without *Dasein* the granting would not have taken place. In that sense it remains true that if no *Dasein* ek-sists, then no world is 'there' either. On the other hand, if it is true that *Dasein* does not have the priority in the coming-to-pass of Being and time, then all that which *Being and Time* tried to describe from *Dasein's* point of view, must now be described from the viewpoint of that mysterious 'It' which

grants Being as well as time. Where in *Being and Time* the horizonal schemata were understood as that which *Dasein's* understanding projects, it is now said that 'It' gives time in such a way that in time the ek-stases grant one another to each other. In other words, where in *Being and Time* the ek-stases were determined by the 'for the sake of which,' the 'in the face of,' and the 'in order to' of *Dasein's* projecting case, they are determined now by the Open which is granted by the 'It' while the three dimensions give themselves over to one another.

2. 'It' Grants Being and Time

We have seen that we must say: There is something which grants Being as well as time. But what now is this 'It?' In answering this question, Heidegger suggests, we must not think of this 'It' as a 'power' or a 'God.' We must try to determine it from Being as Presence and from time as the transcendental domain in which the clearing of the multiform Presence is granted.

The granting which is found in 'It grants Being' manifests itself as a mittence of Presence in its epochal transformations, whereas in the expression 'It grants time,' it appears as a lighting presenting of a four-dimensional domain, the Open, time-space. Taking into consideration that in Being as Presence time manifests itself, one could expect that genuine time, the four-fold granting of the Open, constitutes that mysterious 'It' which grants Being as Presence. Genuine time would then be the 'It' we have in mind when we say 'It grants Being.' The mittence in which Being is granted, would then consist in the granting of time. But is it really true that time is that mysterious 'It' which grants being? By no means, for time itself, too, is the gift of an 'It grants.' Thus this mysterious 'It' is still undetermined.[65]

[64] *Ibid.*, pp. 16–17.
[65] *Ibid.*, pp. 17–18.

Heidegger points out that perhaps we find ourselves in a very difficult situation here in that we have to use sentences of Indogermanic languages which do not have a clear theory about 'impersonal propositions.' He invites the reader, therefore, not to pay too much attention to the propositions, but rather to the 'thing itself' to which they refer. What is meant by the 'It' must be determined from that granting-process which belongs to it, that is the granting which at the same time is mittence (*Geschick*) and lighting presenting (*lichtendes Reichen*).

In the mittence of Being and the presenting of time there manifests itself an ap-propriation making Being as Presence and time as the Open that which they properly are. That which makes both, namely Being and time, what they properly are (*Eigenes*) and makes them belong together, is what Heidegger calls *Ereignis*, aboriginal and ap-propriating Event. The *Ereignis* makes Being and time belong together and brings both to what they properly speaking are. In other words, that mysterious 'It' about which we have spoken is the *Ereignis*. And this *Ereignis* is ontologically prior to Being as well as to time, because it is that which grants to both what they properly are. —This expression is correct and yet it is not completely true, because it hides the original relationship between Being, time, and the Event.

But what then is this ap-propriating Event? Before trying to answer this question we must point once again to two difficulties connected with this question. We have already seen that this typical Event is such that it cannot be captured in a proposition. Furthermore, in asking the question: What is this ap-propriating Event we ask about the quiddity (*Was-sein*), the essence, the mode of Being, the way in which the Event abides and is present. But this presupposes that we already know what Being is and how

Being is to be determined from the viewpoint of time. We have already seen that the mittence of Being rests on the revealing-concealing presenting of the pluriform Presence in the Open domain of time-space. But this presenting as well as that sending belong within the Event, and thus cannot be presupposed in the determination of the Event.[66]

That is why it is perhaps better to say first what Event does not mean. The word 'event' does not have its common meaning here. It usually means occurrence, whereas in this case it means the ap-propriation taken as a presenting and sending. In other words, whereas it does not make sense to speak about the occurrence of Being, it does make sense to speak about Being as Event.

In the past people have tried to conceive of Being as *Idea, actualitas,* Will, and so on. One could think that Heidegger is suggesting here that it is now time to think of Being as Event. That this is not so becomes clear the moment one realizes that any attempt to understand Event as a modifying interpretation of Being is tantamount to trying to understand Being in terms of a typical kind of being, namely an event. One might proceed here along the following lines. Until now we have tried to think about Being in terms of Presence and letting-be-present in its relation to the showing-and-hiding presenting of genuine time. In this way it became clear that Being belongs to the Event. Thus it is from the Event that the granting as well as its gift (Being) must be determined. In this case one could say that Being is a kind of Event, but Event is not a kind of Being. Such a solution of the problem, however, is too cheap in that it hides the original relationship. Event is not a *summum genus* under which one must distinguish Being as well as time. As we have seen, Being has manifested itself as the gift of the mittence of

[66] *Ibid.*, pp. 18–21.

Presence which is granted through the presenting of time. As such Being remains a property (*Eigentum*) of the ap-propriating Event; Being vanishes in the Event. And the same is true for time. In the ap-propriating Event, Being as letting-be-present is sent just as time is presented there. In the Event, Being as well as time are ap-propriated (*ereignet im Ereignis*). But what about the Event itself? Is there anything more we can say about it?

Heidegger is of the opinion that, indeed, one could say more about it. In the preceding pages we came across expressions such as 'denying,' 'withdrawing,' 'withholding,' etc., which made it clear that a certain 'withdrawal' (*Entzug*) is characteristic of the aboriginal Event. This clue can and should be followed up in greater detail. But Heidegger refrains from doing so for purely practical reasons.[67] He concludes the Time-lecture with a few general remarks on certain characteristics of the Event.

We have seen that the sending in the mittence of Being was determined as a granting; that which grants was said to hold to itself, to adhere to itself, to withhold itself; it withdraws from the revealment. A similar statement was made in regard to the presenting characteristic of time. But if it is true that the Event withdraws from revealment we may say that the Event ex-propriates itself from itself and that a certain ex-propriation is characteristic for the ap-propriating Event. This does not mean that the Event gives up itself, but precisely that it preserves its own property.

We have seen, also, that in Being as Presence there manifests itself a process which is going-on and which concerns us men in such a way that the vital characteristic of our humanity is to be found in becoming aware of this procedure and thus taking it over. But this acceptance of Presence's going-on

rests on the fact that we stand in the domain of presenting which the four-dimensional time has passed on to us.

Insofar as Being and time are found only and exclusively in the ap-propriation (*das Ereignen*) there belongs to this as a characteristic the fact that it brings man who receives Being to that which is characteristic of him as he stands within the domain of genuine time. This belonging-to rests on the complete ap-propriation characteristic of the ap-propriating Event. It is this complete ap-propriation which lets man enter this Event. This is why we cannot conceive of the Event as something opposite to us or as something which encompasses everything. Representational thought has as little access to the Event as does a speaking in propositions.

Finally, by going from Being to the mittence of Being and from time to the presenting of time-space we have gained some access to the Event. It is of importance, however, to repeat once again: The Event is not a thing. The Event *is* not, nor is there something which gives the Event. The only thing we can say is: *das Ereignis ereignet.* This tautology points to what hides itself in truth as *a-letheia.*[68]

IV. *Conclusion*

We must now return to the main question Heidegger left unanswered in *Being and Time.* There can be no doubt that his thought has made considerable progress since 1927. Part of this development was already evident in *Letter on Humanism* (1947), where the priority in the coming-to-pass of truth is given to Being and a historicity is attributed to Being itself which is distinguished from, and independent of, *Dasein's* temporality and historicity. In other words, it is stated in *Letter on Humanism* that the historicity of the understanding of Being is not identical with Being's own historicity. In this and other works of the same period it

---

[67] *Ibid.*, pp. 21–23. See for other approaches to the 'Event': *Ibid.*, pp. 44–45.
[68] *Ibid.*, pp. 23–25.

was not yet clear how Heidegger believed he would be able to avoid relativism once the finitude and historicity of the Being-process is explicitly recognized and admitted. In this regard in *Letter on Humanism* Heidegger seems to adopt the following point of view.[69] The thinking of Being thinks Being as this grants itself in mittences. The various mittences taken together constitute Being's history. "That is why thought which thinks upon the truth of Being is as thought historical." [70] When a foundational thinker thinks the mittences of Being and formulates this in words, then his thought is historical. When he retrieves the thought of an earlier foundational thinker than his thought is historical in a second sense, but both these senses are complementary; in both cases Being comes (future) to the thinker as having-been in what is (past) and is made manifest (present) through the articulation of words. That is why the fundamental structure of thought is that of recollection.[71] All thinkers then are engaged in the identical task, namely to think the mittences of Being, but each one accomplishes this in a different way. That is why there is no real progress in foundational thought.[72] That the coming-to-pass of Truth in foundational thought leads to different expressions is connected with the fact that Being discloses itself while partly hiding itself. From this it follows that each expression is equally meaningful provided it understands itself *as* historical. Refutation in foundational thought is absurd.[73] Heidegger himself is aware of the danger of relativism which remains present in this view, also. He believes that one can overcome this danger by realizing that relativism makes sense only within a sub-

ject-object opposition. Once it is realized that the truth of an object is not to be considered as relative to a subject, relativism loses its meaning.[74] But this does not answer the question adequately, and the danger of relativism was not yet completely overcome in 1947. For there can be no doubt that Heidegger does not admit an absolute truth in the sense that there is a truth which is 'eternal' or 'praeter-historical.' Furthermore, in his view there is no necessary link between the various epochs of Being's history. "The epochs never permit themselves to be derived from one another and, indeed, to be reduced to the sequence of a consecutive process." On the other hand, there is a relationship between the epochs in that each later epoch comes "out of the concealment of the mittence." [75]

When later in *Vorträge und Augsätze* (1954) and *Identität und Differenz* (1957) the ambiguity of the *Ereignis* conception as found in *Brief über den Humanismus* is removed, Heidegger was in a position to sharpen his position in regard to the question of relativism. It seems to me that it is one of the main contributions of the Time-lecture that it makes this later view explicit. Heidegger emphasizes once again the finitude of man, the finitude of man's comprehension of Being, the finitude of the coming-to-pass of truth, that is the finitude of the *Ereignis* itself. And yet he asks the question of whether a contemplative turning toward the *Ereignis* could perhaps lead to the end of Being's history. Heidegger says that the experience for which the lecture tried to prepare the reader, does not lead to an identification of Being and thought (Hegel), and yet in some sense this experience does lead

---

[69] Richardson, William J.: *op. cit.*, pp. 545–548.
[70] Heidegger, Martin: *Platons Lehre von der Wahrheit. Mit einem Brief über den 'Humanismus'* (Bern: Francke, 1947), p. 81.
[71] *Ibid.*, p. 111.
[72] *Ibid.*, p. 81.
[73] *Ibid.*, p. 82.
[74] Heidegger, Martin: *Vorträge und Aufsätze* (Pfullingen: Neske, 1954), p. 261.
[75] Heidegger, Martin: *Der Satz vom Grund* (Pfullingen: Neske, 1957), p. 154.

to the end of the history of metaphysics. True, the *Ereignis* contains possibilities of unveilment which thought cannot yet distinguish and even less can push aside as irrelevant; thus the contemplative turning toward the *Ereignis* cannot 'stop' future mittences. But could it perhaps be that after the experience has been lived in that contemplative turning toward the *Ereignis* one can no longer speak of Being's history. Before the experience is lived thought remains either within one of the epochs (relativism), or it tries to transcend this epoch by appealing to the 'God of the philosophers' or another absolute. However, once this experience is lived one can understand each mittence as one possible mittence in which the *Ereignis* itself withdraws.[76]

Heidegger returns to this issue in the question concerning the meaning of the term 'change' as found in the lecture in the expression *Wandlungs-fülle des Seins*. From within classical metaphysics this means the changing forms of expressions in which Being shows itself historically in each epoch. Then the question is: By what is the sequence of the various epochs determined? or, from where is this sequence determined? Why is the sequence the way it actually is? Hegel thought that the sequence is determined by necessity which at the same time is the highest freedom. Heidegger believes that *on this level* one cannot ask and answer this question. One can only say here that the history of Being is the way it is. This 'that' is the only datum which, for thought, is to be accepted inevitably and thus 'with necessity.' One can even indicate then a certain regularity in the sequence and (for instance) claim that the sequence is 'guided' by an increasing forgottenness of Being.[77]

From the viewpoint of the Time-lecture, however, that is to say from the viewpoint of the *experience* for which

it tries to prepare us, the term has a different meaning. In the lecture it is said that Being is changed into *Ereignis*. On that level, the expression does not point to the various manifestations of Being which follow one another, but to the fact that Being (with all its possible, epochal manifestations) is taken back into the *Ereignis*. In other words, if the philosopher looks at the *Wandlungsfülle des Seins* as has always been done in classical metaphysics, then this fullness falls apart in epochs which are no longer related to one another in a way that can be justified with necessity. One can bring a unity to the multiplicity only by introducing the 'God of the philosophers' as the one who gives the series a goal, or eventually who constitutes this goal. One can bring a kind of unity to this multiplicity by setting up a law or rule which somehow justifies the sequence of the epochs, one similar to that suggested by Heidegger. But underlying this way of looking at things there is the classical conception of time which conceives of time in terms of isolated 'now'-moments which as such do not necessarily belong together.

However, if the philosopher looks at this 'fullness' from the viewpoint which Heidegger tries to suggest in this lecture, then the unity of the multiplicity is never broken. The question then is not how this particular and isolated epoch could ever change into another isolated epoch, but how the Being process as a whole 'changes' into the Event in which future and past are held together in the Presence. For in this case one understands, or perhaps more accurately stated, *experiences* that the various epochs are no longer mysteries, but are the necessary consequence of the inherent finitude of an aboriginal Event which presents the Open and grants Being, and in so doing withdraws in favor of this domain and its gift.

---

[76] *Zur Sache des Denkens*, pp. 53–54.
[77] *Ibid.*, pp. 55–57.

CONCERNING EMPTY AND FUL-FILLED TIME*

Hans-Georg Gadamer

Emeritus Professor, University of Heidelberg

The experience is well known which Augustine describes in the 10th Book of his *Confessions,* when he says that he understands precisely what time is when he does not reflect upon it. But as soon as he directs his attention to it and wants to say clearly what time really is, then he is completely nonplussed. This famous description of the problem of time in the introduction of Augustine's analysis appears to me to be the prototype of all genuine philosophical perplexity. Self-concealment in the thoughtlessness of what is self-evident is like a great resistance, which is unconquerable because of its lack of that with which philosophical thought and its desire to comprehend constantly have to contend. To conceive what is self-evident is a task of peculiar difficulty. It is a matter of presenting what is evasive because it is constantly behind one. The behind-the-back experience of such an evasion is the source of the intrinsic uneasiness of philosophical knowledge. Evasion and non-appearance in themselves always have the greater obtrusiveness and conspicuousness, as opposed to the dependable existence of what one is accustomed to. For the philosopher, however, such an evasion has a special structure. It is a withdrawal into what is self-evident, a perplexity which is continually being renewed, which is named by one word, *problem,* and which is taken over from the dialectical situation of conflict. The great fundamental questions of philosophy all have this structure: they do not allow themselves to be held at bay in a way which makes possible an unequivocal answer to them. They seem to evade the grasp of our concepts and nevertheless continue to attract in their evasiveness. To be attracted by something which retracts itself constitutes the basic movement of philosophical interest. This attraction-retraction calls into question the conceptuality in terms of which one inquires. We can indeed say: the philosophical problem is a question which one does not know how to "raise."

Such is also the case with the problem of time. We are greatly perplexed when we attempt to say what time is, because in virtue of a self-evident preconception of what is, what is present is always understood by that preconception. The traditional Greek concepts have conceptually hardened this presupposition. The perplexity in which thought has become entangled is that time appears to have its sole Being in the 'now' of the present, and, nevertheless, it is just as clear that time, precisely in the 'now' of the present, is as such not present. What now is, is always already past. It seems incomprehensible how one is supposed to comprehend what is past, as that which no longer is, and what is future, as that which is not yet, in terms of the being of the 'now,' which alone exists, in such a way that the whole "is" time. The dimensionality of time does not seem to be master of the concept of the being of the present, which deter-

Hans-Georg Gadamer is Professor Emeritus of Philosophy at the University of Heidelberg. He is editor of Die Philosophische Rundschau. *Among his many books are* Wahrheit und Methode *and* Kleine Schriften I *and* II.

* Delivered in June, 1969, in Heidelberg, Germany, at a colloquium honoring Heidegger's 80th birthday. Subsequently published in *Die Frage Martin Heideggers,* ed. Hans Georg Gadamer, Carl Winter, Universitaetsverlag, Heidelberg, 1969. This is a limited publication sponsored by the Heidelberger Akademis der Wissenschaften. Translated by R. Phillip O'Hara.

mines Greek thought of Being. Augustine's great achievement was precisely to sharpen this perplexity of thought and then with his own spiritual depth of experience to show that a mode of reflexive human experience is reflected in the dimensionality of time. To be sure, he thereby follows the reawakening and new interpretation of Platonic thought in late antiquity. But the hierarchy of Being which is developed in the thought of Plotinus and in that of his followers — that the intelligible world descends to the material world via the "soul" and implies that all time has its true place in the "soul"— is transposed by him into his own individual experience. This reinterpretation occurs when he conceives the *distentio animi* as the soul's stretching forth toward the future and ultimately toward the redemption from temporality by divine grace. The soul's stretching forth, its collecting itself out of the dispersed multiplicity which results from corruption through curiosity —this is the point of truth in which Augustine feels superior to the difficulties of Greek thought, even if he is not able conceptually to achieve this superiority.

In truth the question whether time has reality at all is not simply the legacy of Greek thought, but rather is a problem which is raised again and again from the subject matter itself, and it is a question which accompanies thought through the whole tradition of Western philosophy. Is there such a thing as time? Aristotle already touches on this question when he remarks that the designation of time, which he considers as the reckoning of motion, the counted sequence of nows in which motion is unfolded, implies the being of reckoning souls. For him that certainly does not mean that time is less real than, say, "place" ($\tau\acute{o}\pi\sigma s$) or that it exists and occurs only in human apprehension. Such a consequence, however, forces itself to the fore: just as each counted number is only real by the counting of the

human spirit, so time also does not appear to be simply real, and only appears as time in the experience of man. In the famous theses indexed in Paris in the year 1277, it occurs as one of the reprobate false teachings that time is nothing real (*in re*), but exists only *in apprehensions*. It seems to be an unavoidable speculative temptation to raise this question: is there really time? Or is the way in which one thinks that which really is as in time bound to the specific finiteness of consciousness, and is time, therefore, (alongside space) an *a priori* subjective form of intuition as Kant teaches, or in whatever way? Probably every thinking person succumbs to the temptation, contra what is really the case, to think of time as something which can be conceived as suspended. This temptation is stronger regarding time than place, which, in view of what is present, itself appears present and thereby appears to have an incontestable reality. Greek conceptuality seems simply to formulate that which corresponds to all human experience of Being.

These speculative impulses have absolutely nothing to do with the modern scientific concept of time. For in science no assertion concerning the reality or illusion of time is made at all. The scientific concept of time functions simply as that which makes possible temporal measurement and the quantifying observation of processes of motion. When Newton uses the famous expression of absolute time which flows constantly, he simply extrapolates that which is demanded by the immanent conditions of temporal measurement. To be sure the problem of time has from time immemorial been most closely connected with that of temporal measurement; connected so closely, in fact, that the problem of temporal measurement appears actually to diminish and replace the problem of the being of time. In any case the independence of time from what is supposed to be measured in time is a necessary demand of all temporal measurement. Time in this sense is empty in so far as such an expression has any sense at all in relation to the physical concept of time. And it is empty in so far as the more recent development of physics and its analysis of simultaneity have not also relativised the problem of temporal measurement. It is not only modern science which fails to raise the question of the "being" of time —every departure from temporal measurement and temporal calculation obscures the question by keeping in view that by which one measures time. Thus the oldest answer of the Greeks, that time is the heaven, is completely natural. But how much is there already presupposed! As overagainst everything which is "in it," time, which is to be measured, is already conceived as "empty." And the experience of empty time is in any case not an original experience. Given its non-primordial character, one is moved to ask, what are the experiential conditions which allow time to appear to us as the empty time which we fill up.

Among the many statements which Aristotle makes regarding the being of man occurs the statement that man is the creature who has a sense for time (αἴσθησις χρόνου). The context in which Aristotle mentions this sense shows unequivocally what he had in mind: man's having foresight. To have foresight, however, means: seeing anticipatorially that which is not yet and thereby relating in their distance what is foreseen and what is present. One thereby accepts the foreseen as present. A sense for time is primarily a sense for what is future, not for what is present. This sense is present in prolepsis and refers what is present to what is not present. A sense for time means first that we are creatures which can set objectives for ourselves and are able, therefore, to seek means which are appropriate to these objectives. And that presupposes distance from what captivates one for the present moment. To be able to make up one's mind to

do something includes the ability to prefer something which is unpleasant, e.g., a bitter medicine in light of the anticipated purpose of its healing effect. That is an anthropologically reasonable thesis of Aristotle. Man is distinguished from the animal by the fact that the animal is completely occupied and engrossed by the what is present or most imminently expected. The immediate binds him in his instincts. On the other hand, collecting animals like bees and ants are especially interesting for philosophy, because they seem to have something analogous to human foresight, since they prepare themselves for the coming winter. To what extent, however, is that a sense for time? Certainly not as a sense in which time is experienced as time. It is indeed not time as such toward which human expectation or foresight is oriented, but rather toward a future situation as something that is yet to be. Nevertheless, this futurity has its significance for the experience of time. Time "until" the attainment of the purpose is not simply bided as it "passes," but rather this time span is experienced in the same temporal way: as duration. Duration is the mode in which we experience anticipation and the anticipatory disposition as 'time for' and as 'time until.' In this instance time is experienced as free or empty. The view to purposeful action functions as a measure and everything that is not commensurate with it is overshadowed by the anticipated present of the decisive purpose. The penumbral character of everything else which imposes itself as alluring and attractive permits time itself to appear as something of which man can dispose — for the purpose of purposeful action. Time is made free for this purposiveness, and in this light it may be considered empty: when it is viewed in relation to what fills it.

This Aristotelian view is supplemented by the insight of the modern Aristotelian, Hegel. Hegel describes man's ability to restrain his passions as being the distinction of human beings. Restrained passion requires denial in the moment for the benefit of future success. To this extent restrained passion is a basic presupposition for the possibility of there being human culture: it makes work possible. Time is here encountered, therefore, as that which is to be disposed of, as that which can be filled in one way or another, and therefore, as that which is to be administered. The pre-plan of that time which is to be administered constitutes, therefore, the emptiness of time.

The question now is, however, whether this mode of experiencing time as that which we ourselves project as empty, i.e., project with a view to filling up, is the original experience of time. Do not all forms of disposing of time mean an inauthentic temporality, i.e., an experience of time which presupposes a more original temporality: that of the projecting being (*Dasein*) itself, which is itself temporal and which does not simply reckon with its time? Heidegger raised to an ontological theme the essential finiteness of existence (*Dasein*) as the original temporality of human existence to which Augustine already directs our attention. Death is not only something of which every child receives knowledge in such a way that it thenceforth "knows it." Heidegger rather showed how 'knowledge' of death lies at the base of our experience of time and of our reckoning with time. The Greek myth of Prometheus also reflects this same insight, insofar as Prometheus takes from men the exact knowledge of their own deaths in order to provide salvation for them. Such unknowing knowledge of one's own finitude, however, means the failure of the disposability of time. This time is conscious as something which establishes real limits, and this in a final way. For time itself is experienced as the hostile opposition which destroys the illusion of an unlimited continuation of the possibility of disposing of time, and this negative experience of being too

late or past is applicable not only for the end of life, but similarly for every single experience and decision in life. Nevertheless, this insight simply confirms in general that time is understood as that which is at our disposal and which is at our disposal in the sense that it is presence. Its negativity as such becomes unavoidable only in border-line experiences.

In fact we always experience the negativity of time in this context when time is lacking for us or slips between our fingers, and that means that we find no more time *for something*. Thus the expression *hora non ruit* makes sense precisely because it preserves the ghostlike imperceptibility of time's elapsing in the experience of being too late. It appears as if there is something uncanny about it. But is it really time which is experienced in this instance and which is experienced as limited opposition, rather than that for which we strive in time, or which evades us as unreachable? What kind of a reality is time itself as opposed to what is expected of it and in it? Indeed, what kind of an entity is it, in which one can always speak only of vanishing and not of beginning? Our whole sense for language resists the expression that time begins, whereas with respect to the vanishing of something other than time we always have in mind its beginning as the corresponding motion. Is time "something" at all?

The fact that time is something comes out most clearly at that point where nothing is encountered "in the time" towards which human existence or *Dasein* has a future character. Time, in its transience, is then experienced as something present by its emptiness. Something similar is connoted in part by the German expression of *Zeitvertreib* (pastime). What in *Zeitvertreib* is actually passed away (*vertreiben*)? Certainly not the time which passes. And yet time itself is intended, its empty duration, that lingering (*das Weilen*) which as lingering is too long (*lange*) and therefore appears as agonizing boredom (*Langweile*). Here one certainly does not dispose of time, but only because one simply does not know for what purpose to use it. One is bored because one "has" nothing "to do." The disposing of time, its systematic arrangement and filling up, is there, as it were, in privative form. What is lacking are intentions, and thereby the experience of boredom continues to be referred to the reentrance of intentions. Boredom is an extreme form of the experience of time with which one must reckon. Time becomes as it were refractory by nothing being in it, because it does not pass quickly enough. Thus there appears to be no essential difference between boredom and the experience that time becomes long. This experience occurs when we wait for something. When we say "it takes forever" we mean simply that what we expect has still not yet come. The opposite experience, that one would like to make time last longer for the sake of some beautiful moment (in this case the passing of time is in fact experienced as a deprivation), this experience also means something for the sake of which one administers or beguiles time or wants to detain it. This experience is not intended as time itself; it appears as a phantom horizon of the emptiness which is to be filled out. *Non in re, sed in apprehensione.*

Is it not the case in all these experiences, however, that the reality of time is always simultaneously intended? The temporal horizon into which we live may well be our projection, but in the end is it not the case that the conscious projection of an experience of time resides in liveliness as such? When Schelling writes, "The anxiety of life drives the creature from its center," he is alluding with this expression to the basic disposition of the "creature," to preserve itself as "itself." Anxiety here is not so much a state of mind, but rather the *agens*, which resists against life's being constrained and threatened.

It is the reality of time which is so

experienced. In such an experience time is not conscious as the empty horizon which embraces every occurrence in time. Rather it is conscious as primordial temporality, which occurs with an entity as such, and which is there driven by the anxiety of life. Overagainst this primordial time, "world-time" turns out to be secondary. The "reality" of time, however, does not mean that time is something present-at-hand. Since Heidegger's critique of the ontological implications of the concepts of subjectivity and consciousness, that is self-evident. Given Heidegger's derivation of world-time as the horizon of *Dasein's* care which is addicted to the world, it is clear, in light of the primordial temporality of *Dasein* and its essential care-structure, that the question of the reality of time does not ask whether or how it is constituted as an object of consciousness.

This question is basically laid out in *Sein und Zeit*. The transcendental analytic of *Dasein* points out the *a priori* conditions of every human experience of time and of Being in the demonstration of the temporal structure of care. But the book is not limited to developing the ontological distinction of *Dasein*, i.e., that of "understanding" its Being and of constructing the *a priori* presuppositions for all understanding. It was not in vain that *Sein und Zeit* juxtaposed the self-constancy of the "there" as anticipatory resoluteness to the traditional metaphysical question of the self of *Dasein* (*Sein und Zeit*, p. 322). In this book Heidegger did not seek to conceive the "horizon of time" in terms of the self of *Dasein*, but rather in terms of "there" as the ontological structure of resoluteness — which was later to be designated as "event." Primordial temporality, ultimately, is not the being of the futurity of *Dasein*, which understands itself out of its being. It is rather the "event of Being," in which the horizons of the future and the past are permeated in such a way that *"Da-Sein"* takes place. *Dasein*, which projects itself upon its being, is not the only 'reality' that has a temporal structure. *Dasein* is not the only source of the temporal horizon's projection. This temporal horizon is the region in which concern for 'care' understands itself, and this horizon is filled by this understanding. Time is such that Being comes to pass.

When one has learned to detach temporality from the ontological preconception of the present-at-hand and also not to conceive it as the simple horizon-phenomenon of temporal consciousness, then other phenomena press in, in which time likewise appears as "real." These preconceptions have their point of connection, not in the Aristotelian tradition of thought, but in the Platonic tradition. By following Heidegger's elucidation of the ontological conceptuality of metaphysics and of the force of tradition, which this conceptuality perpetuates, we may better recognize these preconceptions in their true meaning.

I begin with the doctrine which Plotinus, following Plato, defended, viz., that time can be understood only from the perspective of eternity. This is revealed in a new light when the customary theological premises are suspended. What we call eternity is thus, as is claimed by the theological tradition of Christianity, a concept which has as background the ontological distinction between creator and creature. Thus concept of eternity does not exist in Greek thought, not even in Platonic thought, which divided the "invisible" world of ideal Being, and ascribed to it timeless Being in the sense of ἀΐδιον, from the visible world of Becoming, which lacks Being. (The latent word-play between ἀΐδες and ἀΐδιον in the "Phaedrus" is to be compared . . . 80d₆.) To be sure it was precisely Plato, who in giving the first definition of time, called it the moved image of eternity. But the word which he used here is *Aion*. *Aion* itself means a temporal phenomenon. The word is used above all for 'lifetime' and then this meaning is transformed to 'unlimited duration.' Aristotle, in order to designate the eternity of the divine mover, had to append συνεχὴς καὶ ἀΐδιος (*Met.* 1072b 29f.). And when Plato in the "Timaeus" designates time as the moved image of eternity, the connecting thought is that "the world" is the organic state of a living creature which rests on the intelligible order that Plato mathematically constructs as the Pythagorean harmony of the universe. This order maintains itself in its movements and is called by him the "world-soul." For "soul" is the principle of self-motion and self-preservation. The myth of the "Timaeus" presents mythically how the world is founded in the being of the soul. *Aion* is thus the life-time of this great world-organism, the superior, unlimited duration of the world enlivened by its "soul." Through its distinction from the changing transitoriness of our appearing reality, the duration of what has been beautifully united acquires the new accent of eternity.

In what follows I will try to adhere to the fact that time is conceived from the perspective of the world's life-time and to keep aloof from all implications which intend an eternity that would no longer be temporality. I am thereby following a motif which originates in Plotinus and which has been developed above all by Franz von Baader and Schelling into the doctrine of "organic time." It will also be important for us that Scholasticism in its doctrine of "Aevum" adhered to its temporal character by distinguishing the angels' time from eternity, which befitted no creature at all. All these questions arise when one exceeds certain designations found in *Sein und Zeit,* viz., its "transcendental" self-interpretation and the primordial temporal experience of *"Dasein"* which knows itself to be finite.

In order to make the problem of organic time perceptible, I will begin with one of the most profound statements that I know from that part of the Greek tradition familiar to me. It is a statement of the Greek doctor Alkmaion: "Human beings therefore have to die because they have not learned to connect the end with the beginning." What is intended by this sentence, the depth of which is terrifying? It is evident that a cyclical structure is implied in it. The fact that life's process is a cycle and that life is above all differentiated from so called dead entities by the fact that it constantly maintains itself in the cycle of its regeneration, is a basic insight, in light of which the doctor Alkmaion surely understood also man's health as an organic being. This cyclical process constitutes the being of living things. It constantly discharges itself back into itself in a process which is rythmically repeated such that there is a continuous restoration of balance.

The phenomenon of balance that appears here points to the broadest associations of early Greek thought. In the cosmological realm it occurs in a series of formulations like *isorropia* or similar words and formulates the conception of the being of *physis*, insofar as the world is not made and not borne by an Atlas, but rather keeps and maintains itself in itself. Such a concept of balance apparently underlies not only Greek medicine, but every uncluttered view of organic life. Thus it seems that Alkmaion had just spoken of *isonomy,* and everything that we know of his doctrine of antitheses confirms that this mysterious sentence from which we are proceeding aims at the rhythmical and basic constitution of life.

It opposes humans to the gods, however, because humans lack this constant self-reconstruction and regeneration that constitutes the wonderful being of the Olympian gods. Since pain only briefly belongs to the gods and the peril of death does not belong to them at all, their individual personalities, which the poet evokes, are dissolved in the continuous self-reproduc-

tion of their power. Thus there are indeed no individuals which, as gods, bear the authentic immortality. Aristotle's verbatim critique of the Olympian gods who enjoy nectar and ambrosia, however, correctly uncovers this contradiction (*Met.* B 1000a 9ff.). The divine figures have more the ontological status of the form of life which reproduces itself as genus in the cycle of natural life and not as individuals. The view of the cyclical character of natural life itself, however, still guides man's primary self-understanding when the immortality of the soul, as occurs in the Platonic "Phaedo," is conceived from the perspective of life's reproduction. This reference is still more interesting not only in the "Symposium," but also in the "Phaedo," where it strangely limits the evidence for immortality, which is based on the doctrine of ideas. Man, however, is, as it were, the fateful creature whose own certainty of life knowingly includes the certainty of death. Alkmaion apparently thinks from the perspective of this life-certainty, which is familiar to the observing eye of the doctor as the constant battle for the preservation of balance, its being jeopardized and its being reclaimed. Life-certainty possesses its own structure of temporality, such that an indwelling sense of lasting Presence belongs to it. That is the basic assurance behind the words of Alkmaion: they point out, as though it were a dereliction or failure, that such continuous presence, like that which characterizes cyclical motion, is not achieved by man.

If this failure belongs to the essential being of man, then the temporality which is inherent to his life-certainty is modified. When, in contrast to the inherent nature of *Physis,* turning back into one's self does not take place in eternal recurrence, past and future are separated, and the "duration" of life is articulated in the unfolding of one's age. Time itself thereby becomes organic, and such a constitution of time is constitutive for the state of organic being. Only that which is separated from the cycle of life and isolated as something separate, "has" time. It has begun "its" time when it begins its life. Schelling once illustrated this point by reference to a seed: the seed does not yet belong to the time of the future plant and therefore is in a certain sense "eternal." But when it germinates and thereby ceases being a simple seed, the time of the developing plant has begun. That means that the seed is now "fixed" as past for the plant. What has been separated from its own past can no longer participate in its return. The primordial separation which in one act occurs in a being which has a past and in a being which is a self, thus poses death. Thereby life-time is articulated in the course of a life. For that is the authentic temporal structure of such a life-time: the present is in formed phases which are constituted in periods of life, each of which has its own dimension as what it may be sooner and what it may be later. Getting older is not a process which corresponds to the flow of passing time. It is not a continual flowing by of time which determines in every moment one's age. This continual flux is rather the way we measure time: We attach that which is in time to the uniform time-lapse of the "clock." But getting older is not an experience of passing time. It is rather a specific determination of that which has its own time, whether this determination is then experienced by someone or by others. Thus such an experience of age does not belong to the temporal consciousness of passing time, which conceives both the open dimensions of future and past as the infinite continuation of passing time. Hegel once described it very beautifully — it is conclusive and correct that the temporal experience of life exists in the fact that a vast quantity of the future slowly melts and a huge quantity of the past grows. And Max Scheler, who has made very profound comments regarding these things, directly derived the naturalness of death, and the affirmation of death, if I may so express it, from this schema of a past which becomes ever more and more. The experience of time which is here transpiring is that of becoming something else — not as something which has changed on a constant substratum, but rather in the immediacy of having become something else. A living creature enters a particular age and leaves another age behind. Its temporality has a discontinuity of a peculiar kind, upon which Heraclitus had apparently already reflected when he conceived as the secret truth of Being the sudden change, the abrupt appearance of what is new and the sinking of what is old: "Children throw away their toys when they grow up" (Reinhardt, From Frgm. 70, and Clemens, Protr. c 10, 78,7 in Hermes 77). Again we must keep in mind that such an experience of change points back to non-change, i.e., to an undifferentiated union of the "present," in which that which lives "maintains" itself. This ontological status of the present belongs to the *Aion* in one's life-time as such, without detriment to all the changes which form one's "course of life."

It is useful here to recall Plotinus. All cosmic geneologies of his system can be set aside. He himself says that one who simply attempts to understand what time is, is led back to the *Aion*. *Aion,* however, means the mode of Being which belongs to the essence of life or, as Plotinus says, the lustre of Being which radiates from life qua life. Plotinus surely follows Plato and has in view intelligible Being, i.e., the realm of ideas, as true Being. But he nevertheless conceives the antithetical construction for time, which Plato intends when he calls time the moved image of eternity. In this instance he does not think of time at all as eternity, but thinks of it totally from the perspective of being moved. Plato himself says of eternity that it remains in one place ($\mu\acute{\epsilon}\nu o\nu$ $\grave{\epsilon}\nu$ $\acute{\epsilon}\nu\acute{\iota}$). Plotinus makes this his point of departure and carefully delineates *Aion*'s state of Being, which is neither pure selfsameness nor self-constancy, neither ταυτότης nor αὐτόστασις, overagainst the intelligible world: the *Aion* is encompassing without encompassing parts. Everything is in it at the same time. It is complete being in the present, in which no future is outstanding and from which no past is missing. Its being is no lifeless presence, but is rather an infinite possibility or power (ἀπείρος δύναμις). In a certain way, it is thus much, even everything, like the seed or point are in their own way.

This *Aion* is like some time before the origin of time, before the negativity implied in the difference between one thing and another and before the progress from one to another. And it may be experienced with and in life's certainty as such. Schelling, who contemplates the problem further, describes this temporality by using the example of undeveloped childhood which "without any distinction" is still momentary fulfillment, i.e., is still before the beginning of time when the past is "posed" and future is opened up.

This analysis of *Aion* plainly describes the temporal structure of that which endures as one and the same in every alteration and articulation of life's phases, namely liveliness. It is thus not necessary that the self-sameness of an identical ego be given along with it, an ego which endures through every alteration and for whom its identity occasionally flashes in the consciousness of recollection or, more likely, as fright. *Aion* is rather the complete identity of life with itself, which fulfills the Present by the constant virtuality of its possibilities. As much as recollection and memory also constitute the self-consciousness of a person, the self-sameness of being alive is more subjacent and more closely resembles the angels' mode of Being in Medieval speculation. Their temporality is the *Aevum* without the continuity of an ego.

If this is right, then we have gained some ground so as also to do justice to the temporal character of historical experience. For the temporality of history is also not originally measured time, and where it is such, it is not an arbitrary co-ordination of an event to the periodicity of nature or of heaven. For the decisive question is in that case, where does such a measurement at any given time begin, i.e., what is to be taken for a chronology? The phenomenon with which it is concerned is that of the epoch. In astronomy a certain constellation was originally designated for chronological purposes, which by its reappearance is a kind of caesura from which a new cycle of celestial movement begins. A similar task of making the event comprehensible is assumed by an historical consciousness when one arranges the process of history by epochal divisions. This always gives the impression that the division into epochs was an arbitrary process of description, classification and ordering of historical facts. The conflict over the division into epochs, however, which is carried on among historians, proves that the claim of the historian is another type of claim, namely that of placing the caesuras there in his historical description where the joints are (to express it Platonically). Thus the experiencing of epochs can not be appropriately described from the stance of a pure nominalistic theory: historical science which interprets nominalistically demonstrates precisely this by its own procedure.

What, then, is an epoch? How does it exist? If we pay attention to the use of language, it gives us a hint. We speak on occasions of an epoch-making event. To be sure this expression is often completely empty. Many epoch-making events are simply announced on the radio. What we mean by an epoch-making event, however, is completely independent of the appropriateness or misuse of this expression. An epoch-making event establishes a caesura. It establishes that which preceded as old, and everything which now comes, as new. In some circumstances the concepts of old and new have a dialectic of profound inner uncertainty. What is new rapidly becomes obsolete, and what is old proves to be new. But when it is a question of the concept of epoch, this dialectic of old and new comes, so to speak, to a halt. For an epoch-making event clearly ordains such a separation between old and new which we ourselves do not create and which we nevertheless must follow. When we become conscious that a new epoch is impinging upon us, or when we arrive at such a judgment in the retrospection of historical experience, that does not mean that the old is simply forgotten and the new welcomed, until the new again becomes obsolete and the old which was forgotten is renewed. When a new epoch dawns, one properly takes leave of the old. That is not forgetting, but is rather cognition. For cognition always occurs in departure. In departing the old is so separated from the indefinite moments of expectation which had bound our existence to it as we were engaged and projected toward the future, that it now first begins to rest completely in itself. What is really separated has acquired a new durability. We are familiar with this experience of departing, especially when we are separated from those near to us by death. When life lines are cut by death, in spite of the anguish of the loss, we do not experience a simple removal, but also a new kind of presence: the image of the one from whom we have departed acquires a lasting character. In experiencing an epoch, wherever it takes place, one also experiences such a departure, or better, one experiences the necessity of taking leave. It is not a chosen departure from something, like so many that we experience, but rather something which concerns time itself: it is experienced as an epoch, as a pause which interrupts the uniform flow of passing time. It is clear that this experience is a discontinuity and is therefore experienced as the downfall of the old. But at the same time it is the experience of a new beginning. All relations appear to be ordered in another way and to be joined to new forms. The old becomes surveyable in itself as something separated or departed, whereas an indefinite future begins, which fills man with fear of the unknown. One no doubt has a presentiment of a new gravitational point, which will result in a new order. But it is not yet to be discerned.

If our observations are right, then the experience of time which we are discussing is determined by the character of *transition*. What again matters is that we resist the anticipations of Greek ontology. The transition of which we speak is not the same as the 'now' that couples together what has preceded and what is to come, while it itself does not endure. It is in another sense that being-in-transition in a strange way simultaneously causes separation and conjunction: transition appears as the true being of time in the sense that everything is in it at the same time such that past and future are together. Whereas the uniform passing of time is a constant flux, it is clear that the experience of transition does not mean such a simple passing of time. It means rather, a definite-indefinite being, which in the experiences of departing and beginning brings the flow of time to a standstill.

Thus we do not understand the dialectic of transition by reckoning transition in terms of what is past as well as what is future. Rather the problem is to show how this intermediate position establishes the distinction between what is past and what is to come and at the same time establishes the union of both. We need to show how one is freed for the new by departing from the old.

Hölderlin's reflections in "Uber das Werden im Vergehen" ("On Becoming in Passing Away"), which go beyond Schelling's insights, become useful. What is transition? Hölderlin in his treatise described the nature of transition from the perspective of his poetical interest. It is a sort of commentary to the Empedocles-Drama. Hölderlin's tragedy presents much difficulty, as is well known to the interpreter who wishes to apply the customary tragical theories of guilt. Within the context of such customary theories, guilt or passing away are completely incomprehensible. Even that theory of verbal offence which Hölderlin at first maintained as the guiding idea for his Empedocles-poetry was later eliminated by him, and in his drama he devised departure and the fulfillment of time as the real agent of tragedy and downfall. His theory of verbal offence is somewhat comparable to the famous Tantalus-motif, according to which Tantalus boasted that he had sat at the table of the gods and by his verbal offence incurred the terrible familial curse which destroyed Agamemnon, Iphigenia and Orestes. Here transition, the change of time, is the only theme. In Empedocles the will of "maturing time" presents itself to the consciousness of an initiate, whereas the one entangled in fate usually suffers only downfall — and awaits with fear the beginning of the new as an "unknown force."

This glance at the poetical symbol of the Empedocles-figure can help us to understand that transition does not mean the dialectical mediation of the old and the new, as the problem of the "now" means in Greek ontology. This misunderstanding, however, is found in Hölderlin's conceptual mode of expression. There the transition "between to be and not to be" is designated as that in which "the possible becomes real and the real, ideal." That sounds as if the point in question were simply whether the two-sidedness of transition permits our interpretation of it to be, as it were, circumvented. If one looks to the old that passes away, the process looks like a downfall. If one looks to the new that arises, the same process looks like an evolution, a genesis, a beginning. That is in truth nothing other than the

old Greek theory of the double-relative Now, which constitutes the continuum of time. But the question does not concern two-sidedness which "transition" has for the interpreter, which constitutes the "maturing" of time. It has to do, rather, with the real uncertainty and the open infinity of the event itself. The point is not that from another perspective the dissolution of what exists is the beginning of something new. The decisive point, rather, is that insight into the necessity of this downfall gives its own existence to both, to what is past in the recollection of the dissolution and to the new, which is supposed to follow what is past. And further, the point is that in this insight, time itself is experienced. The distinguishing characteristic of transition is not that it is both passing away and developing at the same time, but rather that the new comes to be as the old is recollected in its dissolution. Thus Hölderlin in his treatise systematically contrasts the "ideal" dissolution with the "real" dissolution. It is only the "ideal" dissolution, i.e., the recollection of dissolution, that permits the future to be free in its own, yet uncertain determination. Thus with a view to tragedy, Hölderlin speaks of the ideality which the dissolution of the old requires. That means that what departed, the past world, precisely in its being over and done, is affirmed at the same time by the insight into the necessity of its dissolution. He calls the ideal dissolution "fearless" and thereby alludes to the tragical catharsis. It is "comprehending what is uncomprehensible," "of conflict and death itself by that which is harmonic, comprehensible, alive" (Beissner, 4, 1, p. 283, 11 ff.).

What is thus claimed for the "free imitation of art" as the "idealistic" dissolution, appears to me to be in truth one of our most profound forms of temporal experience: only he who can bid farewell, who can leave what lies behind him or what is removed from him beyond his reach, who does not cling fast to what is past as something which he can not relinquish, is at all able to have a future. This was thought through by Schelling with profound insight. We are familiar with this same insight in the theory of neuroses in modern depth psychology, which teaches us that when a person is bound to something, is not free from it, he is prohibited from becoming free for his own possibilities. This is the individual-psychological correspondence to the above mentioned epoch-experience. The ability to bid farewell, just as much as the openness for the new which is undetermined, is in the "all in all" character of transition. This is the justifiable motif in the concept of utopia, that a utopia in its manner of reflection replaces in general the uncertainty of the future which is yet to be determined — just as the Christian proclamation speaks in this context of hope. Hope is only significant when one does not insist upon the old, which is subsiding.

It is significant that Hölderlin views together this experience of departure and of beginning something new with his own poetical experience and unites the epoch-experience with his experience of language. In the Empedocles-figure the will of "maturing time" presents itself to the consciousness of the initiate. This will is otherwise experienced fatefully in a lack of freedom, which takes the form of downfall or the threat of newness. What Hölderlin's reflections attempt to make clear is how downfall is or can be a beginning. In the dissolution of the certainty of an existing world, infinity, which at the same time is the indetermination of what is possible, is the beginning of a new certainty, the "beginning of time and world." "The world of all world, the all in all which always exists, presents itself only in all time or in downfall or in the moment . . ." This sentence implies that transition as "the possibility of all relations," as the "all in all," *is time.*

What takes place as temporal change, similarly takes place in linguistic change. The epoch-making event which bids farewell to the old and becomes the beginning of the new is "expression, sign, presentation of an alive, but particular totality," just as the case is with the linguistic event of poetic work, whose words are "new" in all of its elements. Hölderlin's treatises are peculiarly obstructed, contemplative attempts, which are decoded only with difficulty into exact interpretation. But what it considers can be comprehended from the subject matter. Whether departure or ideal dissolution, the "all in all" of infinite possibilities not only falls to the fated men of a new era, but to every man who attempts to communicate himself totally, and above all it falls to the lot of the poet.

What makes a poet? Certainly that he says something new — in a new language. But the poet succeeds in this only because he does not simply speak further, or better: because language with its stock words and its constructions, as they are at hand for the poet, do not permit him, as it were to speak further. We, who are not poets, know the matter of *e contrario* when we translate. There we experience the same thing. It then sounds almost always like Goethe when we translate Sophocles. And that is because we are not poets, i.e., because we simply speak again a language which is already prepared and given. Hölderlin thus accurately describes the "procedural mode" of the poetic spirit when he says that the poet's word has to dissolve completely all prior factors of linguistic formation and construction. Only then is what he says in advance of that which he confronts as indefinite and yet as something to be said. That 'something which is to be said' then finds its language through him. The poet must find the word which makes possible his poetical statement and which does not possess it as what has already been given. Language is thereby poetical — not by a "poeticizing" of everyday language, but precisely by freeing language from the constraint of non-living convention. This, however, is its freeing for its own infinity. In the creation of the poet, the "all in all" has become a lasting being.

I nevertheless think that in a certain sense we all have the same linguistic experience, which the poet has in a most exemplary way.

Speech attempts to bring something into language. The appropriate word which I wish to say to someone or which someone else says to me must be spoken in such a way, relating as it does to what is not yet conscious and familiar, that one is not benumbed by it as by the metallic sounds of our educational admonitions. On the other hand, we say that we cannot find a language for someone who cannot be reached because he is closed-minded. So it is. Whoever speaks must find the *language* which is not yet there. Every real speaking is a "language event," or, to express it with Hölderlin, "something infinitely new." A real word which is addressed to someone obviously presupposes a readiness to leave behind what one brings along by way of prejudices and prior attitudes, and to be open for the wave into the indeterminate openness of the future, an openness which takes place with every word addressed to us. A theme for further exploration might consider how departure and dissolution are connected with beginning and "new creation" in our human experience, as well as in the linguistic experience of the poet.

Let me make a final general remark, however, to conclude this attempt which is dedicated to a master of thought. If what I have attempted to show is right, viz., that transition is always a strained position between departure and opening into something indeterminately new, then the possibility of something indeterminately new is dependent upon the force with which we are able to bid farewell. But that means, dependent upon the force with which we know. Perhaps I may summarize with a word of Hölderlin which also expresses our temporal feeling of transition and our perception of ful-filled time. It says: "That there is something lasting in a lingering sojourn of time."

HEIDEGGER AND CONSCIOUSNESS

CHARLES E. SCOTT

Vanderbilt University

The topic of this paper concerns the nature of existential awareness, a topic which Heidegger has not developed with explicit thoroughness in his own philosophy. In this light, I should note at the beginning that at its best Heidegger's thought is not designed to encourage its own repetition. He has not attempted to create a school of philosophers who canonize his 'teachings' or make a 'system' out of what he has said, and by his own accounting he has not been concerned to discover a body of stated truths which disciples carefully repeat. My interest in this discussion is not to articulate what might be considered Heidegger's 'doctrine' of consciousness. He does not have such a doctrine, and he does not even use the word 'consciousness' in *Being and Time*. Instead, he has pursued a way of thinking which he hopes will open new insights and appreciations, which will free himself and others from the crystallization of interesting observations and assumptions into dogma and schools. My interest is to consider ways in which human awareness transcends discursive conceptualization and empirical observation, and I find Heidegger's thought helpful in this process.

Because of the necessary limits on a discussion of this length, I shall restrict the study to *Being and Time*. My reason for focusing on this book is that Heidegger's analyses of 'world' and of *Seinsverständnis* provide particularly interesting ways to approach the existential dimensions of consciousness. When we finish, hopefully, we shall have opened the way a little wider for considering human awareness free from the limits placed on our understanding by models based on observing or by models founded on an idealist ontology. We shall not have produced, however, a new way to interpret conclusively Heidegger's own attempts to think

being. Rather, we shall have thought about the nature of human awareness by considering critically several ideas developed in *Being and Time*. My intent, then, is to show how certain of Heidegger's observations help toward understanding consciousness in its existential, pre-conceptual dimensions. I shall also indicate how, in this book, Heidegger's orientation appears to give an unjustifiably unhistorical status to the essential structures of existence, a status which has important implications for one's understanding of the nature of human awareness.

1. Heidegger and Leibniz

Heidegger's last lecture at Marburg in 1928, before he returned to Freiburg, concerned Leibniz. (Note: I am making the following remarks on the basis of "Aus der Letzten Marburger Vorlesung," which Heidegger published in *Zeit und geschichte: Dankesgabe an Rudolf Bultmann zum 80. Geburtstag*, ed. Erich Dinkler, J. C. B. Mohr, Tübingen, 1964.) *Being and Time* was then published. He had taught seminars during the two preceding semesters on the formation of concepts, as well as seminars focused on Kant, Hegel, Aristotle, and Schelling. He wanted, in this lecture, to engage Leibniz' metaphysics, as he had engaged Aristotle, etc., in the seminars, in light of Heidegger's own understanding of human existence as being in the world. His central concern was to see how Leibniz

Charles E. Scott, associate professor of philosophy at Vanderbilt University, received his Ph.D. from Yale in 1965, where he has served as instructor in philosophy and Dean of Berkeley College. He has published in several journals. His main interests are philosophy of religion, existential and phenomenological philosophy, and 19th century German idealism. Professor Scott is co-editor of this special issue of The Southern Journal of Philosophy on Heidegger.

understood the relation between the particularity of the monad and the sameness of all monads, or how Leibniz understood the relation between being and beings. This lecture shows also to what extent Heidegger himself, at this period of his thought, was both instructed and caught by Leibniz' powerful view of reality. It also points up a dilemma to be found at the heart of *Being and Time* and one which later in the paper I want to consider in terms of human consciousness.

Part of Heidegger's interest in *Being and Time* was to understand the nature of human power. He wanted to show that the energy of existence is not to be conceived as a quantum that is in-itself and established independent of the existing subject, but that it is self-moving and 'lived.' Rather than being simply "present at hand" as a given thing independent of its manifestations, human power is always a living occasion and must, consequently, be considered in terms of the fundamental ways in which it is lived. One key to understanding the explicitly existential part of *Being and Time* is understanding the nature of human self-movement as Heidegger conceived it. And this same key, with regard to monads, Heidegger suggests, can be used to unlock Leibniz's grasp of reality.

The monad in Leibniz's philosophy is an originating power. (Note: The interpretation of Leibniz which follows is Heidegger's. My purpose in this section is to understand something about Heidegger's philosophy through his understanding of Leibniz. Hence, I will not attempt to relate Heidegger's interpretation to other interpretations of his great predecessor.) It is an irreducible entity, and thus its energy brings it to *individual* expression. The monad's activity isolates in the sense that its action *expresses* an irreducible nature. Its actions in relation to other particulars thus always sets itself apart from the action of other monads.

The monad is a simple unity. Its energy in relation to other things does not disperse the monad, but expresses its own self-harmony. That this harmony is not essentially discordant with all other monads will be noted in detail later. As a point of departure, we should hold in mind that the creating energy of the universe, for Leibniz, originates in radically single realities, and that this energy is the *identity*, the *presence* of individual realities that cannot be reduced further to a common, non-individualized substance.

What, then, is the nature of this energy? Heidegger stresses that it is not a potentiality which needs an external mover to set it into action. It is self-motivating. And it is distinctly purposeful rather than random in nature. It is in the service of nothing else. The monad's purposiveness comes from itself. It is itself a tendency-toward. . . . It is urgency (*Drang*) with an indwelling and immediate mission. Its direction is not given to it from outside itself. To be a monad is to be in a distinct direction, to have specifying inclination, to be immediately and individually purposive. Thus, it is correct to say that the monad's power and purposiveness are identical with itself, that they are indwelling rather than externally supplied. They do not 'wait' for anything, but are always in act.

Nothing else, then, can be a surrogate for the monad's own self-urgency. To use the terminology of *Being and Time*, which Heidegger does not use in this lecture, the urgency of the monad is radically *its own*. The monad's urgency is "eigentlich." It is the irreducible individuality of the monad, that without which the monad would be nothing at all. The monad's energy is the monad in its self-expression. Or, to use other words, it expresses its own self-harmony through the particulars with which it relates. The point of stress here is that the monad, qua its individuality, is always different from and impenetrable by the particular things and occasions which it confronts. *It expresses itself only from its own self-originating power and never from external powers.* The monad gives harmony to its relations. It is never given harmony by powers originating in these relations, because it already is its own harmony and unity. We shall return to this fascinating relation between self-originating power and self-manifestation when we consider the 'existentials' as forms of awareness and when we examine critically the question whether existentials are subject to change.

Thus, when Leibniz sought to understand the nature of being he did not look to relations among monads, but rather to the nature of self-origination within the monad. The entree, Heidegger states, for understanding being is thus something like an "I". It is the subjectivity, the active self-identity of the monad. For man the self is the model for understanding the monad, because man's being himself is the only privileged access he has to self-origination. Everything else is externally related, while the "I" is "beyond sense and matter." (Note: Quoted by Heidegger, p. 497.) *It moves itself by providing the unity that it is for the particulars that it confronts.*

The difficult idea here is that for Leibniz the monad, and for Heidegger human existence, is found as a purposeful unity. Being one's own identity, whether we speak of a monad or of human existence, is being 'this' kind of energy and no other. It is a tendency toward itself through other things. It is *limited* energy in the sense that it is a living *identity*. It does what its identity is. Since it is itself and no other, and since it is itself in all of its actions, the monad (or, for Heidegger, human existence) already "understands" itself. That means simply that it is its own purposiveness, its own tendencies. Or, it is its own being and is never some other being. As such it already is a structured unity only within the context of which other things have relation and, in the case of human existence, meaning.

Heidegger's word for living one's own

fundamental state is *Seinsverständnis.* By it he intends to designate in part a being which is purposeful, self-originating, and self-relating, a structure that is immediately lived and is never merely passively on hand. "Understanding being" means *existing* one's being, as distinct from considering it at a distance. As I shall show later, this term designates a form of awareness which conditions all other forms of awareness. Presently, we need to see that for Heidegger's Leibniz all reality is characterized by individual, purposive energy, and this purposiveness is unavoidable, immediate, and creative solely on its own terms.

Heidegger notes that Leibniz did not see clearly the import of this part of his monadology for understanding the nature of human action. Indeed, Leibniz never focused clearly on lived, human subjectivity. But, adding this focus which Leibniz lacked, Heidegger develops part of his predecessor's ideas in relation to human existence. Even as the monad orders its relations according to its own unity, and thereby imprints itself indelibly in the order that it creates, man also "presents himself" through his ordering actions. The actions are certainly conditioned by what is acted on and by the situation of the action. But the existence of man, his 'unity,' his fundamental and self-identical state, is presented through his actions and is not created by any relative conditions. Man "ranges out" and "encompasses" as he lives, and thereby he "presents" himself, he puts forward his limited and indwelling purposiveness through what he orders. The being that one is is thereby manifest in the order that he creates, because his being is the only unity and source of order that man 'has.' Hence, although Leibniz did not say so, human existence is one way through which monadic nature is presented (Note: ibid., pp. 499–501). Existence, like the monad, speaks out of itself, and what it imparts is necessarily in its own likeness.

At the center of Leibniz' monadology

is the concept of appetite. Monads "strive." They seek their own order. That is one important meaning for "urgency" or *Drang.* "Urgency is the nature, i.e., the essence of substance." (Note: ibid., p. 502.) Hence, monads are immediately inclined toward the creation of order out of the manifold to which they relate. We have seen that creation in this context means self-presentation. It means, for Leibniz, striving with multiple things and situations in the direction of a unity which the monad already is. A monad "puts itself over there" by means of things upon which it imprints its image. That is the way the monad lives its individuality.

[Note: The similarity between *Drang* and Heidegger's concept of *Sorge* is clear. The urgency of human existence is named "care," the finite appetite of man toward order centered in his own neediness. *All* ordering actions are founded in this neediness, and all orders bring man's being to relative expression. The lived structures or limits of human urgency are named "existentials," and they are given finite unity by birth and death.]

The point I wish to emphasize with regard to Heidegger is one that he emphasizes with regard to Leibniz: the limits of self-originating urgency compose a fundamental "perspective" which is always lived by the entity in question. Heidegger contends that for Leibniz the monad is an "Augen-punkt" which is expressed in its ordering action. Were the monad unformed or were it not self-moving there could be no self-expressive perspective. There would be either a totally unformed indiscriminateness or discrimination imposed on the monad distinct from what would be its own purposelessness. But the monad is limited and purposeful. Hence, the monad itself composes a "position" in terms of which it gives position to all its relations. It "individualizes" and "isolates" its relations in terms of its own individuality and active self-sameness. The monad is "energetic self-concentration" through its relations with other realities.

We may direct this contention to Heidegger's own analysis of Dasein, by noting that human existence is an "Augen-punkt" which transcends man's particular and historically relative perspectives. Human existence is itself a perspective, and the structure of this perspective is articulated by Heidegger in terms of existentials, limits and possibilities which are fundamental to existence. This point will be developed in the following section, where we shall discuss existentials as forms of awareness. Further, since man, like the monads of Leibniz, creates order in terms of his own unity, and since man, in contrast to individual monads, has the power of intelligent reflective relation, his world is the occasion for self-understanding. Man is "open to himself" by means of the world around him which he experiences always in the image of his own being.

Finally, the individuality and isolation of the monads does not mean chaos according to Leibniz, because the order enjoyed individually by each monad is in a pre-established harmony with all other monads. For Leibniz this means divine providence. For Heidegger the sameness of human existence is given and not explained. For Leibniz pre-established harmony means cosmic order. For Heidegger the sameness of human existence means that a community of authentic persons is possible. For both, the given harmony of individual structures means that the final principles of order among finite entities are not primordially created through communication and tradition which, as we shall see, causes one to wonder in what sense of the term 'existentials' are finite in Heidegger's understanding of them.

2. Awareness in the World and Transcending the World.

There are two suggestions elaborated in the above section which I should like to develop further. One is that being, now we need to say human being, is expressed through the orders created by self-moving entities, i.e., by human beings. I shall contend that such orders *in their efficacy* compose one kind of awareness which does not arise from conceptual action. The second suggestion is that *Seinsverständnis* is intrinsic to individual human existence. I shall contend that "Seinsverständnis" designates a form of human awareness which is independent of the interests and purposes of conceptualization and which transcends the historical relativity of existence in the world.

It has been remarked frequently that in *Being and Time* Heidegger understands human existence as radically alone in the world. That particular way of interpreting Heidegger's concept of human existence is mistaken, because being in the world means, for Heidegger, being *intrinsically* related to persons and things. One is always within traditions and societies which give him his language and his ways of existence. (Note: See as illustration of this claim Heidegger's discussion of interpretation, pp. 150, 326–8.) Man is his social and cultural relations with persons and things. He lives *in* relations, not external to them. Human existence is thus 'extensive' in the sense that lived individuality, far from being a capsule outside of space and time, is radically innerworldly. Man finds himself and understands himself through his creation of worldly relations, institutions, and artifacts. And, conversely, the structures and persons in a man's world immediately give him directions, purposes, and forms which direct and give identification to his energy. (Note: See, for example, his discussions of world and worldliness, pp. 63ff; 'mitwelt', pp. 117ff; throwness, pp. 192, 228; everydayness, pp. 113–125; and refutations in Dilthey, pp. 46–47, 209–11.)

It would thus be incorrect to say that human existence is like a Leibnizian monad in the sense of being totally unpenetrated by influence. Man is indeed always disclosed with things and events. Human existence is always pro-

jective through worldly structures. It is always in the process of creating its own place for inhabitance according to its needs and interests. But it is also intrinsically "open" to the inhabitable place that it makes in the sense that it lives through its own creations. Human existence gains form and direction by means of what it creates (i.e., it is intrinsically 'traditional.' It "projects" itself or "presents" itself through the language and other cultural forms which it inherits. Or, it creates culture out of the culture by which it is already in significant measure created. (Note: See pp. 150ff, 326ff.)

This contention is expressed clearly in *Being and Time* through Heidegger's analysis of 'world.' The world is constituted in part by things which have their own 'drifts' and 'tendencies.' It coheres through complicated systems of reference which define what is appropriate and inappropriate for things. Or stated another way, man creates instruments and situations 'for the sake' of certain concerns, and the particular individual is aware prethematically in his world as he *employs* instruments and *manages* situations which are not created de novo by him, but which have their own historically developed and often enormously complicated demands and possibilities. We usually are aware of things by *using* them or by relating to them within the functional purposes which *they* have in the culture. The world, then, is characterized by purposes and means and possibilities which originated through human concerns and which, once created, *express* human concern and solutions vis-à-vis particular needs.

That 'world' names a domain that is intrinsically related to human concern seems clear. (Note: Heidegger's concept of 'world' does not deny that nature enjoys an independence of what man does, as some critics seem to think. It is rather a concept through which Heidegger attempts to understand human significance and meaning. Hence when he discusses 'world' he is discussing the context in which human existence lives significantly and meaningfully not only in relation to itself, but also in relation to what is quite independent of it.) It is equally clear that for Heidegger the various significations found in the world are to be explained by reference to human energy and by reference to no other source of energy. But that does not mean that one cannot run up against real objects or that things evaporate when they are not used. It means, rather, that what we bump into or discover express worldly meanings, that the things found in the world are thoroughly 'alive' for us by virtue of the form and place they have gained through man's living with them. We have already confronted Heidegger's contention that man presents himself through worldly order. We may now carry that contention further by saying that the functions and interrelations among things and events manifest both the specifying interests of man and his *need* to order and concern himself with his place of habitation. And that means, given our present point of interest, that man comes to understand himself and other things and persons by means of the structures of the world *as he lives with them*. World- and self-understanding without a life structured by functions and interactions could not occur according to Heidegger. The world is the place where man comes to understand himself explicitly, because it is there that both his particular interests and his most fundamental existential structure gain expression through forms which give him purpose, direction, and significance.

This means that the term 'world' as Heidegger uses it names a domain of awareness which is independent of the particular individual who lives in it. Language, for example, gives form and direction to the person who uses it. Symbols instill loyalty or adversion in persons. Tradition and cultural environment create discriminations in a person who functions with instruments and institutions. It would be too much

to say that the world is itself conscious, if one had in mind an independently subsisting entity 'out there' which he called 'world.' But it is correct to say that the world *as lived* both manifests and creates forms of awareness in persons. That is, the historical structures and relations which make up the world embody intentions which, when lived, add dimensions of awareness to a person's life, dimensions of which he is not the author but which give significance and purposiveness to his life as he functions with them. To use Heidegger's language, things and events, as 'present at hand,' are quite abstract and lifeless. But when one works and plays with instruments and lives through culturally structured situations among people, the instruments, situations, and personal relations are not simply present at hand. They are moments of life with which one is immediately involved, and as such they are living forms of energy, i.e., they are directional events. In that way they constitute moments of awareness which cannot be reduced to an object 'over there' or a subject 'in here.' They are rather events of interaction which have their own structures of significance, meaning, and direction and which form 'my' energy. They give significance, meaning, and direction to one who becomes involved in them, even as he may well modify them. One is aware preconceptually, then, in his use of 'worldly' forms, such as tools, institutions, and customs. The 'world' is characterized by drifts and tendencies, significances, inter-relations, and discriminations which give place and time to all that occurs. Things and events disclose meanings by virtue of being intrinsically meaningful, such that living with things and events means being in interaction with purposes and interests which one inherits rather than makes and which in part make up his consciousness whether he knows it or not and whether he explicitly chooses them or not.

In the world, then, one is motivated by possibilities and limits which are not specifically one's own. We have seen that lived structures of the world have "their own drifts and tendencies" which are intentionally founded and which have a created independence. We find them to be forms of awareness because, by virtue of their lived purposiveness, they constitute forms of discrimination which give significance and place to other things and events. One finds himself with these inheritances, and he lives through them as he projects himself into the future, i.e., as he plans organizes, thinks, speaks, etc. One thus finds himself always with a relative identity of which he is not the sole creator. The worldly forms of existence constitute lived perspectives which are relative to place and time and are potent and creative. They also constitute what Heidegger calls a "fall" away from being because their power is communal in nature and not founded in the particular intentionality of the individual. We shall return to this idea later in the discussion.

We can thus say that human existence is not a lonely island that is cut off from the presence of others. To the contrary, human existence is "being in the world," and that means that it is created out of history, culture, and human relations. Whatever man does, he does within a cultural-historical-social context that gives him a domain which defines what is significant and meaningful, a range of limited possibilities and means for modifying this very context within which he finds himself. To be in the world, i.e., to exist, is to be made aware by the structures intrinsic to the world in which and through which one lives. This process does not appear to be the result of conceptual action, but the result of using the language, tools, etc., of one's culture such that a conceptual framework may develop.

But human being transcends everyday existence. 'Care,' according to Heidegger, is the being of man. It names human urgency, or the analogue to *Drang* in the Leibniz lecture. Being is

not identical with existence, although it, as the self-presentation of existence, is intrinsically related to existence. The word *transcend* in this context means 'always present with worldly existence, but not identical with it.' We have seen that 'being in the world' means that one is always conscious of himself and others through structures of significance and meaning which both arise in and define relations among men and among men and things. Worldly consciousness, far from being radically individual, is always a living relation for which no single individual is solely responsible. Our task now is to see how human being is a form of awareness which transcends worldly relations. (Note: When a commonly understood term is being reinterpreted, one feels the frustration of seeing the common meaning altered, while the word itself remains the same. This is presently the case with the terms 'consciousness' and 'awareness.' I use the terms interchangeably, and their meaning in this discussion, as distinct from some of their traditional and ordinary meanings, will have to become clear through our process of investigation. In any case, it should be abundantly clear that sensual perception or discursive understanding are inadequate models for understanding consciousness as we have discussed it so far. Both sensual perception and discursive understanding are, of course, types of awareness, but neither should be taken as definitive of what it means to be aware in all or even in most cases. It should be further noted that while *"form* of awareness" seems legitimate terminology here, Heidegger's post-*Being and Time* reflections make "form" a difficult term to use in any context with sole regard to being. We shall discuss why later in this paper.)

We touched on *Seinsverständnis*, or understanding being, above when we discussed the self-purposive and the consequently self-presentational nature of the monad. 'Care' names for Heidegger the lived inevitability of human self-projection, that is, it names the 'nature' of human purposiveness. A being that were utterly sufficient would not be one of care. It would need nothing in addition to itself. Human energy, on the other hand, is always in need of projecting itself out of its past and its presence with others. Instead of being already and completely actual, human existence is always 'on the road,' i.e., it is always incomplete and it always relates to itself in terms of its incompleteness. 'Care' means that man is a self-relation that inevitably seeks to actualize himself out of his own limitedness. His being is potentiality for self-realization rather than an established and adequate form for existential identity.

Man's being is also a unity. It is not 'scattered' through existential relations, but is his unity, his presence, in the midst of relations for which he is not solely responsible. Heidegger's term for existential unity is *Jemeinigkeit* or my-ownness. Through this characteristic of existence he wants to account for the irreducibleness of human presence. Man is more than his relations to others. He is a being for whom no other, ultimately, can be a surrogate. Hence, 'my-ownness' designates, not simply a psychological state, but the very potentiality for having states for which and to which one is himself accountable. It means that human existence, along with its historical-social dimensions, is a locale with its own urgency and presence. Its presence cannot be adequately explained by tallying up influences, because all influences on it depend already on its presence. To make this point in different terms, man is historical and social in his existence because he is a self-relation that makes possible historical and social forms of existence.

Given man's *Jemeinigkeit*, Heidegger discusses awareness which transcends worldly influences through such concepts as anxiety, call of conscience, and resoluteness. Indeed, as I hope will become clear, all "existentials" compose both the lived possibilities for meaning

and also the lived and immediate purposiveness of human existence, such that to exist is to be aware preconceptually of one's own being. In his early years, through his dissertation and Habilitationsschrift, Heidegger concerned himself with the mental context for signification and meaning. (Note: His dissertation title is *Die Lehre vom Urteil im Psychologismus. Ein kritisch-positiver Beitrag zur Logik*. His *Habilitationsschrift, Die Kategorien und Bedeutungslehre des Duns Scotus*. Neither manuscript is available outside of Germany, as far as I know, but one can read a careful account of them in Otto Pöggeler's *Der Denkweg Martin Heideggers*, Neske, 1963, pp. 17–26.) At that time he thought that a priori and changeless structures provide the context for signification in all synthetic mental relations. He sought, under the influence of Kant and Husserl, a "pure" grammar which gives the universal form for all languages, i.e., a "steady" structure which defines the possibilities and limits for all meaning. He came to see that this approach left out of account the life and energy as well as the historicity of the structure which he was analyzing. When he wrote *Being and Time*, he had not given up the conviction that human existence composes its own horizons for meaning and significance, but he had come to see that these horizons must be understood as self-moving and that the movement was intrinsic to the horizon. He had been dissatisfied with the 'rigidity' of Kant's rational a priori structure, and he sought through his own existential-phenomenological approach to account for the self-identical and self-presentational nature of human energy. Hence, he dropped the term 'categories' as used by Aristotle, Kant, and Husserl in their individual ways, and used instead the term 'existentials' to name the self-empowering structures of human existence. By emphasizing the living nature of human structures he emphasized that they are their own drift, their own power. To *be* a structure is to be on one's own way, an insight which he thought Aristotle and Leibniz had already developed in limited ways, and an insight which led to his own concept of *Seinsverständnis*. If a structure is considered without intrinsic reference to its self-realization, one loses an understanding of its self-presentational power. And self-presentational power is what makes a structure a form of awareness.

By analyzing human existence as being in the world, Heidegger showed in a remarkably penetrating way that man is not only always within an historical-social context, but that that context, far from being simply external to him, is existential, is lived by him. Hence, we have seen that everyday, worldly structures are 'ontic' forms of awareness, i.e., they are particular ways in which one is aware of persons and things. Now the move is from 'categories' which provide stark boundaries seemingly independent of the energy they bound, to existentials which one is in his existence. One does not possess existentials as something which comes into his power, but may leave. One lives them. But now he lives, not simply historical and social relations, but his own, irreducible potential for existence, his *Seinkönnen*.

The idea to be understood is as follows: Human existence is self-presentational in the sense that it creates through (i.e., lives through) its own limits and possibilities and thereby presents itself in the forms of life that it creates; and since one is his fundamental limits and possibilities, i.e., since he *lives* his self-presentation, he is primordially aware of his being.

Man's primoridial understanding of being, his *Seinsverständnis,* is found in his inclination toward his own self-manifestations. This heavy language means that man comes inevitably toward himself through his worldly relations by virtue of his own purposiveness. When we say in English that this is an understanding *of* being we are immediately involved in a prepositional

embarrassment. 'Of' usually, though not necessarily, implies an object separate from the subject. In this case 'of' must be understood as a subjective genative which does not imply an object separate from the subject. Being purposive in a certain fundamental way is a way of being aware, because this native drift or inclination is the lived, unavoidable context for all meanings and significances. It composes a primordial 'Augen-punkt,' a native stance with regard to all things. One is thereby his own possibility for meaning and significance. He is primordially aware of the domain within which all reality will occur as far as he is concerned, because he *is* already the structure which provides the horizons for all particular relations that might occur. Whenever he conceptually understands himself, he finds that he is already acting purposively and with an intuitive grasp of the limits and possibilities which he is.

This language about existential situations sounds initially and uncomfortably as though Heidegger, in spite of his protestations, still has precisely what he criticized Kant for conceiving — a "logical subject" that provides "steadiness of identity," but lacks temporal existence. (Note: *Being and Time,* p. 319.) But for Heidegger, 'care' is not an identity. It is an horizon for identity. And 'temporality,' the meaning of 'care,' does not describe a logical subject, but the lived inevitability that all particular forms of identity and subjectivity do not exhaust human being. Human being is not an individual identity, but is the inevitability for finite identities and for the inadequacy of any identity to make man non-finite. In a word, 'temporality' means that human energy finds only historical expression and that no historical expression will completely exhaust human being. Man will always *have* to project himself further, in spite of all the security and strength of identity which he may find for himself. He always, qua his being, transcends his specific existing state. (Note: Heidegger's own discussion of transcendence, which I have largely presupposed here, is developed in his discussion of care, Sections 39–44, and being to death, Sections 46–53.)

How, then, can one have a preconceptual understanding of his being if his being is no one thing and not even a fundamental identity? How can one be aware primordially of his inevitably transcending his accomplished, worldly selfhood? One form taken by this awareness is 'flight' to the everyday world. The very absence of a final identity *inclines* one, qua his worldly identity, to shore up what he has accomplished and to ignore as best he can the finitude which he also is in relation to his existing self. The mood of anxiety is a closely related type of awareness characteristic of man *in* his finiteness. It is the primordial grasp that no accomplished state of existence is final as far as man's being is concerned. It is the lived inclination toward self-projection and self-concentration. Without 'anxiety' man would feel no urgency toward the future. With it he grasps immediately that he is finite and ungrounded in any accomplishment or finally securing state. By virtue of anxiety, man seeks to possess and defend. He seeks to give himself a future which at least in some measure is significant in terms of who he is and what he has in the world. Further, in his existence one is also inclined toward his being. He experiences inadequacy regarding all that he has and is, a fundamental drift away from securities, a drift expressed well in Rilke's *Duino Elegies*. And this awareness may reach intentional explicitness when one, through his attitudes and perspectives, affirms his own finiteness by anticipating the inevitably provisory nature of human accomplishment. When he sees the world free of the expectation that more possessions, relations, or existential concreteness will give him a sense of utter at-homeness in the world, he is, as we shall show in a moment, 'clear' that he is primordially finite. (Note: cf. Heidegger's discussion of *vorlaufende Ent-*

schlossenheit, Section 62.)

A thorough study would need to show exactly how these moods and attitudes express a primordial awareness of being. Such a study would also be a long treatise. It must suffice here to state that a primordial awareness of being self-relational, finite, self-moving, and always unfinished takes the form of inescapable moods, 'perspectives,' and tendencies which one lives and which can be analyzed, but which are not themselves the result of analysis or self-conscious interpretation. These moods and tendencies do not express, as many philosophers have thought, an immediate trans-human "ground" of being. (Note: For example, the early Schelling, Schleiermacher, as well as Tillich.) They express, rather, man's own being, his 'urgency,' his lived inevitability which are empowered, which are tendencies and drifts intrinsic to human existence.

Finally, the forms taken by the finite urgency of human being are always self-presentational. Or, human being is an urgency toward creating a world structured through concerns. The moods and attitudes mentioned above are not simply passive states. They do not provide information about what is the case in particular circumstances, certainly, and thus are not ways of knowing about things. But they are modes of urgency toward creation which express themselves in what is created. Even as worldly meanings and significances are in the direction of . . . , or are for the sake of . . . , the existential structures of man are living inclinations toward self-expression. Care means: man is always inclined toward making cultural and environmental dwelling places for himself; man always, by virtue of his finitude, transcends the particularities of his existence; man must create out of his own resources. There is no plenum uncreated by man on the basis of which man can find out what he is supposed to do, and given this absence of information, man creates out of his culture and out of his own, given existentials. He thereby "presents" himself as a creature of care in the world that he makes inhabitable.

The peculiar Heideggerian idea is that "presentation" in this context is disclosive of being, and since one is his presentation, he is a *Seinsverständnis*. He is a primordial form of awareness because of the way human existence "proposes" itself in the world, and this awareness is preconceptual in the sense that man is already caring when he begins intentionally to clarify what is the case by means of discursive structures. One lives with self-presentational energy which creates meanings and significances, and creation, rather than occuring in a vacuum, occurs through human intentions and concerns, that are already expressed and structured in the world. *That* one always concerns himself with things and presents himself as a creature of care expresses a primordial awareness that he is a creature of finite care. To be aware is to be one's own inclinations and purposiveness, and finite care names the purposiveness that man always is in his own being.

Through the concepts of 'being in a world' and 'existentials,' then, we have found two modes of awareness which provide meaning, significance, place, mood, attitude, and purpose, which are not initially *objects* of consciousness, which are not modes of rational observation, which do not arise out of a specific intention to clarify what is the case, and which are not structured according to the logic of conceptualization. We have discussed two forms of awareness that are immediately lived rather than discursively grasped. The implication which is inherent in these observations is that if we are to understand human consciousness we must often begin with the events in which the individual and the world occur together, that consciousness is an event in which man is preconceptually given direction through his culture and in which his existence is preconceptually

presented through its own limited energy.

3. Concepts and Preconceptual Awareness

I have contended that when one lives a drift or a tendency he is aware, be such a drift or tendency or culturally relative phenomenon or a structure of existence. We have seen that one kind of awareness originates historically in used, worldly structures such as are found in grammars, social customs, institutions, etc. Another kind of awareness is found in the presented structure of human being, a structure which is interpreted as manifested in the world, transcending the relativities of the world, intrinsically and finitely energetic. Why call this awareness preconceptual and what is the philosophical import of thinking about it? In order to answer these questions, we shall first note some of the ways in which Heidegger uses concepts in *Being and Time*.

Being and Time has the dual purpose of *describing* existential structures and *pointing* the way toward being. Existential structures are ways of being in the world which are given with existence and which are discovered as they are lived. They are not the products of conceptual interpretation or of any intention to order logically, clarify, or explicate. Hence, they are independent of discursive interests, although they may be discursively focused, viz., *Being and Time*. What is happening when Heidegger provides a conceptual framework for understanding human existence through his descriptions and analyses? (Note: Heidegger does not show carefully how concepts arise out of *Seinsverständnis* in *Being and Time*, and in order to treat this question thoroughly, we would need to consider some of his later essays. We can, however, note how concepts function in this book and see how far that will take us toward understanding the relation between conceptual and preconceptual awareness.)

In *Being and Time* Heidegger describes what is present and lived, but what is not 'theoretical' in its primary state. A lived function or inclination is not oriented around theoretical purposes and is not intended to be a conceptual interpretation of something else. The structures of both our relative ways of existing and of human existentials do not originate in discursively schematizing interests and in that sense are not conceptual in nature. In *Being and Time,* then, Heidegger is attempting to describe thematically what is not conceptually thematic in nature, and thereby we can see that he uses concepts to make understandable lived structures which do not come theoretically packaged. On the one hand he abstracts himself from the lived world by means of his conceptual scheme. On the other hand, he uses concepts, such as "Vorhandenheit," "Auslegung," etc., in order to point out the difference between his descriptive structure and the structure which he is describing. Primarily, he seems to me to clarify the difference between the intention to clarify and the complex purposiveness of the world and of human existence such that the *interest in clarification* is seen to be only one form of human purposiveness and hence as only one way of being conscious. By conceiving this difference, he places one in a position to affirm the integrity of the world and existence which is distinct from the intentions which lead to its conceptual recognition. And this affirmation, as we have seen, is possible because one lives the difference between conceptual and preconceptual purposiveness, a difference that is now clear to him conceptually.

But what prevents Heidegger's conceptual scheme from being purely arbitrary on his own terms? Why is his analysis not simply a subjectivistic theme played against a formless horizon of being? Human being, according to *Being and Time,* is not formless in its preconceptual manifestation. We have distinguished the conceptual and the preconceptual according to the different purposiveness of the structures involved, not according to a presence and absence of structures. The preconceptual, we have seen, is a lived structure which has direction and relations independent of discursive intent. (Note: One might be inclined to define as conceptual all structures which can be recognized by means of concepts. That seems to me to be misleading, because one is then inclined to think of various forms of discursive logic as the final criterion for clarity and truth and to consider conceptual structures as necessarily definitive of existential acts. Neither of these assumptions appear to me as to be true. It seems preferable, rather, to reserve the term 'conceptual' solely for one kind of mental activity, and thereby emphasize the difference between what is recognized and the act of recognition. I am contending that preconceptual awareness, which is self-relational and worldly, is the state which allows and justifies one's recognition of what is different from conceptual activity.) Heidegger's analysis in *Being and Time* is an attempt to describe and interpret what man lives. Human being is given conceptual form as one clarifies the structures that give form to his life. The question of authenticity and inauthenticity in relation to a conceptual scheme, for example, has to do with whether the concepts bring to self-conscious expression one's own potentiality for being, i.e., his own existentials. or whether they bring to expression rather one's tradition's potentiality as it is expressed in social, artistic, linguistic forms, etc., without intrinsic and now self-conscious reference to Dasein. Concepts, then, are structures designed to clarify, describe, and explain. They compose a specific way to be concerned with the world and thus manifest at least indirectly 'care' and all the other existentials. When self-understanding is the issue, concepts can and ought to describe the forms of existence which one lives.

Being and Time, then, is in part an essay in self-understanding which proposes to place the self in the context of its being. As a conceptual scheme it proposes a direction for conceptual self-determination, i.e., it proposes a way of understanding the self in which one recognizes that the meaning of his being is finite care and hence that certain attitudes toward himself (such as "anticipatory resoluteness") are appropriate and others (such as absolutizing some achievement) are inappropriate. Heidegger sought in this book to describe the existential nature of the self by developing concepts and conceptual relations which interpret their own limits and possibilities. These limits and possibilities, as we have seen, are lived structures, not simply an amorphous light.

On the other hand, *Being and Time* does not attempt to capture being in concepts. It attempts to show that being, while manifest through existential structures and concepts, escapes conceptual structures. Heidegger attempts to make this point by an analysis of the structural way in which being is manifested, but never exhausted by existence. Hence, a schematic understanding of existence cannot, in principle, be a complete understanding of being. It may well be that being is finally an amorphous light vis à vis concepts, but that is not what Heidegger attempts to describe in *Being and Time*. It is the case, rather, that Heidegger *points toward* being in this book, but he points toward it by *describing lived structures* which constitute human existence. Hence, he does not, in this essay, push on to what may be called, with regard to his later work, 'nonconceptual thought.'

Concepts thus both describe and determine human existence. They may describe: 1) the cultural forms which are lived and which provide an historical, traditional, common structure for the existence of men together, and 2) the existential forms, shared by men, but self-moving and hence individualizing rather than communally originated.

Concepts *determine* the self as ways through which one directs himself explicitly and discursively toward what has already given him direction. They may either incline one toward or away from the structures he lives. In either case, they can never replace the lived structures (i.e., they always presuppose these structures), and they can never become men's fundamental "openness" to the world. Their value is clearly immense, but they are never a surrogate for either world or being. The fundamental power and meaning of concepts are found in lived, preconceptual structures and hence structures which transcend both conceptual intent and discursive logic. On the other hand, concepts provide uniquely human access to both the power and meaning which man lives, and the way one develops this access is the way in which he explains and clarifies what his world is like, who man is, and what men should do with regard to the world.

We may delineate the function of concepts in *Being and Time* under five headings: 1) they describe how things are manifest in the world; 2) they describe how human existence is disclosed through worldly structures; 3) they name the meaning of human existence and describe how that meaning becomes known; 4) they point out the transcendence of being in relation to existence; and 5) they manifest what is described or pointed out. The first four of these points have to do with interpretation and may be discussed together. The fifth designates the relation between conceiving and being, and we shall consider it separately from the others.

With regard to the first four functions we may observe that an interpretation of existence through concepts is clearly an historical endeavor. The concepts that are used will always have a history of development and use, and new concepts will always arise in relation to others that made possible the new one. We have seen that a conceptual, interpretative scheme has the intent to clarify and predicate. It is an attempt at communication in which a lived situation is specifically focused and delineated. The interpretation, qua its historicity, presupposes a tradition of interests and ideas, and the interests and ideas give rise to the interpretative effort. Hence, culture and history as well as individual, personal intentions are brought to bear in an interpretation. In addition, that which is interpreted through description and naming is, as we have seen, historical and intrinsically related to human existence. Consequently, when Heidegger names and describes worldly existential structures, he names and describes what is already existentially active. His concepts develop and refer to lived situations. What is interpreted in this case is also being lived with, and his interpretation of world and man arises self-consciously out of the preconceptual, lived involvement with world and self. Heidegger's concepts, then, function at one level as descriptions of how the world and things in the world are experienced, and as descriptions of how man discloses his own possibilities and potentiality in the world. His interpretation of the meaning of human being arises as he analyzes worldly functions, how man intends, how man experiences space, things, other persons, etc. To exist in 'this' way and to find the world 'this' way means that finitude and not some pre-established identity or plan is the meaning of human being.

But a description or an interpretation of human existence does more than describe and name. It also manifests what it describes. This central idea sways between the obvious and the obscure. It is clear that one expresses to some degree his 'age' or his 'times' in his interpretations. That means that he expresses in his endeavors those common interests and ideas which enable him to carry out publicly and meaningfully what he does. Hence, one may come to understand an era or a movement through a person of genius who reflects imaginatively and with unusual

power both the history and the destiny of certain fundamental convictions and pursuits which have formed a society or culture. Analogously, Heidegger contends that a description of the world as lived arises out of worldly life. The description is situated in time and reflects the situations that it describes. Further, the fundamental structures of worldly existence, its historicity, not only its own history, its intentionality, not simply its particular intentions, its temporality, not simply its own time, etc., are also manifest. "Knowledge does not first create a 'commercium' of the subject with the world, nor does it arise out of an action of the world on a subject." (Note: Translated in English edition of *Being and Time,* tr. Macquarrie and Robinson, SCM Press, 1962, p. 62.) We have already noted the inseparability of self and world. Likewise, an interpretation of the self does not create self-relatedness. It presupposes that the self is related to itself, and this self-relation is manifest in, not created by, the self-interpretative act. Hence, in describing the world and the self one gives expression to the world and the self that he describes. (Note: One might ask about, say, science fiction. Does one have to live in that world in order to describe it? No, of course, if one thinks of what is described as a 'place over there beyond our world.' But that is not what is described. What is described is quite 'worldly' in the sense that it is an imaginative projection founded very much in what one experiences.)

Finally, interpretations manifest human being. As we have seen, Heidegger is not attempting to describe being, and the point now is not that what is described is also manifest in the description. He names the *meaning* of human being and the other ways in which being is manifest in human existence. The meaning of being is descriptive of human existence — Dasein — and not of being as such. Being transcends existence, i.e., it is never exhausted in or identical with existence. That means simply that it cannot be adequately described. But it is present in existence. It is "manifest" in human existence. In a broad sense of the word, it is partially *experienced*. At this point, Heidegger's most characteristic and most difficult employment of concepts is one of pointing to being in such a way that the interpretation manifests what it cannot describe.

In order to understand what 'point to being' might mean we must keep in mind our discussion of *Seinsverständnis*: man lives the manifestation of being—he is an event that is—and hence he is aware of being in the form of a "Seinstendenz," which is found through anxiety, openness to one's future, etc. We have also seen that interpreting is a way of intending, i.e., it is a way of existing, and as such should be understood as a human act and not as a transtemporal event. When one 'points to' being he points to the presentness of his world, his existence, and his interpretation. Being is thus manifest through its interpretation, but is not susceptible to interpretative objectivity. Negatively, this means that concepts do not function as mediating structures between being and world, because being is not an objective or a subjective pole needing such mediation. Positively, Heidegger's position means that posing questions about human being and attending to the unfinished nature of human existence 'point out' being in a way which makes a difference in how one views conceptual certainty and in how one relates to his future. It is clear that this position involves a concept of preconceptual awareness, but in *Being and Time* it is not at all clear how this awareness of being comes to relevant conceptual expression such that one can *conceptually* clarify his preconceptual state vis à vis being. The absence of any explicit analysis of the relation between concepts and being probably explains in significant measure why, while *Being and Time* has had an enormous effect on existential and phenomenological analysis, it has had much

less effect on the predominant philosophical concepts concerning being. The essay develops with power the relation between world and self, but leaves unfinished the relation between being and thought.

Heidegger's contention concerning the manifest nature of being is not intended to create conceptual satisfaction. It is intended to state that the *event* of human existence, its presence, is not fully understandable although it is lived. To say that one *points* to being, however, means that one *enables* further questions about existence and being by *placing in question* all conceptual certainties about existence in relation to being. When one points to being, he orients philosophical discussion around the openness of existence. He countenances the disclosedness of human existence in historical situations, none of which sufficiently accounts for the presence of human existence. Heidegger is attempting to point out the lived awareness that no explanation of existence is adequate as an 'explanation' of the disclosedness of existence, that the being of interpretative acts transcends its own interpretative structure. Hence, one points to what escapes meaning and yet is manifest through meaning.

Conceptual interpretations, then, are ways in which man projects himself through clarifying, historically developed structures. Conceptual schemes have their own drifts. They are intellectual orientations which open up areas of interest and give direction for further thought. They interrelate the past, present, and future through the way they bring human traditions to bear on issues and problems, and thereby they open the way for plans, projects, experiments, corrections, etc. How we describe and qualify things provides us with motivations and possibilities for confronting ourselves and our world. Our concepts are ways of 'going on' out of our past and in our present. They manifest where and who we are, even if without specific self-reference. They *express*, in a word, our *temporality*, our human presence, as they constitute memories and reminders, directions for action, bases for hope or despair, present recognitions, and ways of recovering what was once experienced but is now lost except for the remaining conceptual structure.

4. Leibniz Revisited

Heidegger has clearly developed a distinctly non-solipsistic, existential view of the way man understands in his world. He has shown why 'understanding' should not mean only 'conceptually grasped' but also 'lived.' He has shown that 'awareness' cannot mean an isolated, private presence to one's self, because awareness is historical and worldly,' as well as because 'understanding being' does not have reference primarily to a structure of selfhood. Hence, the concept of consciousness which we have been discussing denies the primacy of the individual self as an interpretative principle, as well as denies the interpretative primacy of both sensual perception and discursive understanding. It affirms the primacy of world and the transcendance of being for an understanding of human consciousness, when these elements are grasped as an event of disclosure.

Heidegger's debt to Leibniz (and Kant) is seen with particular clarity when we recall his central contention that, in the context of our discussion, awareness is always 'fallen' when it occurs through worldly powers and structures. Only that awareness is 'authentic' which originates in and articulates one's own care in relation to the world. When we are moved and directed primarily through cultural and social forms, we are created in significant measure by our tradition and culture. We are living witnesses to the ways men have sought to give order to their surroundings and voice to the otherwise silent state of matter. Unlike Leibniz' monad, human existence is penetrated deeply by influences external to its own power for self-presentation. But like Leibniz' monad, 'Care' and the

existentials, though always manifest in historical situations, are not themselves products of history. Human urgency is 'jemeines,' and that means that a person is authentic when he existentially affirms his transcendence of all 'external' powers, when he 'runs toward' his future by affirming his own finite openness which is not replaceable by any other influence or force. This means that for Heidegger existential awareness of being, being one's own finitude and one's own urgency, is individualizing and transcends all other forms of urgency.

One can easily misconceive what Heidegger means in this regard. He is talking about *openness* to the world, not about closedness to it. Existential affirmation (*vorlaufende Entschlossenheit*) involves a thorough acceptance of one's *own* finite presence which has its own urgency and which cannot be resolved into any one existential form of accomplishment or cultural identity. One is thus always open to the world because he is finite and specifically undetermined in his being.

But human openness, human transcendence of all forms of existential accomplishment—all states, grammars, and . interpretations — is also formed. The existentials are given. They are not a priori forms of intelligence or impersonal structures of intention which bracket out the world. They are lived forms found only in worldly interactions. Yet when one is authentic and orients himself toward his future through his finite openness and not through what he is or has in particular in the world, he conforms his attitudes and interests to his potentiality for being which transcends his historical state and all historical creations. He "attunes" himself to his own power of self-presentation.

Heidegger's position means that there is a type of human awareness (though not, of course, an interpretation) that is trans-cultural, that human existentials as given, not out of the past, but as *susceptible* to past and present creations, are experienced, as far as the person himself is concerned, as uncreatable and unmodifiable. Consequently, the existentials are not conceived by Heidegger as created out of temporal processes. Human existence in its particularity is indeed created by interactions, but the existentials — human potentiality — enjoy a paradoxical sufficiency. Heidegger has in fact radically redefined human sufficiency, giving primacy to finitude and openness instead of to a pre-historical and stable identity. But existentials appear to be a form of sufficiency nonetheless, insofar as they are uncreated by history and culture and are the lived criteria for the meaning of authenticity. They seem to be understood by Heidegger as immune to change, as finite, but within existence as changeless forms of self-presentation. It is significant that he never discusses even the possibility that the existentials, which we have found to compose a type of awareness, develop or change.

There thus appears to be a harmful tension between the openness of being and the unhistorical givenness of the existentials. (Note: By "unhistorical" I mean that the existentials are not experienced as historically created, although they are *found* only in historical situations.) The event of being in the world is characterized by potentiality which transcends worldly processes. These existentials serve as lived criteria for what it means to be authentic, and as such they appear to be given, but not historically processing powers for self-realization. They do not "fall away" from being like everyday life does. But when they occur they transcend the temporal nature of their occurrence. They are the conditions for change and process, and as such it would seem that they cannot be understood finally as events, although that is the way I think that Heidegger wants to understand them. Rather, they appear to be potencies which make events possible. And this position seriously disturbs the pri-

macy Heidegger gives to being as occurrence.

We may observe as a point for future departure that man is certainly an experiential unity that is, as Heidegger has shown, open to and in part constituted by his world, and that he is *intrinsically* finite and hence radically open to change and development. We can also see that to exist one's own being, to be one's own limits and possibilities, is a mode of awareness which is prior to conceptualization, but available for conceptual recognition. But Heidegger has not shown how one's being an open unity is an awareness through *uncreated* existentials, i.e., existentials which are not subject to change. He has contended that all forms of awareness that are created historically and culturally are 'fallen' to the extent that they do not originate solely in one's own "potentiality for being." This analysis is incomplete until the nature of the givenness of existentials is itself interpreted such that one sees whether or not human potentiality for existence, in its transcendence of the particularity of existence, is in principle uncreatable by progressive stages of historical interaction. Are the existentials themselves traditional in nature? My own belief is that *Seinsverständnis* is also intrinsically historical in the sense that lived human limitations and possibilities, i.e., the existentials, which constitute human presence in the world and which condition human potentiality for being (*Seinkönnen*), are themselves subject to creation and decay through worldly and physical interactions and developments. This means that 'care' and 'finitude' are probably not adequate to account for the meaning of creation and decay either in the world or in human being, that human urgency is not simply a radically individualizing energy, because it does not originate solely in the creating individual, but, for example, originates in part through spoken language. We may ask if it is not the case that in his being man is aware not simply of his own potentiality for being, but also of the process in which potentiality is created, viz., again language. If one answers affirmatively, then potency and temporality are themselves found to be within the sovereignty of history, an insight I believe that Heidegger grasped only partially in *Being and Time* because of the enormous shadows cast by Leibniz, Kant, and Husserl.

We have found that Heidegger's analyses of instrumental functions, language, tradition, and existential structures constitute a significant turn away from the primacy of the knowing self and the primacy of discursive intelligence when consciousness is considered. Although we have not considered in depth his contention that being is best understood as event, we can see that the event of being, rather than the individual subject, is the right point of departure when preconceptual awareness is to be understood. And we have seen that Heidegger's understanding of existentials must be re-thought with regard to their *intrinsic* historicity if we are to understand that awareness is an event which is thoroughly historical and finite in nature.

THE MATHEMATICAL AND THE HERMENEUTICAL: ON HEIDEGGER'S NOTION OF THE APRIORI

THEODORE KISIEL

Northern Illinois University

Heidegger's most penetrating reflections on the essence of mathematical physics inevitably turn on the sense in which it is mathematical. And in a fashion which has come to be known as "Heideggerian," he bases his reflections on the original Greek sense of *mathesis* and *mathemata*, so that the notion of the "mathematical" is thereby broadened from its current reference to the "apriori" discipline that deals with number, quantity and the like, to the comprehensive sense of a process of learning in which we come to know what we already know, where the *mathemata*, what is thereby known, refers to any apriori knowledge whatsoever. *Mathesis*, the genuine essence and most difficult kind of learning, is a taking cognizance of this prior knowledge: of bodies—the corporeal; of plants—the vegetative; of animals—the animate; of man—the human; and of things—their thingness.[1]

Heidegger distinguishes this "most difficult learning" from lesser kinds by means of an example. Learning to use a rifle is based on a prior acquaintance of what a rifle and a tool in general is. But this is only a general and indefinite kind of knowledge. Only when we truly make this general knowledge our own, for example, the producer of the rifle who must become thoroughly and explicitly acquainted with its workings and operative purposes (*Bewandtnis*), do we arrive at the most original learning process which bears the proper title of the "mathematical," whereby we "get to the very bottom"[2] of what we already know and explicitly take cognizance of it. In more familiar terms, the "mathematical" is first of all a learning directed toward "principles" and their formulation, knowledge "from the ground up." It is only by extension that the "mathematical" then comes to refer to knowledge "deduced" from principles thus established, and that the mathematical ideal of knowledge finds its locus in deduction.

Heidegger's choice of example already suggests the problem of this paper. For in *Being and Time*, the explicit articulation of the ontological constitution of handy tools, i.e. their most basic deployment (*Bewandtnis*), is discussed more in hermeneutical terms. These purposive relationships are exposed by a process of interpretation (*Auslegung*), first in a circumspective-

Theodore Kisiel, after working in nuclear engineering for several years, took his Ph.D. in philosophy at Duquesne University in 1962 and is currently associate professor of philosophy at Northern Illinois University. He is coeditor of Phenomenology and the Natural Sciences *and co-translator of Werner Marx's* Heidegger and the Tradition. *His numerous article are chiefly in the areas of phenomenological philosophy of science and hermeneutics.*

---

[1] *Die Frage nach dem Ding* (Tübingen: Niemeyer, 1962) p. 56. Cf. *What is a Thing?*, trans. W. B. Barton, Jr. and Vera Deutsch (Chicago: Regnery, 1967) p. 73. Hereafter *FD*, with corresponding pagination of English translation inserted in parentheses after the pagination to the German text. Cf. also *Holzwege* (Frankfurt a.M.: Klostermann, ³1957) p. 72.

[2] *Ibid.* '...bis zum Grunde.'

everyday way[3] and perhaps later in a scientific-thematic elaboration, as *Being and Time* itself has done. In more ways than one, there seems to be an overlap between the mathematical and the hermeneutical as conceived by Heidegger. In its apriori knowledge, in its making explicit of something that is already implicit, in its circular structure, in its "always saying the same about the same,"[4] the mathematical is strongly reminiscent of Heidegger's own way of thinking, which he is more prone to call hermeneutical than mathematical. And yet, at least one interpreter has been led to assert that *Being and Time* itself is in fact mathematical in Heidegger's own sense.[5] The issue becomes even more crucial when the respective historical developments of the mathematical and the hermeneutical diverge into the later Heideggerian distinction between calculative and fundamental thinking. In Heidegger's own schema, the mathematical path leads to the demise of metaphysics; the hermeneutical path takes us to a new beginning in thought. Their respective issues accordingly suggest that radically divergent conceptions of rationality (ground) are at work in them.

The Mathematical

Heidegger nowhere makes explicit reference to the most blatant precedent of his interpretation of *mathesis*: the Platonic doctrine of learning as reminiscence. Socrates alias Plato slips between the horns of Meno's "eristic" dilemma of complete knowledge versus total ignorance, both of which would render learning and inquiry impossible, by positing the intermediate alternative of a prior but latent knowledge (*Meno* 80 B-E). His solution in the soul's prior participation in the Ideas (Whatnesses) is nevertheless decisive for the direction later taken by modern philosophy, which is where the burden of Heidegger's discussion of the mathematical falls. For the latent knowledge which makes learning and inquiry possible is not taken out of things but rather out of oneself, as Plato explicitly states (85 D), and the one point from the *Meno* that Heidegger duly notes.[6]

It is in this sense that the spirit of the mathematical becomes the basis of the spirit of modernity. "A light broke upon all students of nature" with the realization that nature is best understood according to a plan of one's own making projected out of "reason's own determining."[7] When compared to ancient and medieval science, the distinctive trait of modern science does not lie in its emphasis on facts, experiment or measurement, as it is often said, but rather in the apriori projection of its domain of investigation. It is this ground plan, with its fundamental decisions on how this domain is to be approached and the basic conceptual structure within which its judgments are to be formulated, that determines the acceptable procedures for providing grounds and proofs within the science, and accordingly how facts are to be found and exact measurements are to be obtained, as well as, the manner in which experimental tests are to be devised. "The essence of science consists in such presupposing, in such pre-judgments about its objects."[8] Accordingly, not only is there no presuppositionless science, but also just how scientific a science is is measured by the degree of explicitness and definiteness with which it concerns itself with its presuppositions.

---

[3] *Sein und Zeit* (Tübingen: Niemeyer, 81957) p. 150. Hereafter *SZ*.
[4] *FD* 57, 62 (74, 80).
[5] Laszlo Versenyi, *Heidegger, Being, and Truth* (New Haven: Yale UP, 1965) pp. 78–79.
[6] *FD* 70 (91).
[7] Immanuel Kant, *Critique of Pure Reason*, trans. Norman Kemp Smith (New York: St. Martin's Press, 1965) B XIII, p. 20. Hereafter *CPR*.
[8] *FD* 141 (180).

The above description suggests once again various senses of the "mathematical." It applies both to the projective process out of oneself toward things as well as to the apriori knowledge which makes this possible. But more basically, it refers to the "metaphysical" attempt to "get to the very bottom" and explicate the scope and limits of that apriori knowledge which one possesses. "Only when thinking thinks itself is it absolutely mathematical."[9] The purest adherence to the mathematical is therefore to be found in Descartes' *Cogito* proposition, which brought to light a new essence of "ground" and of "principium."[10] And because the "I think" is essentially an "I posit," the basic principles take the form of ground propositions which form a closed system (*Mathesis universalis*) around the supreme principle of self-position. This *mathesis* is to be grounded in terms of its own inner requirements so as to be self-consistent. i.e. free from contradiction, self-evident and therefore absolutely certain, and self-founded while founding all knowledge and determining all of being through its categories and principles, which are "a pure self-giving of that which thinking in its essence already *has* in itself."[11] The *mathesis* is the realm of pure reason independent of experience, which in its projects and from its concepts alone decides in advance what a thing is, without consideration of things encountered in the confusion of experience. Whence Leibniz could so pithily mark of this domain by his famous emendation to the Aristotelian dictum: "There is nothing in the intellect which is not first in the senses... except the intellect itself." For Kant, "this domain is an island, enclosed by nature itself within unalterable limits. It is the land of truth—enchanting name!—surrounded by a wide and stormy ocean."

And before venturing out to sea, Kant first endeavors "to cast a glance upon the map of the land."[12] In this endeavor to define the exhaustive system of the synthetic apriori principles of pure reason (understanding), Kant remains within the "mathematical" tradition. And yet his conception of these principles inaugurates a revolution which foreshadows a breach of the mathematical. For one thing, even though synthetic apriori propositions are still subject to the principle of contradiction, it is no longer their supreme principle.[13] For another, such principles are no longer self-evident, i.e., intelligible in and from themselves, they acquire their intelligibility only in relation to a possible experience. Accordingly, to the same extent, they are not self-founded, even though they do found all objectively valid knowledge and determine what things are to be, and so still deserving of the appellation of "principle."

The inner strains that Kant introduces into the modern tradition of the "mathematical," which sought to found knowledge in principles derived from pure reason alone, are rooted in the seemingly contradictory character of his notion of the "synthetic apriori." In Kant's reading of this tradition, every prior metaphysics based on pure reason, e.g., the "rational" metaphysics of Wolff and Baumgarten, sought a knowledge out of concepts alone (hence apriori in the analytic sense) which nevertheless claimed to extend our knowledge of the world, man and God (hence synthetic). It therefore claimed to add to our knowledge of objects without moving beyond the concepts and letting objects have their say. But

---

[9] *FD* 80 (104).
[10] *Nietzsche* (Pfullingen: Neske, 1961) II, 167.
[11] *FD* 84 (108).
[12] *CPR*, A236=B295; N.K.S., p. 267.
[13] *FD* 144 (184–5).

111

because it pursued the contradictory task of developing synthetic judgments in an analytic way (or aposteriori judgments in an apriori way),[14] the claims of dogmatic metaphysics remained without objective validity. The analytic judgment considers the object only according to its concept and not as a object of experience, i.e., a temporally determined object.[15]

But then how are synthetic apriori judgments possible, if not logically? If the ground of their possibility is not logical, it must be ontological (or in Kant's terms, "transcendental"), in that they must maintain some sort of relation to experience and its objects. But what sort of relation can this be, since, insofar as they are apriori, such judgments are to say something about objects prior to their actually being given? Kant's answer: Synthetic apriori judgments are to find their basis in their relation to "possible experience," or better, to the "possibility of experience." Thus, the highest forms of synthetic apriori judgments, the principles of pure understanding, are to be made secure, i.e., "proved" "not directly from concepts alone, but always only indirectly through relation of these concepts to something altogether contingent, namely, *possible experience.*"[16]

The issue hinges upon further specifications of this "relation," which is the central task of a "transcendental logic."[17] But at least one thing is now clear: The ground has begun to shift from the tautological identity of analytic judgments toward the correlation of judgments with objects of experience, i.e. from truth as consistency to truth as conformity. However, it is not clear whether this change of place

in any way takes us out of the realm of the mathematical. Perhaps we have merely gone into the area of "applied mathematics." The procedure of the *Critique of Pure Reason* suggests as much. After establishing the purely formal conditions of experience, i.e. the schematized categories and the forms of intuition, Kant now asks how they are to be applied to experience. The ultimate result is the articulation of rules of employment, the synthetic apriori principles of understanding, which express and describe these conditions of experience, "contain nothing but...the pure schema of possible experience"[18] without which no experience of objects would be possible. And yet, as already indicated, these principles themselves require proof, which consists in showing that they do in fact apply to every possible object of experience. In other words, one must show that "the conditions of the *possibility of experience* in general are at the same time conditions of the *possibility of the objects of experience.*"[19] This supreme principle of all synthetic judgments is the new "principle of identity" which supplants the tautological principle of non-contradiction as the more fundamental ground for propositions which add to our previous knowledge. Each proof of the principles of understanding thus always comes back to the supreme principle and each principle does no more than to express it in another way.[20]

Hence, when it comes to synthetic principles and the concepts from which they are derived, "their employment and their relation to their professed objects can in the end be sought nowhere but in experience, of whose possibility they contain the

---

[14] *FD* 131–2 (168).
[15] *FD* 137 (175).
[16] *CPR*, A737=B765; N.K.S., p. 592.
[17] *FD* 138 (176).
[18] *CPR*, A237=B296; N.K.S., p. 258.
[19] *CPR*, A158=B197; N.K.S., p. 194.
[20] *FD* 151, 188 (193, 243).

formal conditions."[21] But if the principles find the ground of their proof in experience, which in turn necessarily presupposes the principles, are we not proceeding in a circle in our "proof"? Kant himself points to this peculiarity of each of the principles when he notes "that it makes possible the very experience which is its own ground of proof, and that in this experience it must always itself be presupposed."[22] What Heidegger has to say about the hermeneutical circle inherent in the question of the meaning of being applies equally well here, that this involves "no 'circular reasoning,' but a remarkable 'back and forth relatedness'."[23] "The principles are proved by going *back* to that whose coming *forth* they enable, for these propositions are intended to bring out nothing other than this circular movement, which constitutes the essence of experience."[24] Kant's transcendental reflection, which first found its locus in the movement of thought to its object, now finds itself drawn into a movement of reciprocal grounding between the subjectivity of the subject and the objectivity of the object, where the "between" suggests the ground of a more original unity as the essence of transcendence (experience). Going *back* to this ground would then be a more basic transcendental reflection, one which Heidegger assumes as his own task. The stage is accordingly set for a transition from the mathematical to the hermeneutical, inasmuch as, in the course of his own reflection, Heidegger identifies the relation under study as "the hermeneutic relation."[25] In short, by way of the transcendental, the mathematical ripens into the hermeneutical.

Transition

Kant is the ambiguous intermediary who paves the way for this transition from self-grounding to the ground "between," although he himself remained within the tradition of the mathematical, insofar as he attempts to determine the being of beings (thingness of things, objectivity of objects) in advance out of principles derived from the subjectivity of the subject. The determination of the thingness of things finds its locus in the categories, which, in specifying the kind of *ratio* that is ultimately expressed in the various "ratios" of the form "something as something," embody an "incipient interpretation of the being of beings."[26] Since every kind of assertion has its anticipatory preconception (*Vorgriff*)[27] in one of the apriori concepts of the understanding Heidegger's reading of Kant insinuates that the Kantian categories incorporate what he himself calls the hermeneutical "as" preceding every apophantic "as." But the existential-hermeneutical "as" finds its deeper roots in the prethematic interpretations of the everyday world of gear before it develops into the thematic objectifications of the theoretical world of natural science, which determines Kant's model of a thing.[28] Heidegger's "way up" from the existentials to the categories is not Kant's way. Instead, Kant follows the "way down" of imposing categorial forms upon the matter of sensation. The language of "subsuming" the manifold of intu-

---

[21] *CPR*, A420=B299, N.K.S., p. 260.
[22] *CPR*, A737=B765, N.K.S., p. 592.
[23] *SZ* 8.
[24] *FD* 187 (242): *Rückgang, Hervorgang, Kreisgang* – my emphasis.
[25] *Unterwegs zur Sprache* (Pfullingen: Neske, 1959) pp. 122, 125–8, 136, 150–1. Cf. *On the Way to Language*, trans. Peter D. Hertz (New York: Harper, 1971) pp. 30, 32–4, 40, 51.
[26] *FD* 49 (64).
[27] *FD* 146 (187).
[28] *SZ* 158, 357–364; *FD* 100–1, 110 (128–9, 141).

ition under concepts is the language of mathematical application rather than that of hermeneutic exposition. Meaning is imposed from above, from the self, and not drawn from below, from the situation in which the self finds itself. The meaningful context within which any particular experience becomes meaningful is to be found in the structures of pure reason, not in the world in which man finds himself "thrown." The mathematical project is therefore not seen in its full "facticity" or "throwness,"

To acknowledge the presence of meaning *in* experience would be to shift the locus of the apriori from pure reason to that "between" which reaches back behind man as well as before things. By being thus plunged into the matter of experience, the apriori is demathematized and the search for the apriori takes on a different character. If intentional or existential structures are first found in the thick of experience, they then must first be uncovered *from* it before they are projected *upon* it. In this vein, Heidegger spoke early of the need for a "hermeneutic of facticity." But if we conceive the hermeneutical broadly, so that it pertains to any process of exposing hidden meanings, then the *Critique of Pure Reason* would also have to be included. That this is to a certain extent acceptable and even unavoidable has already been suggested above under the rubric of a certain overlap between the hermeneutical and the mathematical. The operative word here is really "facticity," and the significant feature lies in how *it* necessitates a hermeneutic more fundamental than the hermeneutics of judgment in which Kant finds his starting point. As an initial indicator of where this more fundamental sense of the hermeneutical resides, it might be noted that Heidegger's shift of the

locus of truth from the judgment to existence ultimately focuses on the "fact" that human understanding always takes place through *language* within a *tradition*, and that these two axes of the human situation (one structural and the other dynamic in emphasis) have always been manifest considerations in hermenutical thinking. Moreover, both are manifestly "meaning-giving" factors, and so bear on the problem of an apriori context within which particular experiences can become meaningful. They are therefore "conditions of the possibility of experience." But when Heidegger employs this Kantian locution, he is prone to prefix it with adjectives like "existential-ontological" or "existential-temporal,"[29] in order to distinguish his apriori from the logical and epistemological ones which Kant has uncovered for the cognitive and scientific "experience."

To render experience possible is thus to confer meaning upon it. In order for any synthetic judgment to be possible, it must have "objective validity." Under the influence of Neo-Kantians like Hermann Lotze and Emil Lask as well as Husserl's critique of psychologism, the earliest Heidegger identified the "objective validity" of a judgment with the phenomenon of meaning, where meaning was considered to be the immanent content of judgments, hence ideal and therefore independent of the real psychic acts that form judgments.[30] But Husserl counterbalanced this overly logicist sense of meaning with his intentional theory of consciousness, and Heidegger in his own fashion follows suit. The search for a transcendental and ontological foundation for the "objective validity" of judgments is particularly manifest in the way he exploits certain facets of Kant's formulation of the supreme

---

[29] *SZ* 87, 357, 365.
[30] Heidegger's survey of research in logic (1912) and his dissertation on psychologism (1914) clearly adopt such a theory of meaning. Cf. his 'retraction' in *SZ* 155–6.

principle of synthetic judgments. Kant states: "These pure synthetic judgments therefore relate, though only mediately, to possible experience, or rather to the possibility of experience; and upon that alone is founded the objective validity of their synthesis."[31] When one concept is compared synthetically with another in a judgment, a *tertium* is required as the medium within which the object ("something altogether different") in accord with the judgment may be encountered and an empirical synthesis may take place. The mediating role is played by the transcendental imagination and its medium is the apriori form of time. Together they constitute the unified totality (*Inbegriff*) that makes experience possible. But what is the "object" of experience in its pure possibility? Heidegger identifies Kant's "transcendental object = X" with the pure horizon against which particular objects take their stand, itself not an object and therefore "nothing."[32] And in *Being and Time*, this "nothing" is identified with the "world as such,"[33] the space of significance within which particular things assume their meaning. It is a world that "worlds" and therefore structured dynamically by time. The phenomenon of meaning now finds its locus in the future of the being which projects the world in which it finds itself and seeks to understand what it means to be. Meaning thereby finds its locus in the "apriori forms" of space and time in a more existentially grounded fashion than in Kant. Nevertheless, the apriori knowledge that Kant described "mathematically" is in its way the same "antecedent understanding of the being of beings"[34] which forms the

basis of Heidegger's hermeneutic of facticity. But now, understanding "is not simply a mode of knowing, but primarily a fundamental moment of existing."[35]

The Hermeneutical

Manthanein not only means "to learn" but also "to understand," which since Schleiermacher and Dilthey has been a central concern of hermeneutics. But if we interpretively understand what we already implicitly understand, as Heidegger's discussion of the hermeneutic circle suggests, then the hermeneutical parallels the mathematical "learning what we already know." Whether it is circumspective or thematic, interpretation "lays out" and explicitly appropriates its own preunderstanding. As already indicated, the only difference with the mathematical tradition seems to be the depth at which the "already" is placed. If the immediate and unreflective understanding is first a moment of existing before it is a mode of cognition, therefore more an understanding that we *are* rather than have, then it enters into and even constitutes the definition of human existence. If the term "knowledge" still applies here, it is more the immediate "know how" of existence, a knack or feel for what it means to be and what we can do that comes from "experience." From a long familiarity with the world, we already know how to "get along" with people and "deal" with the things of the world in "going about our business." We already know what the world is "about." In short, we already know how to live, and this skill of Being is a "knowledge" *in actu exercitu* which expresses itself through

---

[31] *CPR*, A157=B196, N.K.S., p. 194.
[32] *Kant und das Problem der Metaphysik* (Frankfurt a.m.: Klostermann, ²1951), sections 24 and 25. Cf. *Kant and the Problem of Metaphysics*, trans. James S. Churchill (Bloomington: Indiana UP, 1962). Hereafter *KM*.
[33] *SZ* 187.
[34] *KM* 20 (15).
[35] *KM* 210 (240–1).

our attitudes and styles of action.

But all this is understood "as a matter of course," without reflection, and if someone should articulate one or another facet of this knowledge that comes from familiarity, we are naturally inclined to reply "Of course!" (*Selbstverständlich!*). And yet, what is familiar may not always be really understood, and this in direct proportion to the depth of its familiarity, so that what is most familiar to us can in its unobtrusiveness be what is most likely to be overlooked. What is nearest experientially can at once be the furthest from our mind.[36] We can be oblivious of our most intimate experiences. For example, in our concern for the particularities of daily existence, the more comprehensive sense that we have of what it means to be can easily lapse into oblivion. In fact, in terms of time spent in this way and in view of the human inertia that encourages this tendency, the oblivion of our sense of being must be acknowledged to be one of the most characteristic and dominant features of human existence. There is so much in life that conspires us to do so that one might even say that it is natural and normal and ultimately not of our own doing. The very variety of life militates against the simplicity of this sense. And the very simplicity of this sense militates against a clear-cut expression of it. It is therefore to this above all that Polanyi's maxim might apply: "We know more than we can tell." To which Wittgenstein might add: "What we cannot speak about we must pass over in silence."

And yet we have already suggested that our basic sense of what it means to be *expresses itself* in our attitudes and styles of action, and so finds an outlet in more particular manifestations. The tone of an assertion,[37] the tenor of a speech, the inflections of a voice, the modulations of an interchange, the *genius loci* of a university, the temper of an age: All of these serve to illustrate how a global phenomenon, however muted and evanescent, may nevertheless betray itself in its more particular manifestations. Such is the phenomenon *par excellence* of phenomenology, which "in the first instance and for the most part does *not* show itself at all ...but which at the same time is something that belongs so essentially to what in the first instance and for the most part does show itself, that it indeed constitutes its sense and ground."[38] In order to divine this most basic sense, in order to detect its fleeting innuendoes and often disguised nuances in the more manifest phenomena, the *logos* of phenomenology assumes a hermeneutical character.[39] This applies particularly to the phenomenology of human existence. If the meaning of human existence is first sensed as an atmosphere, as in a mood, if our most basic "assumptions" assume an atmospheric quality pervading the fabric of our existence, then a most subtle hermeneutic must be developed in order to make manifest this medium in which and by which we live, move, and assume our being. If, in contrast, the mathematical reaches its optimum in an apophantic system of truths on the basis of an architectonic of principles, then the hermeneutic now being proposed is doomed to a never-ending reading between its lines, as it were, in order to grasp something of the meaning pervading the interstices of its manifest

---

36 'Being is the nearest. Yet the nearness remains farthest from man.' *Über den Humanismus* (Frankfurt a.M.: Klostermann, 1947) p. 20. Cf. translation by Edgar Lohner, in *Philosophy in the Twentieth Century*, ed. Wm. Barrett and H. D. Aiken (New York: Random House, 1962) Vol. III, p. 282. Hereafter *BH*.
37 *WD* 13 (37).
38 *SZ* 35.
39 *SZ* 37.

structure without actually being said.

This is in fact the basis of Heidegger's own approach to the texts of the history of philosophy. It is likewise the experience of the tradition with regard to the texts that over the years have become "classic," which have repeatedly lent themselves to new and productive interpretations and thus seem inexhaustible in their yield. Great poets and thinkers have somehow managed to find words which somehow intimate the ineffable, so that the text transmitted to us seems to speak for itself out of a surplus of sense. Whence the mysterious temporal structure of "repetition," whereby the same text always says something different in different contexts and at different times.

Thus, contrary to the early Wittgenstein's dictum "to say nothing except what can be said" (*Tractatus*, 6.53), Heidegger seeks to orient the efforts of human existence and its tradition toward saying the unsaid and even its impossible asymptote, the unsayable, and moreover to define the grounds of the possibility for doing so (thus using Kant against Kant). But if "the sayable word receives its determination from the unsayable,"[40] so that the ineffable, the "silent power of the possible,"[41] lies at the basis of the long conversation of the tradition, this recognition does not mean to recommend a direct assault on "what we cannot speak about." The proper response is rather more paradoxical. Models taken from the tradition suggest that "every incipient and authentic naming utters the unspoken in such a way that it remains unspoken."[42]

Accordingly, the greatest gift of a thinker lies in not what he says but what he does not say.[43] Hence, "the course of such a discourse must have its own character, according to which it would be more silent than spoken."[44] Reticence and not abjudication is the prescription, especially when we talk and write about silence, which has produced "the most obnoxious chatter."[45]

With this precautionary corollary, it might be well to re-emphasize the main point by invoking John Wisdom's recommendation: "Philosophers should be continually trying to say what cannot be said."[46] In its absolute refusal even to try under the polemical guise of a rejection of "metaphysics," which is pilloried by the standards of a logical absolutism, positivism is a betrayal of philosophy. In the face of the ineffable, the philosopher may find himself at a loss for words, he may stammer his way into self-contradictions, he may be forced into long periods of silence, but he must *try*.

But how can one speak of a dearth of words,[47] if, in its best moments, the entire tradition of poets and thinkers has directed itself toward the same end? It seems more appropriate here to speak of a feast rather than the famine of language. But in this context, both "language" and "tradition" are equivocal terms, and the point of crisis lies precisely in the phrase "in its best moments." For our usual stance toward these gross realities (or better, "transcendental magnitudes") which constitute the most basic presuppositions of our experience is unthinking and "matter of fact," and this natural attitude of *Selbstverständ-*

---

40 *N* II 484.
41 *BH* 8 (273).
42 *WD* 119 (196)
43 *WD* 72 (76)
44 *US* 152 (52).
45 *Ibid.*
46 John Wisdom, *Philosophy and Psychoanalysis* (New York: Philosophical Library, 1965) p. 50.
47 On the *Sprachnot* of philosophy, see Hans-Georg Gadamer, 'Die Begriffsgeschichte und die Sprache der Philosophie' (Opladen: Westdeutscher Verlag, 1971).

lichkeit is the greatest obstacle to thinking. Not that daily life and more reflective activities like science and politics proceed in total unawareness of their "self-evident" principles. But the relatively narrow and tentative presuppositional base of common sense or of the prevalent paradigm or world-view is made manifest only when a more radical question intrudes to "destroy" the hardened "deposit" of tradition and challenge the spontaneous self-forgetfulness of "ordinary language." The need to revise initiates the search for new directions and new modes of expression, which, in view of their fundamental and encompassing character, still develops out of the "sources"[48] of tradition within the "living" language, both of which constitute the meaningful context without which we would not understand anything at all. It is in this sense that review and revision always involve a "repetition" and that the reversal of the spontaneous tendency toward forgetfulness is a "reminiscence."[49]

Accordingly, the reversal is not simply a return to the self but more basically to the historical and linguistic situation in which one finds oneself. The "hermeneutic relation" is not that of a soul to eternal Ideas or of rational faculties to universal and necessary categories but of a "Being-in-the-world" structured by the concrete universals of language and tradition. Accordingly, "as the situation is new we must think anew and act anew." Even the unknowns and therefore our responses to them are thoroughly historical. For the very sense of our questions is conditioned by the

"thickness" of our particular "hermeneutical situation," the totality of historical presuppositions in which we find ourselves.[50] Each epoch thus has its own unsaid in what is already said which it alone is called upon to say; i.e. it has its own mission of what it means to be.[51]

Which is why the repetition of the tradition is not rote and mechanical, but rather an encounter with precedents which involves a countering and a countermanding of what in them is past and gone in order to expose their bearing on the unprecedented.[52] In order to demarcate its own possibilities and limits from other epochs, it must first execute a "demystifying" critique ("destruction") of what it takes for granted. We must therefore learn what we already know in order to unlearn it, so that we may learn what we do not know.[53]

Our response to the novelty of our own hermeneutical situation thus institutes a translation that reaches even into its presuppositional bases. The circular movement between preunderstanding and its exposition through interpretation is therefore more than an explication of perduring implications. Even the lesser tasks of adapting the tradition to the exigencies of the time contribute to transmuting this seemingly closed circle into a temporal spiral. Almost as a "spin-off" from our particular interpretations of texts, dramas, music, etc., a reshaping of our tacit assumptions takes place, subtle shifts in our fundamental ways of thinking which in due time can open up unexpected new horizons of understanding. In view of this tacit temporal development of the presuppositions

---

[48] *SZ* 21.

[49] *KM* 211 (242).

[50] *SZ* 232. Cf. Hans-Georg Gadamer, *Le Problème de la conscience historique* (Louvain: Publications Universitaires de Louvain, 1963) p. 76.

[51] *Der Satz vom Grund* (Pfullingen: Neske, 1957) p. 187. Here *das Ungesagte* is identified with *Seinsgeschick*.

[52] *SZ* 386.

[53] *WD* 5 (8). The issue here is what it means to think, suggesting another difference of the hermeneutical from the mathematical, that of learning a way to be rather than a 'what' (essence).

themselves, the direction of interpretation will at times have to be
reversed in order to uncover this new
ground of presuppositions. As already
indicated, this first step involves a
demystification of the doxic, the
clearing away of presuppositions which
have become obsolete but which are
nevertheless maintained in public par-
lance by a sort of "cultural lag."
Hermeneutic conceived radically always incorporates the art of taking
away[54] knowledge in order to reveal
the basis from which it can then
proceed to new knowledge.

But how is a radical hermeneutic to
describe this translatory movement, if
the basis is no longer the security of a
fundamental self in cognitive touch
with eternal verities? For the process
of backtracking into known presuppositions may conceivably reach a point
at which it veritably cuts all established ground from under it, and
the only possibility left is to shift
ground radically. Accordingly, to describe the movement of thought at the
nadir of absolute groundlessness, Heidegger speaks of a leap into an abyss
(*Abgrund*) that brings the thinker into
the proximity (*Nähe*) of potentially
new ground. Here is the point of
departure of radical thinking from
academic scholarship, which remains
within the jurisdiction of the mathematical prescription inscribed over the
portals of the Academy.[55] To experience "the difference between an
object of scholarship and a matter of
thought"[56] is to experience the change
in priority and direction between
controlled research from ultimately
firm ground toward definite goals as

opposed to a state of finding oneself
under the control of something beyond
our ken, where the paths "to the
things themselves" sometimes abruptly
trail off into obscurity, in which
thoughts come to us rather than we to
them, where the only appropriate
stance is to "let things speak for themselves," so that the hermeneutical now
refers first to "the bearing of message
and tidings"[57] that precedes and
underlies interpretive exposition.

Viewed from this direction, the
hermeneutical process does not yield
merely what is already known by us,
even latently, but what is transmitted
to us in the course of the process. It is
this "gift" character of the hermeneutical that clearly distinguishes it from
the mathematical. The latency of the
hermeneutical situation is not limited
to the latent knowledge already possessed by us.

Where, then, is the surplus of sense,
the source of novelty, to be situated?
The recurring allusion to "the things
themselves" suggests where the "heart
of the matter" lies: in *die Sache selbst*, in
the mystery of Being, that unspeci-
fiable totality of meaning which the
long conversation of human existence
attempts again and again to say and
which the language thus transmitted
to us has somehow managed to say
without being able to say it totally.
"Language once in one great moment
says something unique, which remains
inexhaustible because it is always incipient and therefore beyond the reach
of any kind of levelling."[58] Tradition
at its most profound is eternal inci-
pience;[59] it transmits, i.e. has an
inexhaustible "give," insofar as it is

---

[54] Cf. Søren Kierkegaard, *Concluding Unscientific Postscript*, trans. David F. Swenson and Walter
Lowrie (Princeton UP, 1941) p. 245 n. Akin to Heidegger, Kierkegaard's critique of the inner-
directedness of the Platonic doctrine of reminiscence leads to the positing of an outer-directed
'leap' of faith.
[55] *FD* 58 (75).
[56] *Aus der Erfahrung des Denkens* (Tübingen, Neske, 1954) p. 9. Translated by Albert Hofstadter in
Poetry, Language, Thought (New York: Harper and Row, 1971) p. 5.
[57] *US* 122 (29).
[58] *WD* 168 (191–2).
[59] *Nietzsche* II, 29.

developed "out of the things themselves."[60] Whence the Heideggerian superlatives for Being *itself*: a hidden treasure of fullness, the wealth of the simple, inexhaustible wellspring of the ineffable, aboriginal gathering of essence, the dynamic stillness that is the source of history, so old yet ever so new.

In addressing themselves to the same source, the great poets and thinkers always say the same; but in view of its inexhaustibility, what they say is never uniformly the same. In ever returning to this source, philosophy does not progress; but in the face of its ineffability, philosophy's task is never done. Once having been said, it has yet to be said. The tradition must be "repeated." Whence the peculiar temporal structure of the hermeneutic circle, of "pre"-suppositions which lie ahead of us.[61] If existential apriori are "perfect tense apriori,"[62] the tense is not simply past perfect, for the past here is still forthcoming. If thinking never first comes to its thoughts, it is because thinking stems from a more archaic "thought" (*Gedanc*) out of which its thoughts are forthcoming.[63]

Inasmuch as this "thought" which calls upon us to think is the gathering place of what has been and still endures, it may be called "memory" (*Gedächtnis*). This would be a reversion to the Platonic doctrine of reminiscence only if memory here were simply a human capacity. It is that, but it is something more, namely, the place ("house") in which man dwells, that treasury of the past which we call "language." Language is the storehouse of Mnemosyne, the mother of the Muses that prompt us to thought. Language has the capacity to hold what has already been said, out of which it yields the unsaid that is yet to be said. Language thus deserves the title "hold of all holds, relation of all relations"[64]: on the one hand, thesaurus of Being and food for thought; on the other, the focal point of the essence of man, where "the soul ignites" (Eckhart) in recall to thought —hence the milieu of history, the atmosphere of comprehensibility which enables the whole of a tradition to speak through a great thought and thus stay alive. Without this "element of thinking," man could not function as a man; removed from his medium, he would become like the proverbial fish out of water.

Perhaps one might then hazard the following supreme principle of all hermeneutical judgments, i.e. their ultimate *locus veritatis*: The condition of the possibility of human experience is at the same time the condition of the possibility of the historical world.

The linguisticality of human existence: the language of Being—the colon suggests the simple center which is the heart of the matter of the hermeneutic relation, the apriori of all aprioris.

---

[60] *SZ* 153.
[61] *SZ* 327.
[62] *SZ* 85.
[63] *WD* 91–99, 157–9 (138–153). The English translators have translated the archaic German *Gedanc* by the Old English *thanc*. The text develops the complexity of relations between *Gedanke*, *Gedenken*, *Gedächtnis*, and *Dank*, the latter suggesting the 'gift' character of the hermeneutical process, as well as their bearing on *Gewesen* as *Verwahrnis*, the 'keep' where truth is held in trust, which in turn bear on Heidegger's discussion in other places of the *Ver-hältnis* (see note 64).
[64] *US* 267 (135). Here the essence of language is identified with 'the primeval tidings of the event of appropriation,' which holds to itself as it holds us in its reticent appropriation.

THE PROBLEM OF LANGUAGE*

K.-H. Volkmann-Schluck

University of Cologne

The problem of language will be initiated and dealt with in this paper in a manner fundamentally different from the way in which it is presented in a wide variety of perspectives. The following attempt at an exposition of the problem makes its way via the question of myth. The most immediate cause for a philosophical treatment of myth is given by the works of Walter F. Otto, Karl Kerenyi and the structural myth-research inaugurated by Levi-Strauss. These are lines of thought which, no matter how different in their points of departure, methods, and intentions, make the problem of language their object, or in the end arrive at this problem. The actual motivation for a philosophical interest in myth, however lies in Schelling's philosophy of mythology. Schelling's constructions of the history of mythical polytheism, as well as his discovery and securing of their principles, are guided by the sole intent of furnishing evidence for the fact that myth contains truth such that it is precisely the mythical character as such that constitutes the truth of myth. Truth, however, according to Schelling's own words (WW II 2, pp. 142ff.) is "a law that demands that nothing remain hidden, that everything be revealed, that everything be clear, definite and determined, so that every enemy be overcome and, in this way, perfect, composed being may first be established." Schelling, therefore, conceives the history of mythical polytheism as the process of truth's coming into being, as the necessary path on which the unconditioned will for disclosure, clarity, definiteness and decisiveness acquires what it wants and thereby comes to itself. Since, however, all desiring, i.e., every instance of self-realization, requires a resisting object on and in which it is realized, what is disclosed and determined necessarily presupposes what is non-disclosed and undetermined. Thus at the beginning of history monotheism was only in essence, but not yet in reality. If this essential monotheism is to become real, it requires the opposite of itself, the overcoming of which is the means of its realizing itself. This opposite (*Gegenteil*), the object (*Gegenstand*), is mythical polytheism.

According to Schelling, the truth of myth, like all truth in general, has its place in consciousness, but not in such a way that consciousness itself were already the truth. Consciousness, taken for itself, is simply the formal part of self-knowledge. It has its reality in that to which it refers, in its object. But it is indeed the place where truth alone can be realized, provided the highest world law demands that everything be revealed, clear, definite and determined. Therefore realized truth exists in consciousness which knows itself as knowing reality in accordance with its essence. Hence, idealized truth exists in absolute *Logos,* which has comprehended the mythological process as the necessary means of its own realization through constructing a philosophy of mythology.

The following consideration begins by questioning the place of mythical

Karl-Heinz Volkmann-Schluck is professor of philosophy at the University of Cologne. His published works include: Plotin als Interpret der Ontologie Platons, Einfuhrung in die philosophischen Denken, *and* Interpretationen zur Philosophie Nietzsches.

---

* Delivered in June, 1969, in Heidelberg, Germany, at a colloquium honoring Heidegger's 80th birthday. Subsequently published in *Die Frage Martin Heideggers, op. cit.* Translated by R. Phillip O'Hara.

truth. Indeed, the view according to which this place is consciousness is of modern origin. And even those who go so far as to see an "unreflected prefiguration of consciousness" in being, because of its relationship to *Nous,* as conceived by Plato and Aristotle as idea and *Eidos,* will hesitate to expand this interpretation to Heraclitus as well. As to Heraclitus, the notion could rather be entertained that truth is determined from the opposing relationship between God and man. For in the thought of Heraclitus man appears in his opposing relationship with the divine as its antitype, i.e., as mortal, and thus permits the converse of life and death, the antithesis of all antitheses, to appear. Those who are immortal, who live forever, however, first come to light in their turn because death as such is co-existent in the life of mortals in such a way that man, by virtue of his mortality, is the indispensable partner in this world drama.

We may thus ask this question: Supposing that myth is true — and the fact it is true is Schelling's judgment which forms the constant point of departure for the following discussion — what then is the place of mythical truth?

As said, this question is always already decided for Schelling. The content of myth is fashioned by the divine powers, from whose interaction nature originates. These powers arise again in consciousness as spiritual powers and involve consciousness in a theogonic process. We will now drop this concept of consciousness and simply raise the question: Where does that which the myth relates appear?

The first answer runs as follows: Everything which myth relates occurs in mythical speech itself. Mythical speech provides the realm in which everything it says takes place. To be sure cultic activity also belongs to mythical religion. But there is no cult which is not based on a divine history. We would therefore be able to approach the place of mythical truth if we could succeed in determining the mythical

mode of speech itself. But a conception which has understandably dominated us for a long time at once obstructs the path of this endeavor. We have always and without examination taken speech to be already a communication, a communication of feelings, aspirations, opinions, thoughts, recognitions. Expressed generally, we take speech to be a communication of ideas which we have construed and construe of ourselves and things. Speech is for us a communication of ideas by means of expressions, which for their part can be fixed and given durability in something written. This conception seems to correspond to a completely natural view of language. It is, in fact, philosophical in origin, and it appears for the first time in the passage with which Aristotle in $\pi\epsilon\rho\grave{\iota}$ $\dot{\epsilon}\rho\mu\epsilon\nu\epsilon\dot{\iota}\alpha s$ begins his investigation of *Logos* in the sense of an attributing and negating expression. But since *Logos,* as viewed by Plato, presents an interweaving of $\check{o}\nu o\mu\alpha$ and $\dot{\rho}\hat{\eta}\mu\alpha$, Aristotle first makes both these parts of speech the theme of his reflection and thus co-articulates the essence of language:

"What takes place in the voice is the characteristic sign ($\sigma\dot{\upsilon}\mu\beta o\lambda o\nu$) of occurrences ($\pi\dot{\alpha}\theta\eta\mu\alpha$) in the soul, and what is written is the characteristic sign of what occurs in the voice. And just as writing is not the same for everyone, so also are vocal expressions not the same with everyone. That, however, of which these are primarily signs ($\sigma\eta\mu\epsilon\hat{\iota}o\nu$), the incidents of the soul, are the same with everyone, and that of which they (the conditions of the soul) are representative approximations ($\dot{o}\mu o\dot{\iota}\omega\mu\alpha$), namely the objects, are likewise the same."

We will here dispense with an interpretation of this passage and call attention only to three circumstances: 1. Language here appears to be a totality of references which are characterized in various ways: $\sigma\dot{\upsilon}\mu\beta o\lambda o\nu$ $\sigma\eta\mu\epsilon\hat{\iota}o\nu$, $\dot{o}\mu o\dot{\iota}\omega\mu\alpha$. 2. Language comes into view as what and how it primarily shows itself. It shows itself, however, in speaking, as that which occurs in the voice, and above all, as something written.

3. This first characteristic of language already points to possible modifications of the basic conception concerning language: language as spiritual-mental expression, as a manifestation or activity of the spirit, as a reaction to the pressure of what is real, as a system of signs or of information, as a symbol, as literature.

The Greek word μῦθος means simply discourse, narration, speech. But with the conception according to which all speech is a proclamation of mental images, we do not approach mythical speech. For if speech is exhausted in proclaiming mental images, which man makes more or less exactly regarding things, then how could the relationships appear there, in which the gods and men reach each other? Did Hesiod, when he narrated in his theogony the history of divine succession up to the eternally enduring dominion of Zeus, want to communicate mental images which he, Hesiod, had made of these processes, and about which no one knows when and where they took place? The mythical poets themselves state that their speech is of another kind. The Greek epic poets begin their poems with an appeal to the Muses, which is no superficial ornament and decoration with which the poets wish to gain greater esteem, but which rather expresses the manner of their speech itself. According to this, the actual speakers are not the poets, but the Muses, daughters of the highest god.

Nevertheless, this self-testimony of the mythical poets does not directly help us. For the Muses themselves are mythical figures, the daughters of Zeus, and the place of their appearance is mythical speech. In order to be able to perceive to what extent they are the actual speakers, we would need to have acquired clarity regarding the nature of mythical speech. We, however, gain least of all by speaking of "poetic in-spiration" — it is a word used as a last resort which expresses nothing in the face of poetic creativity and even less with reference to mythical poems. Mythical composition of poetry, according to the testimony of its poets, occurs when what is to be said is open to being said (sich-sagen-lassen). Such a mode of speech has long since withdrawn into silence. The question, therefore, is whether we are capable of even undertaking an attempted reflection on the mythical mode of speech. As is usually the case with thinking, it depends on making an attempt.

We, too, if we are reasonable, frequently let ourselves be told what we have to say, e.g., when a difficult situation is before us in which we are inexperienced and for which we therefore obtain advice from someone who is experienced. Even then our speaking is not a simple reiteration. This openness to being said includes for our part that we recognize advice and that we are able to make free use of what we were advised to say in the discussion. But such an openness to being said, which is familiar to us, remains infinitely far behind what occurs in mythical speech: the appearance of divine and human relationships which ordain the totality of existence.

We stand under the domination of a conception of speech that stems from 'Logos,' which was conceived as the foundation which penetrates the existing thing in its 'what' and 'how' and 'whereby.' We therefore might never succeed in attaining to the mythical mode of speech, if we are unable to create a transition which permits us to attain to myth. We sense such a transition in the basic passage of Heraclitus. The 'Logos' of Heraclitus points forward to the domination of 'Logos' which began with Plato and Aristotle, as well as backwards to myth. Logos is the togetherness of what is converse (ἐναντία). It is the one presence out of the contra-relationship (Gegenverhältnis) of the one vis à vis the other. But there is indeed no doubt that *Logos* means speaking and what is said at the same time. If that be the case, then what is the essence of speaking that *Logos* conceals in itself? It is the union of what is converse in the one presence, out of which each appears as itself. What appears primarily are the divine and the human, which first come to each other in the contra-relationship. But when we speak this way, we must at the same time add that by *Logos* Heraclitus did not conceive the essence of speaking, but the unity of the being of every entity.

Thus in the basic passage of Heraclitus we have not yet attained to mythical speech, but it could form the transition which permits us to attain to it, if we are successful in showing that the essence of speech is what is contained, though not conceived in the *Logos* of Heraclitus. In order to acquire the decisive reference for mythical speech, we must add an essential thought which Heidegger was the first to conceive. The mythical poets of the Greeks testify that their poetic composition rests in an openness to being said. We do not know what that means, because the Muses themselves are mythical figures. But we can raise the question whether we are not also able in our speaking to experience an 'openness to being said.' In fact such a feature is revealed to us in the essence of speaking, if we pay attention to the circumstances which Heidegger, above all, caught sight of and expanded in his essay "Der Weg zur Sprache." When we say something, we present a circumstance according to this or that view, namely for us, the speakers, as well as for those who have heard what was said. But at the same time that we say something, we listen to the language we speak. This listening accompanies our speaking everywhere. It usually goes unnoticed that all our speaking is also always a listening to the language spoken by us. But listening immediately comes to the fore when the appropriate word does not occur to us,

when the right syntax will not come to us. It is just in such an absence of what we would like to say that we can experience our speaking itself as listening to the language we speak. Even more: this revocation of language in the absence of the appropriate word testifies that our speaking is not only accompanied by a listening to the language spoken by us, but that this listening even precedes speaking. This simple fact is irrefutable, and everyone can experience it if he once pays attention to his speaking. All of our speaking is—is what it is—from listening to the language which we at the moment speak. But a speaking of language corresponds to this listening to language. Thus language itself does the speaking. "Language speaks." This sentence of Heidegger does not spread abroad any mystic profundity concerning language, it does not obscure the obvious notion that language is the organ of communication and information. But it expresses a simple, as well as enigmatical matter.

Thus we can experience an 'openness to being said' when we pay attention to the fact that all of our speaking rests on an incitement on the part of the language we speak. If the language revokes its incitement, then we are not able to say anything, then language stays away from us.

Our speaking is an interpretation. We interpret what we address and discuss from this or that perspective, take it to be this or that, in this way or some other way. This interpretation forms the theme of hermeneutics. And it is already clear that interpretation can not be something primordial, that hermeneutics must still take an essential step beyond itself if it wishes to arrive at the essence of language. We always live through an intelligible interpretation of the world, and an interpretation is based on a speaking of language, on its incitement and its revocation. But how is the speaking of language related to interpretative understanding? Can we at least attempt to settle something regarding this question by considering the *Logos* of Heraclitus and by paying attention to the fact that *Logos* means language and what is spoken, speaking and what is said?

The *Logos* permits each thing to appear as itself out of the contra-relationship. Thus a clearness holds sway in the *Logos,* from which something present can first of all reveal itself from itself. But *we* have a comprehending interpretation of what is before us only when what is present appears. That is the hermeneutical situation in which human speech occurs. We may now raise the question: Could it be that the primordial essence of language exists in the *Logos* of Heraclitus? That would mean that language, whose address we hear when we speak, produces and extends the clearness in which everything present is first revealed from itself. In that case our speaking can be an interpretation of that which reveals itself as this or that. Then the speaking of language would not only be what is nearest, but nearness itself which first conveys to us what is near and far as such. And even we ourselves in all of our enduring and changing relations to everything would be first near and then far from ourselves out of the speaking of language. The nature of language, which conveys clearness, and our speaking the comprehending interpretation of the world, belong together in an essential unity. There is no human speaking, or interpreting comprehension, without the speaking of language. And language does not endure as language unless it has freed human speaking for itself. Where something existing appears as something existing, where a world clears itself, there language already speaks, there man is already the one who speaks, who, speaking, listens to language.

This attempt to gain insight into the essence of language consists in joining together several thoughts: that our speaking is a listening to the language we speak, that the nature of language is concealed in the *Logos* of Heraclitus, that the *Logos,* the contra-relationship of what is converse, conveys clearness, in which each thing first appears as something present, so that we are able to address it, discuss it and talk it out.

These deliberations were undertaken, then, with the intention of finding a transition to the mythical mode of speaking. But if we now attempt to use the results of our deliberations for a demarcation of mythical speaking, it is immediately clear that it is not sufficient. We sought a basic characteristic of mythical speaking, 'openness to being said,' and found that 'openness to being said' determines all our speaking, since our speaking can only be what it is in so far as it is admitted to a speaking of language. Nevertheless, we are able to conceive mythical speaking in a totally preliminary approximation as follows: it is a speaking in which what it says itself takes place, i.e., the appearance of the divine and human in their dissimilar essence and elucidation of essential relationships which ordain existence (*Dasein*). Mythical speaking is capable of this kind of communication because it is already admitted to a speaking of language, which imparts to man what it has to say by conveying the clearness in which gods and men appear. But when we point this out, we must also add that such speaking has long become silent and that for this reason everything which myth narrates no longer takes place. To be sure we too are familiar with that speaking in light of which everything appears again and again as if for the first time, i.e., poetical speaking. But no matter how highly one might esteem poetry, no one will assert that poetry bears existence as myth once did, even if poetry does play an essential part in bringing forth existence. For *Logos* has already dominated for a long time as that thinking which fathoms and grounds everything, and its essential history had already begun, as Heraclitus conceived in the *Logos,* not the essence of language, but the Being of existing things. The *Logos* relegates poetry to the second rank, if it does not even expel it, as Plato's *Logos* does. Philosophy dominates, and today that means: the sciences, discharged from the ranks of philosophy, dominate, and they govern what is real. Science dominates even poetry in the form of literary science. That poetry has become an object of literary science proves unequivocally the domination of *Logos*.

But Heraclitus conceived of Being as in *Logos*. He conceived of *Logos* as a basic word for speaking and saying. If we take his perspective, and if we permit, above all, the experience of language, for which we are indebted to Heidegger, to play a role with Heraclitus' conception, then the notion is possible that a speaking has sway in Being itself, which by bringing one thing to another, first permits what is present to appear. And then the question suggests itself whether the speaking which has sway in Being, i.e., *Logos,* is not the speaking of that language by listening to which we are speakers. There is much in favor of this relation. Viewed hermeneutically, our speaking is a comprehending interpretation of that which reveals itself from itself. If everything were to remain in the darkness of absence, there would be nothing to understand and to interpret. But we are indeed everywhere approached by entities in various modes and levels of manifestation and concealment such that we interpret the world in a comprehensible way, i.e., we speak by listening to the language we speak.

Let us inquire further in this direction: How are myth and *Logos* related to the essence of language? In myth, language addresses to man in a unique way what he is to put into words and what he is to preserve in them: the opposition of the gods and man, their agreement and their conflict, human fate which, since man is the antitype of the divine, comes as much from man as it is sent by the gods. But if language speaks in this way in mythical speaking, does that mean that the essence of language itself is articulated? By no means. What myth says is the fullness of that which comes to light in articulately hearing the address of language. The divine is foremost. It is to be comprehended such that man in face of the divine achieves the correct state and conducts himself appropriately overagainst divinity, because he is the opposite of the divine. The event in which the world is illuminated through the speaking of language takes place in myth, but that event itself is not what is said — with the exception that the mythical poets testify that their speaking is an 'openness to being said' on the part of the Muses, the daughters of the highest god.

How is the other mode of speaking, the *Logos,* related to language? How is speaking related to the essence of language, which is a speaking and thinking of Being? Heraclitus conceives of *Logos* as Being, but not as the essence of language. For this reason the relation of *Logos* to human speaking remains concealed in his thought. The conceiving of Being becomes for Plato and Aristotle the question of *what* each thing is, of the *Logos* of *Eidos.* The question, what is language? also needs to be raised within the range of this thought. Language appears as a common One which determines the multiplicity of the various languages and which later turns out to be the concept of language. The essence of language is thus articulated in the radius of *Logos,* in fact decisively so in the sense of answering the question, what is? — an answer which determines the essence of language. But whatever turn this thought takes with reference to language, the essence of language itself is lacking when language is comprehended within this *Logos.* And this absence allows to *Logos* first and formost the uninhibited development of its own essential characterization of language: a promulga-

126

tion of ideas in the soul or in consciousness, and this promulgation occasions the objectification of language through theories of information.

The fact, however, that language retains its essence and thereby even withdraws by ceding its pre-eminence to one of its characteristics appropriate to the *Logos,* does not depend on a human failure. Neither the mythical poets nor the thinkers of *Logos* were wanting in anything. Absence and withdrawal are essential modes of language itself. Language is that which collects in clearing, which does not refer back to itself, but rather points away from itself to that which, by its pointing, rises into visibility, just as light itself withdraws into invisibility so that things can become visible in their appearance in the light.

But if this is the case with language, one final question arises, which we shall consider as we conclude this discussion: If language continues in this mode of self-withdrawal, then how can we contemplate it? How can we determine something about an object of which we at the same time assert that it evades thought and speech? How is such a thing even possible? Simply because it is possible to experience the self-withdrawal of language as such. But this is possible only when self-withdrawal has already taken place. That, however, has already happened. For the essence of language is utterly concealed, because *Logos* has established the dominion of its own notion of language. But thought would first be able to *experience* language's self-withdrawal and the completed fact of its withdrawal when it is concerned with and affected by this accomplished withdrawal.

One possible way of contemplatively experiencing the clearing self-withdrawal of language could be as follows: The fact of withdrawal as such would have to happen in the realm which withdrawal itself has opened up. That is the realm of the *Logos,* which comprehends itself as the essence of exist-

ing things. The contemplation of the absolute *Logos* becomes a philosophy of mythology in accord with essential necessity. Myth begins to appear within the realm of *Logos,* first, indeed, as the self-engendered truth of the *Logos* in its self-generation, as posing the opposite to itself in which it realizes itself. And then much depends on the answer to the question: Does the truth of the absolute *Logos* conceal something questionable in itself, given the fact that it is the law according to which complete Being is posed, Being which is finally pacified by the overcoming of every opponent? Is there something questionable in this law that causes us to raise questions which do not arise externally, but which rather arise out of the law of truth which necessitates that the absolute *Logos,* qua thinking, project a philosophy of mythology? Indeed, we accept Schelling's recognition of the truth of myth, which is founded in the certainty of absolute knowledge, and if we at the same time permit the place of truth, with regard to myth, to become the object of inquiry, then we are compelled to accept myth even more literally than Schelling. We must accept it as a saying which as saying contains the truth itself of what is said. And overagainst this saying, the conception of language cannot hold its own when it is grounded in the soul of man or in his consciousness, instead of in the essence of language itself. We are rather constrained to abandon the realm of *Logos* in order to be able to conceive an essence of language which gives us an insight into a kind of speaking, which in itself makes apparent what it says. That was the reason for the attempt to expound the problem of language by way of the question of myth.

We may assume that when language itself 'comes to word,' speaking could be altered in the event. That, however, does not mean that mythical speech simply returns as poetry. To think this would be a misunderstanding for several reasons: the determining and elemental characteristic of myth is precisely that it retains the essence of language in what is left unsaid and articulates the divine and human relationships in which man has to find himself. But then poetry would have to articulate the essence of language itself. Furthermore: since the first awakening of thought, man in his essence was determined by the thinking of Being, which is still retained in myth with its conceivability and its speakability. Therefore, speech which changes will retain for itself the *Logos,* the conceivability and speakability of Being, and will remain therefore a thinking, but a thinking which takes over the task of thinking Being from clearing-collected speech, from the event of language. Whether poetry is successful in articulating language itself will thus depend on whether thought is prepared and able to ground itself in the essence of language, rather than simply conceiving language from the perspective of the soul, consciousness, spirit or a structure of signs.

One can anticipate least of all the possible alterations of speech by conceptions about language. These alterations depend on the experiences which we are prepared to have with language —experiences which arise from language. Nevertheless the beginning of a contemplative experience of language has already been made. And according to Aristotle the beginning is more than half the task.

LANGUAGE AND REVERSAL

JOHN SALLIS

Duquesne University

I. The Problem of Language and Reversal

The way on which Heidegger's thinking has moved is a way with which the question of language is intertwined, not just in the sense that language is one of those questions that is encountered on that way but also in the sense that language is the medium of that endowment with which anything like a way first opens up. How is this intertwining of language and way to be understood, especially in light of the fact that this way proves to be such that the movement appropriate to it is one of reversal? How is it that language and reversal belong together?

In *Sein und Zeit* Heidegger bears witness to the importance which the question of language had for his way even at that stage. Here he writes: "It is, in the end, the business of philosophy to preserve the *force of the most elemental words* in which Dasein expresses itself. . . ."[1] Already, however, this statement betrays the curious character of Heidegger's involvement with the question of language by the way in which it construes the relation between language and philosophy. Rather than assigning to philosophy the task of determining the essence of language, of developing, as it were, a theory of language, he projects the task of philosophy with respect to language as one of preservation: it is the business of philosophy to preserve language, to preserve the force of the most elemental words. What is that way by entrance onto which the question of language comes to present itself in the guise of a demand for preservation? We need to see that what is at issue is a way on which thinking is drawn back into its element, a way on which thinking lets itself be engaged in a movement of reversal. We need to understand how the problem of language becomes in Heidegger's thinking the problem of language and reversal.

The peculiar way in which the question of language enters into Heidegger's thinking is again indicated in Heidegger's denial that he is engaged in "philosophy of language."[2] Obviously, this denial is not to be taken as indicating that for Heidegger the question of language lacks sufficient importance to warrant an engagement in philosophy of language; on the contrary, this issue is so fundamental for his problematic that justice could not be done to it by engaging in mere philosophy of language. Heidegger says that the question of the essence of language "is something other than philosophy of language."[3] To engage straightforwardly in philosophy of language would be already to presume that language is, as it were, one item among others

John C. Sallis is professor of philosophy at Duquesne University, Pittsburgh, Pa. He received the Ph.D. from Tulane University in 1962. His primary interests are in phenomenology and existential philosophy and in Kant and German idealism. Having published numerous papers in the area of modern and contemporary philosophy, he is the editor of Heidegger and the Path of Thinking, *a Festschrift dedicated to Heidegger on his 80th birthday.*

---

[1] Heidegger, Martin: *Sein und Zeit* (9th Ed.; Tübingen: Max Niemeyer Verlag, 1960), p. 220, Heidegger has pointed out that even earlier, in the *Habilitationsschrift* of 1915, he was already engaged with the question of language, specifically with "the metaphysical reflection on language in its relation to Being." *Unterwegs zur Sprache* (Pfullingen: Verlag Günther Neske, 1959), pp. 91–92.

[2] *Über den Humanismus* (Frankfurt a.M.: Vittorio Klostermann), p. 9.

[3] *Was Heisst Denken?* (Tübingen: Max Niemeyer Verlag, 1954), p. 100.

129

to be interrogated in terms of an already established framework of interrogation, capable, in particular, of assuring us as to what is at issue in every search for an essence. But, as Heidegger says, "Not only does language stand in question now, but also what essence means [*heisst*]—more still: it stands in question whether and how essence and language belong to one another."[4] A framework would need to be presupposed—hence, we cannot proceed immediately to a philosophy of language. Also, however, Heidegger's statement makes it clear that it is not a matter simply of suspending the question of language in order to turn to the question of the framework, to the question of essence, as though it were a prior question. The question of the meaning of essence is not just a question to be taken up by a questioning already assured of its own possibilities and directives but rather has, since Plato, belonged together with the question of the meaning of philosophical thinking as such; and this latter question directs us, in turn, back into the question of language inasmuch as philosophy is itself a distinctive way of speaking. Heidegger writes: "Without a sufficient meditation on language we never truly know what philosophy is as a distinctive re-sponse [*Ent-sprechen*], what philosophy is as a distinctive way of speaking."[5] The questions of language and of essence meet in the question *"Was heisst Denken?"* and it is only within the compass of this question that we can properly respond to the question "whether and how essence and language belong to one another." The question *"Was heisst Denken?"* in its most decisive sense asks: "What calls us to think?"[6] To hear the question

in this, its decisive sense is to be led into the movement of reversal.[7] The problem of language enters into Heidegger's thinking not in the form of a philosophy of language but as the problem of language and reversal.

II. The Structure of the Problem

The problem of language and reversal enters into Heidegger's thinking in two ways. The first of these ways is expressed in the fact that the very possibility of reversal is tied somehow to language—to such a degree as to allow Heidegger to say that that division of *Sein und Zeit* which was to have carried through the reversal originally proposed, the reversal from "Being and time" to "time and Being," was held back because the language was lacking, because "it did not succeed with the help of the language of metaphysics."[8] Language is, Heidegger says, that originary dimension in which man is first able to enter into that conformity by which he is engaged in the domain of the reversal.[9] It is in the dimension of language that the movement of reversal is granted to him. This movement of reversal is a step out of metaphysics back into the ground of metaphysics,[10] and for this movement the language of metaphysics — that is, language as dominated by metaphysics, language as it shows itself within the compass of the metaphysics of language — is insufficient. Language under the domination of metaphysics has fallen "out of its element"[11]; it has come into a condition in which precisely its character as the originating dimension capable of granting entry into the movement of reversal is concealed. Hence, the language of metaphysics cannot but

---

[4] *Unterwegs zur Sprache*, p. 174.
[5] *Was ist das—die Philosophie?* (Pfullingen: Verlag Günther Neske, 1956), p. 45.
[6] *Was Heisst Denken?* pp. 79–80.
[7] Heidegger writes "Dass das Fragen nicht die eigentliche Gebärde des Denkens ist, sondern —das Hören der Zusage dessen, was in die Frage kommen soll." *Unterwegs zur Sprache*, p. 175.
[8] *Über den Humanismus*, p. 17.
[9] *Die Technik und die Kehre* (Pfullingen: Verlag Günther Neske, 1962), p. 40.
[10] See *Was Ist Metaphysik?* (8th Ed.; Frankfurt a. M.: Vittorio Klostermann, 1960), p. 9.
[11] *Über den Humanismus*, p. 9.

fail to grant entry into the movement of reversal. What is called for, however, by this situation is not a mere exchanging of the language of metaphysics for another language but rather, more fundamentally, "a transformed relationship to the essence of language." [12]

How is this transformation with which language would be brought back into its element to be accomplished? The terms of this transformation, its "from which" and "to which," are expressed in a statement from Heidegger's essay *"Bauen, Wohnen, Denken."* He writes: "Man behaves as though he were the moulder and master of language, but *it* nevertheless remains the master of man." [13] The transformation moves from a relationship to the essence of language in which this essence remains concealed and language gets taken as an activity of man [14] *to* one in which language reveals itself as the master of man, as the "clearing-concealing advent of Being itself" by which man is overpowered. [15] But this transformation is, then, nothing less than the reversal itself. The reversal requires a transformation of our relationship to the essence of language, yet this transformation is itself identical with the reversal. Thus, there is here no question of simple priority; it is not a matter of the reversal having as its pre-condition the transformation demanded with respect to language; neither does this transformation, on the other hand, require the reversal as its pre-condition. Each requires the other. It is a matter of intertwining; the problem of reversal and that of language *belong together.*

The second of the two ways in which the problem of language and reversal enters into Heidegger's thinking provides a means for articulating that intertwining, that belonging-together, to which the first way leads. What is the character of this second way? Here the problem arises from the apparent discontinuity, even conflict, between what Heidegger says regarding language in *Sein und Zeit* and what he says of it in his later writings. Within the architectonic of *Sein und Zeit*, language occupies a rather inconspicuous position. The only explicit discussion of it occurs in the chapter entitled "Being-in as such," specifically in the portion of that chapter that is entitled "The Existential Constitution of the 'There.'" In this section Heidegger is involved in uncovering the constitutive structures, the existentials, by virtue of which Dasein is able to be its "there" (*Da*), by virtue of which Dasein is "in-the-world" in such a way as to be capable of encountering beings "within-in-the-world." There are three such constitutive structures, disposition (*Befindlichkeit*), understanding (*Verstehen*), and discourse (*Rede*). Language (*Sprache*) is introduced in subordination to the third of these existentials, discourse, which is defined as "the articulation of intelligibility." He writes: "The existential-ontological foundation of language is discourse." Language itself he describes as "the way in which discourse gets expressed." [16]

This apparent confinement of the issue of language seems almost totally out of keeping with the importance which language so obviously assumes in Heidegger's later writings. For example, in *Uber den Humanismus* he discusses what he calls the nearness of Being (*die Nähe des Seins*) and proceeds to identify this nearness with the *Da* of Dasein. This nearness, he then

---

[12] *Zur Seinsfrage* (Frankfurt a. M.: Vittorio Klostermann, 1956), p. 25.
[13] *Vorträge und Aufsätze* (Pfullingen: Verlag Günther Neske, 1954), p. 146.
[14] See *Unterwegs zur Sprache,* pp. 14 ff.
[15] "Sprache ist lichtend-verbergende Ankunft des Seins selbst." *Uber den Humanismus,* p. 16. On the "overpowering" see *Einführung in die Metaphysik* (Tübingen: Max Niemeyer Verlag, 1958), pp. 114–115.
[16] *Sein und Zeit,* pp. 160–161.

insists, takes place (*west*) as language.[17] What is obviously suggested is that language is not, as in *Sein und Zeit,* a mere derivative of the third of the three constituents of the *Da* but, rather, precisely *the* constituent of the *Da*. Language alone, it seems, is now regarded as enabling Dasein to be its *Da*. Much the same is suggested in *Unterwegs zur Sprache* when Heidegger writes that "Language first enables man to be that creature which he is as man." [18] Language, it seems, is quite simply what makes man to be what he is. But, we feel compelled to ask, what about the other constituents of the *Da* which Heidegger elaborated with such care in *Sein und Zeit?*

There is still a further, even more fundamental difference between what is said regarding language in *Sein und Zeit* and what is said in the later writings. According to the former, language is the way in which discourse, the articulation of intelligibility, gets expressed. There is virtually nothing to suggest that such expression is anything other than an activity of man, something accomplished by man. Language, it seems, is simply an activity of man. But in the later writings, to state it in the boldest fashion, "language is the language of Being," and man is called only to respond to "the unspoken word of Being": *"Die Sprache spricht."* [19]

Between what Heidegger says regarding language in *Sein und Zeit* and what he says in the later writings stands the reversal in Heidegger's thinking. Hence, it is only through a reflection on the reversal, only through an effort to understand in what sense the reversal "stands between" *Sein und Zeit* and the later writings—it is only thus that we can approach the problem of the coherence of what Heidegger says regarding language. Does the transi-

tion from the discussion of language in *Sein und Zeit* to the discussion in the later writings become intelligible in light of the reversal, in light of the way in which the issue of the reversal allows us to understand the movement from *Sein und Zeit* to the later writings? It is through this question that we shall attempt to take up the problem of language and reversal.

III. Language in *Sein und Zeit*

Before considering the question of the reversal we need to ascertain more specifically what Heidegger says about language in *Sein und Zeit* and what is at issue behind what he says. We focus on two sections of Division I: (1) the section in Chapter 3 where Heidegger offers a description of signs and (2) the section in Chapter 5, referred to above, which deals with the constituents of the "there."

In the first of these sections there is a statement which comes directly to the point that is relevant to our problem. Heidegger writes: "A sign is not a thing which stands to another thing in the relationship of indicating; it is rather an item of equipment which explicitly raises a totality of equipment into our circumspection so that together with it the worldly character of the ready-to-hand announces itself." [20] Signs, presumably also linguistic signs, are not mere things. Like the other beings encountered within the *Umwelt* they are items of equipment bound up in an equipment-totality. A sign, however, is not just another item of equipment but rather has a distinctive function which distinguishes it from all other equipment. This distinctive function Heidegger calls "indicating" (*Zeigen*). Indicating, however, is not a matter of a co-ordination of certain pieces of equipment, namely signs, in a one-to-one correspondence with other pieces of equipment, namely what is

---

[17] *Uber den Humanismus*, pp. 21, 25.
[18] *Unterwegs zur Sprache*, p. 11.
[19] *Uber den Humanismus*, pp. 47, 45; *Unterwegs zur Sprache* p. 12.
[20] *Sein und Zeit*, pp. 79–80.

indicated by the sign. Rather, a sign, as indicating, raises the total meaning-context, the referential totality, into our circumspection.

It follows, then, that language is not to be regarded in terms of individual words or linguistic units correlated in some fashion or other either with discrete meaning-contents or with individual things. Rather, linguistic signs are bound up in a total meaning-context in the sense of bringing that total context to light. The way in which language indicates needs to be understood in reference to the total meaning-context rather than in terms of correspondence between words and things or words and meanings. Heidegger thus attempts to get beneath the traditional understanding of language in terms of correspondence and thereby to undercut the classical alternatives of correspondence by nature and correspondence by convention. This is not to say that the understanding of language in terms of correspondence is incorrect; it has its rights, but it is not primordial. Heidegger wants to point beneath it to a more primordial dimension where language is, first of all, a lighting-up which lets the world, the total meaning-context, announce itself.

In the discussion of the constituents of the "there" in Chapter 5, the issue of language enters much more explicitly. We have referred already to the way in which Heidegger takes up this issue in the context of his account of discourse, the third existential constituent of the "there," and describes language as the way in which discourse gets expressed. However, it is not only in relation to discourse that the issue of language is taken up; Heidegger refers to it also, though briefly, in the course of his elaboration of the structures which derive from the first of the three basic constituents of the "there," understanding (*Verstehen*).

Let us briefly review this elaboration in order to place the issue of language within it. Understanding is described by Heidegger as the projection of Dasein's Being upon possibilities, upon what Heidegger calls a "for-the-sake-of-which" (*Worumwillen*).[21] In projection Dasein throws before itself possibilities as possibilities, lets possibilities be its possibilities, and is itself these possibilities as possibilities. Possibilities, in turn, prescribe a referential totality, a totality of involvements, a world, in which ready-to-hand beings or equipment can be involved and thereby be what they are.[22] However, in understanding, neither the possibilities nor the prescribed totality of involvements are grasped thematically, and understanding thus has itself the possibility of developing itself into a thematic grasp of the possibilities which it has thrown before itself. This development, this appropriation of what is already understood, Heidegger calls interpretation (*Auslegung*). In interpretation, items of equipment are made explicit with respect to their "as-structure," with respect to their involvement in the referential totality, in the totality of signifying references which make up the structure of Dasein's world. Interpretation is an articulation prior to all thematic assertion, an articulation of what has been understood, of that upon which Dasein, in understanding, has projected.[23] The upon-which of a projection Heidegger identifies as meaning (*Sinn*).[24] Interpretation is an articulation of meaning prior to thematic assertion. Finally, there is the structure which Heidegger calls assertion (*Aussage*), which derives from the further development of interpretation. Assertion is not, however, merely an

[21] *Ibid.*, p. 145.
[22] *Ibid.*, p. 86.
[23] *Ibid.*, p. 149.
[24] "Meaning is that wherein the intelligibility [*Verständlichkeit*] of something maintains itself . . . Meaning is the upon-which [*Woraufhin*] of the projection from out of which something becomes intelligible [*verständlich*] as something. . . ." *Ibid.*, p. 151.

extension of interpretation but involves a decisive change, the transformation of the "hermeneutical as" — the as-structure based in the referential totality — by which interpretation lets itself be guided *into* the "apophantical as" under the guidance of which beings are now articulated with respect to definite characteristics. It is only with assertion that we gain access to such things as properties, and it is here that Heidegger sees the origination of presence-at-hand (*Vorhandenheit*) out of readiness-to-hand (*Zuhandenheit*). Heidegger assigns to "assertion" three interconnected significations: "pointing out," "predication," and "communication." [25] With the last of these the analysis has obviously reached the plane of language. But Heidegger does not elaborate.

The dual locus of the issue of language in Heidegger's account of the constituents of the "there" raises two problems. Through these problems, we can see what is at issue behind what Heidegger says begins to take shape. First, we have seen that Heidegger states explicitly that discourse, the third basic existential constituent, is the foundation of language. We have seen, further, that language also is involved in the derivative structures which originate from understanding, specifically in assertion as communication. The problem is: How is it possible for discourse to be the foundation of language if language is also involved in another existential constituent, namely understanding — specifically in what develops from understanding? How can language be grounded in discourse and yet have one foot, as it were, in another of the three basic constituents of the "there"? Presumably, this is possible only if the two basic constituents, understanding and discourse, are themselves fundamentally connected. This, then, is the second problem:

What is the character of this connection? What is the character of the unity by which understanding and discourse belong together?

Let us try to formulate this problem more precisely. Heidegger defines discourse as the articulation of intelligibility or meaning. Thus, language, as the way in which discourse gets expressed, is the expression of an already accomplished articulation. Discourse provides something pre-given to the act of expression. What is crucial here, however, is that this definition of discourse corresponds precisely with the definition which Heidegger gives of interpretation. The latter too is an articulation of meaning. What, then, is the difference between interpretation and discourse? Heidegger writes: "The intelligibility of something has always been articulated even before there is an appropriative interpretation of it." [26] There is, in other words, an articulation of meaning prior to that articulation that occurs in interpretation. What is this prior articulation? Heidegger proceeds to identify it as discourse. [27] Discourse as articulation of meaning is prior to the articulation of meaning in interpretation. When meaning is articulated in interpretation, such articulation takes place against the background of a prior articulation already accomplished by discourse. What is the character of the prior articulation?

We have seen that in the development of understanding into interpretation and assertion the question of language first enters in connection with the third signification of assertion, namely communication. In the context in which communication is discussed, Heidegger alludes to a link between communication and what he calls "fore-conception" and then makes the following crucial statement: "The fore-conception which is always implied in an assertion remains for the most part

---

[25] *Aufzeigen, Prädikation, Mitteilung. Ibid.*, pp. 154–157.
[26] *Ibid.*, p. 161.
[27] "That which can be articulated in interpretation, and thus *even more primordially in discourse*, is what we have called 'meaning.' *Ibid.* (Italics mine.)

inconspicuous, because language already conceals in itself a developed way of conceiving [*eine ausgebildete Begrifflichkeit*]." [28] This statement provides a solution to our problem, for it points to the fact that that articulation of meaning which is prior to interpretation and which Heidegger calls discourse is precisely that articulation — that "developed way of conceiving" — which is always already accomplished by language itself but which remains concealed, hidden away in the language. Discourse is not, therefore, primarily an articulation of meaning which *we* perform but rather an articulation which is always already performed for us, an articulation which is, of necessity, already delivered over to us, which we have already taken over inadvertently, by virtue of our living in a language — by virtue of our having been thrown into a language with its concealed, yet already developed ways of conceiving.

Now it is clear also how interpretation, as operating always within the compass of the prior articulation (discourse), can stand in a relation to language. Interpretation always takes place against the background of articulation already accomplished by language. And *Sein und Zeit* itself, as an interpretation,[29] is likewise bound to the pre-articulation hidden away in language. What Heidegger's work uncovers as regards language reflects back upon the character of the work itself and requires that *Sein und Zeit,* in its character as a work, be understood in its relation to language, as bound to what is handed over in language. Here is a clue for understanding Heidegger's description of the business of philosophy as one of preserving the force of words.

We need to draw out a further conclusion implicit in this development of the problem of language in *Sein und*

Zeit. In order to do so we call attention to a significant ambiguity centered in Heidegger's account of understanding. This ambiguity is evident in the two fundamentally different ways in which Heidegger describes understanding: In the one instance, understanding is described as a projecting of Dasein's Being *upon* possibilities, in the sense of letting possibilities be possibilities for Dasein, in the sense that Dasein assigns itself to possibilities so as to be these possibilities;[30] in the other instance, understanding is described as a projecting *of* possibilities, Heidegger writing explicitly of "possibilities projected in understanding." [31] The difference between possibilities projected *upon* by Dasein and possibilities projected *by* Dasein is, if taken without further refinement, immense, and it is especially crucial granted the context of the project of *Sein und Zeit*. Since a possibility related to Dasein's projection is a "for-the-sake-of-which" and, hence, prescribes a totality of involvements that constitute the structure of world, nothing less is at stake than the origination of world. If Dasein quite simply projects its own possibilities, bringing them forth, as it were, entirely out of its own resources, then it would follow that world is, in the end, something which Dasein projects. But it is precisely the referential totality, constitutive of world, which allows ready-to-hand beings within-the-world to be what they are, which, consequently, is the Being of these beings.[32] It would follow, then, that the Being of the ready-to-hand is nothing more than something projected by Dasein.

This conclusion is fundamentally at odds with the very project of *Sein und Zeit*. Heidegger repeatedly emphasizes in his various commentary statements on *Sein und Zeit* what was already evident in the work itself: that it al-

[28] *Ibid.,* p. 157.
[29] See *Ibid.,* p. 37.
[30] *Ibid.,* pp. 145, 147.
[31] *Ibid.,* p. 148.
[32] *Ibid.,* p. 87.

ready is involved in the step back out of metaphysics and specifically out of the subjectivism that characterizes modern metaphysics. But what is subjectivism if not the locating of the ground of objectivity, of the Being of beings, in the subject? [33] And if it is objected that, nevertheless, Dasein is not a subject in the modern metaphysical sense, then the problem is only re-stated; for it remains to be determined how Dasein is distinguishable from a subject if, indeed, Dasein projects its world and thereby the Being of what is encounterable within the world.

Clearly this alternative—that Dasein projects its possibilities — can be retained only if we grant that there is something else involved that serves to modify the most immediate sense suggested by such a notion of projection. Indeed, Heidegger himself indicates this when he writes:

> In every case Dasein, as essentially dispositional [befindliches], has already gotten into definite possibilities; as the potentiality-for-Being [Seinkönnen] which it is, it has let such possibilities pass by; it constantly sets about the possibilities of its Being, grasps them, and makes mistakes. But this means that Dasein is Being-possible which has been delivered over to itself—*thrown possibility* through and through. . . . By way of having a mood, Dasein 'sees' possibilities, in terms of which it is. In the projective disclosure of such possibilities, it already has a mood in

every case. The projection of its ownmost potentiality-for-Being has been delivered over to the fact of its thrownness into the "there." [34] These statements call attention to the fact that understanding is not the sole constituent of the "there" and indicate that the various constituents do not simply stand, as it were, alongside one another but belong essentially together. Dasein as projecting is thrown-projecting, a projecting executed within thrownness, a projecting of world only from out of its situation of being already engaged in a world already disclosed in disposition. Heidegger writes: "Indeed *from the ontological point of view* we must as a general principle leave the primary discovery of the world to 'bare mood.' " [35] It is this discovery which always lurks behind every projection. Again, Heidegger writes: "As something factical, Dasein's projection of itself understandingly is in each case already alongside a world that has been discovered. From this world it takes its possibilities. . . ." [36] It is, in other words, primarily in disposition that possibilities are first delivered over to Dasein in order that Dasein might project these possibilities as possibilities, in order that it might assign itself to them, thus throwing them before itself and letting them *be* as possibilities. Dasein indeed projects *upon* possibilities in that Dasein "has already gotten into definite possibilities," in that possibilities are already, by way of disposition, disclosed as delivered over to Dasein; yet, in the same measure, pos-

---

[33] "One need only observe the simple fact that in *Sein und Zeit* the problem is set up outside the sphere of subjectivism . . . for it to become strikingly clear that the 'Being' into which *Sein und Zeit* inquired can not long remain something that the human subject posits." Heidegger's "Preface" to William J. Richardson, *Heidegger: Through Phenomenology to Thought* (The Hague: Martinus Nijhoff, 1963), p. xviii.

Again, Heidegger speaks of his attempt "to liberate the essential determination of man from subjectivity. . . . " He adds: "Any attempt, therefore, to re-think *Sein und Zeit* is thwarted as long as one is satisfied with the observation that, in this study, the term 'Dasein' is used in place of 'consciousness.' " *Was Ist Metaphysik?* pp. 13–14.

See also *Uber den Humanismus*, especially p. 25 where Heidegger states explicitly, in reference to *Sein und Zeit*, that the "projection does not create Being."

In *Sein und Zeit* itself see ¶ 13, ¶ 43(a) and note especially that Heidegger originally projected a "destruction" of Decartes' *Cogito Sum* (pp. 24f.).

[34] *Sein und Zeit*, pp. 144, 148.
[35] *Ibid.*, p. 138.
[36] *Ibid.*, p. 194.

sibilities are projected *by* Dasein in that it is through Dasein as projecting, through Dasein's assigning itself, that they are thrown ahead and allowed to rule as possibilities, allowed to be as possibilities. Hence, Heidegger can speak indifferently of possibilities as being projected *upon* by Dasein and as being projected *by* Dasein.

The ambiguity is thus resolved, but beneath it a further problem opens up: the problem of how disposition and understanding belong together. It is on this problem that the development of the issue of language in *Sein und Zeit* has a crucial bearing. Discourse, we have seen, is, in the final analysis, that articulation of intelligibility which is already bound up and hidden away in language. Discourse is not simply an articulation which we perform but rather is an articulation which is always already in effect, delivered over to us insofar as we *find ourselves* in a language. Thus, discourse refers to a kind of finding-oneself-as-thrown (*Befindlichkeit*) which, as involving us in an articulation of intelligibility (*Verständlichkeit*), is inherently linked to interpretation and understanding (*Verstehen*). It involves a finding-oneself-as-thrown into a certain medium of intelligibility, into a certain already established way of articulation. It is discourse which points back to the unitary, yet complex, ground from which the multiple constituents of the "there" arise. It is discourse as itself this "common root" in which understanding and disposition meet — without, however, necessarily having their distinctive characters dissolved—it is this which forms the bridge from the analytic of *Sein und Zeit* to the insistence in the later writings that the "there" takes place as language.

IV. Reversal

Between what is said regarding lan-

guage in *Sein und Zeit* and what is said in the later writings stands the reversal (*Kehre*). It is to this that we must now turn in order to be able to come to terms with the question of the coherence of what Heidegger says regarding language.

Heidegger uses the term "reversal" in describing the relation between what is accomplished in the published portion of *Sein und Zeit* and what was to have been accomplished in the unpublished final section of Part I. In this final section, which was to have carried the title "Zeit und Sein" everything would, Heidegger tells us, have been reversed. He describes the reversal as a reversal from "Being and time" to "time and Being." [37] Inasmuch as the later writings remain underway to what was still unaccomplished in *Sein und Zeit* as published, the term "reversal" is used to describe the transition from *Sein und Zeit* to the later writings. What is the character of this transition that is here underway? What does Heidegger mean in speaking of reversal?

In the attempt to think through what is at issue in the reversal everything depends upon understanding the proper locus of the reversal. The reversal is not, Heidegger insists, "a change of the standpoint of *Sein und Zeit*," [38] not a shift to a different, presumably more adequate, point of view in principle discontinuous with that which defined the project of *Sein und Zeit*. Nevertheless, he writes: "The thinking of the reversal *is* a change in my thought." [39] The reversal involves a change but one which is not to be construed as a shift from one standpoint to another — nor, indeed, as any other kind of shift executed merely within the movement of thinking: "The reversal is above all not an operation of interrogative thought." [40] The proper locus of the reversal lies rather in what is to be

---

[37] *Über den Humanismus*, p. 17.
[38] *Ibid.*
[39] Heidegger's "Preface" to Richardson, *Heidegger*, p. xvi.
[40] *Ibid.*, p. xviii.

thought; in Heidegger's words, "The reversal is in play within the matter itself"[41]; there is a reversal in the medium of thought, a change in Heidegger's thinking, only insofar as this thinking is led into the movement of reversal by letting itself be bound in essential cor-respondence to what evokes thought, to what calls it forth, and hence, to the reversal which is "in play within the matter itself."

A thinking which is able to let itself be bound by what calls forth thinking, by its sustaining source, is a thinking which, indeed, has undergone a change' but which has not, as it were, executed that change out of its own resources. In order for it to be able to come to bind itself to what genuinely sustains it, the sustaining source must have shown itself in its capacity as granting sustenance to thinking. That which sustains thinking cannot, however, be posed before thinking as an object which could be made wholly transparent, from which all concealment could be banished, but rather is able to sustain thinking only in that it simultaneously withdraws from thinking. The source sustains thinking by drawing it along in this withdrawal.[42] The sustaining source could show itself to thinking in such a way as to allow thinking to be bound to it, drawn along in the withdrawal, only by showing itself as withdrawing.

If thinking comes to be bound to what sustains it, it does so always from out of its situation of having been cast into an age determined by its characteristic mittence of Being (*Seinsgeschick*), by the way in which the source grants itself to and witholds itself from those cast into that age.[43] It is in the mittence of Being which gov-

erns our age that the source must reveal itself in order that, in thinking, we may be bound to it. Yet our age, the age of technology, is determined precisely by a radical self-concealment of the source; our age is the age in which the forgottenness of Being reaches its culmination so that "it appears as though there were no such thing as Being"[44] — as though Being were only "a vapor and a fallacy."[45] Ours is the age in which it comes to appear as though there were no sustaining source or, rather, as though thinking were its own sustenance, as though thinking were capable of providing its own sufficient ground, capable of executing that self-grounding for which it has strived at least since the beginning of modern metaphysics.[46] The source not only withdraws, not only conceals itself, but in our age has come to the point of concealing its concealment; it has come to conceal precisely that withdrawing in which thinking is drawn along and thereby sustained. Our age is determined by a radical self-concealment of Being, not because Being remains simply concealed from us, but rather because this concealment is itself concealed to such a degree that we are cast into utter obliviousness to Being. What is decisive is not that the source is concealed but rather that the fact of the source is concealed — the fact that thinking is sustained by a source and not by itself. Yet even in its obliviousness to its sustaining source thinking continues to be sustained by this source, and what is called for is that, in the midst of the effort on the part of thinking to be its own source, this effort reveal itself as violating what it would establish, that this effort reveal itself as sustained precisely by that

[41] "Die Kehre spielt im Sachverhalt selbst." *Ibid.*
[42] *Was Heisst Denken?* p. 5.
[43] See *Der Satz vom Grund* (Pfullingen: Verlag Günther Neske, 1957), p. 108 ff.
[44] *Zur Seinsfrage,* p. 34.
[45] *Einführung in die Metaphysik,* p. 27.
[46] See *Die Frage nach dem Ding: Zu Kants Lehre von den Transzendentalen Grundsätzen* (Tübingen: Max Niemeyer Verlag, 1962), pp. 74–83. See also my paper "Towards the Movement of Reversal: Science, Technology, and the Language of Homecoming," in *Heidegger and the Path of Thinking* (Pittsburgh: Duquesne University Press, 1970).

whose sustenance it would deny. What is called for is that man's belongingness to Being break through at just that point at which the most radical concealment prevails — at the point of what Heidegger calls the highest danger. This is the reversal: "In the essence of the danger a favor takes place and dwells, namely the favor of a reversal of the forgottenness of Being into the truth of Being." [47]

What calls for and calls forth this reversal is not, however, man himself. As sustained in his thinking by the source and as cast into an age of radical self-concealment of this source, man is able to enter into the movement of reversal only through being led into and sustained in it by the source itself. The reversal has its proper locus in the clearing-concealing advent of Being itself. There is a reversal in thinking only insofar as thinking succeeds in cor-responding to this *"Ereignis der Kehre im Sein."* [48]

The proper locus of the reversal is the clearing-concealing advent of Being itself. Now we can begin to understand the involvement of the problem of language in the reversal, for, Heidegger says, "language is the clearing-concealing advent of Being itself." [49] Language is the proper locus of the reversal. This is why, in discussing the fact that that portion of *Sein und Zeit* in which the reversal would have become explicit was not carried through, Heidegger calls attention to the issue of language. This also is why the reversal requires "a transformed relationship to the essence of language." But this transformation is no mere prerequisite to the reversal; it is the reversal. And it is a transformation of which we are capable only by cor-responding to what is granted to our thinking.

This conclusion — that language is

the proper locus of the reversal — goes beyond what we have said thus far regarding language; we have been led to it only by introducing a cryptic statement from the later writings — that language is the clearing-concealing advent of Being itself — a statement which remains largely unintelligible as long as we have not understood the way in which the problem of language is taken up in Heidegger's later writings. But, then, it was precisely in order to move from what is said about language in *Sein und Zeit* to what is said in the later writings that we found it necessary to take up the question of reversal. The problem of language directs us into that of the reversal, and conversely. The two problems are intertwined; they *belong together*.

In order to lead back into the question of the coherence of what Heidegger says regarding language, we need now to try to understand, more generally, how the project of *Sein und Zeit* coheres with the thinking of the reversal that is underway in the later writings.

At first it appeared that the reversal stood between *Sein und Zeit* and the later writings, that it represented the point of transition. Now it is evident, however, that the reversal is not something once accomplished or undergone and then left behind for the sake of something else to which it is only a bridge. It is significant that Heidegger speaks not of the thinking *after* the reversal but, instead, of the thinking *of* the reversal. Thinking, when it enters into the movement of reversal, remains, as always, bound to that which calls forth thought but which does so only in that it simultaneously withdraws. Being incessantly withholds itself even in the midst of showing itself in that advent into which the reversal leads. The reversal does not terminate in a

[47] "Im Wesen der Gefahr west und wohnt eine Gunst, nämlich die Gunst der Kehre der Vergessenheit des Seins in die Wahrheit des Seins." *Die Technik und die Kehre,* p. 42.
[48] *Ibid.*, p. 44. This issue is discussed at length in my paper "Towards the Movement of Reversal," *Heidegger and the Path of Thinking.*
[49] *Über den Humanismus*, p. 16.

total revealment with which thinking could be brought to completion but rather issues in a recalling of Being as withdrawing. Heidegger's later works remain, and must remain, *in* the movement of reversal: "Thinking itself is a way. We respond to the way only by remaining underway"; "What remains in thinking is the way." [50]

Granted that the later works are engaged in the movement of reversal, how, then, are we to understand their relation to *Sein und Zeit?* Is this engagement already in effect even in *Sein und Zeit,* or is it only initiated in the later works? If the latter, then does *Sein und Zeit* in some fashion prepare the way to such engagement, or is it, on the contrary, simply left behind once Heidegger's thinking has entered into the reversal?

This final alternative is already virtually excluded by Heidegger's statement that the transition to the later writings does not involve an alteration of standpoint. Heidegger elaborates what is meant in this statement:

The thinking of the reversal *is* a change in my thought. But this change is not a consequence of altering the standpoint, much less of abandoning the fundamental issue, of *Sein und Zeit.* The thinking of the reversal results from the fact that I stayed with the matter-for-thought [of] "Being and time" [*bei der zu denkenden Sache "Sein und Zeit"*], sc. by inquiring into that perspective which already in *Sein und Zeit* (p. 39) was designated as "Time and Being." [51]

The entry into the movement of reversal is, therefore, not an abandonment of *Sein und Zeit* but, on the contrary, is the outcome of staying with its fundamental issue. It came about through inquiring into the domain of the reversal already proposed in *Sein*

und Zeit, the reversal from "Being and time" to "time and Being." Heidegger's later works remain on the way to which *Sein und Zeit* pointed.

We have seen that the entry of thinking into the movement of reversal takes place only in a cor-responding in which thinking is able to let itself be drawn along by its sustaining source. The way of this entry is not something which is established by thinking but rather something granted to thinking. Thinking is of itself able to build no bridge by which it could pass over into the movement of reversal. Rather this entry is, regarded from the side of thinking, a leap. But, Heidegger insists, in the leap of thinking that from which it leaps is carried over: "The leap of thinking does not leave behind that from which it leaps, but rather appropriates it in a more primordial way." [52] Not only, then, does the thinking of the reversal not abandon the fundamental issue of *Sein und Zeit,* but furthermore it is precisely the fulfillment of what was there undertaken: "The question of *Sein und Zeit* is decisively ful-filled in the thinking of the reversal." [53] In the thinking of the reversal what was undertaken in *Sein und Zeit* is fulfilled by being appropriated in a more primordial way.

Sein und Zeit already points ahead into the movement of reversal. Already it is engaged in the step back out of metaphysics through the fact that "the problem is set up outside the sphere of subjectivism." Already it keeps its distance from the effort by thinking to be its own sustaining source: ". . . the 'Being' into which *Sein und Zeit* inquired can not long remain something that the human subject posits." On the other hand, the thinking of the reversal appropriates in a more primordial way what was accomplished in *Sein und Zeit* and, hence, as Heidegger

---

[50] *Was Heisst Denken?,* p. 164; *Unterwegs zur Sprache,* p. 99.
[51] Heidegger's "Preface" to Richardson, *Heidegger,* p. xvi.
[52] *Der Satz vom Grund,* p. 107.
[53] Heidegger's "Preface" to Richardson, *Heidegger,* p. xviii.

says "furnishes for the first time an adequate characterization of Dasein."[54] It is this way of understanding the coherence of his work which Heidegger expressed in his response to the distinction which Fr. Richardson formulated between "Heidegger I" (the Heidegger of *Sein und Zeit*) and "Heidegger II" (the Heidegger of the later works): "only by way of what Heidegger I has thought does one gain access to what is to-be-thought by Heidegger II. But [the thought of] Heidegger I becomes possible only if it is contained in Heidegger II."[55]

IV. Language in the Thinking of the Reversal

The thinking of the reversal involves an appropriation in a more primordial way of what was accomplished in *Sein und Zeit*. Presumably, this holds, specifically, of the problem of language, and it is in this connection that we turn, finally, to what Heidegger says regarding language in the later writings. We need to try to understand the way in which the issue of language is taken up in the thinking of the reversal as a fulfillment of what was undertaken with regard to language in *Sein und Zeit*, as an appropriation in a more primordial way.

In the thinking of the reversal the issues of *Sein und Zeit* are appropriated. However, they are not just appropriated in the sense of being taken over; rather, they are, Heidegger says, appropriated in a more primordial way, in such a way as to be brought, through this appropriation, to their fulfillment. This means that the issues of *Sein und Zeit* are, in the thinking of the reversal, brought explicitly into the compass of the fundamental issue their relation to which remained implicit in *Sein und Zeit*. This fundamental issue is that for the sake of which the entire analytic of Dasein was undertaken; it is the question of the meaning of Being. *Sein*

und Zeit, however, failed to carry through the reversal in which this analytic would have been led back into the fundamental issue, and the connection of the analytic of Dasein to the question of the meaning of Being remained largely implicit. But in the thinking of the reversal this connection can come into the light. This thinking is enabled to take the step back out of metaphysics, to recover (*verwinden*) from the incessant effort on the part of thinking to be its own sustaining source. It is a thinking to which is granted the transition *from* utter obliviousness as regards Being, for which Being is simply nothing, *to* an experience of this nothing of Being as precisely the double self-concealment of Being, the concealment of concealment. It is thus that Heidegger writes: "We must prepare ourselves to experience in the nothing the vastness of that which gives every being the warrant to be. That is Being itself."[56] But, to be led to experience the nothing as the double self-concealment of Being is to be led from the concealment of self-withdrawing Being to the recalling of self-withdrawing Being, of the truth (clearing-concealing) of Being. The thinking of the reversal is a being drawn along in the withdrawal of Being itself, its withdrawal from every effort to set it back upon a ground in subjectivity. To appropriate the issues of *Sein und Zeit* in a more primordial way is to let them come into the compass of the recalling of Being as withdrawing. We need to understand how what is said about language in the thinking of the reversal is an appropriation of what was said in *Sein und Zeit* — and *also* how it is constituted as a more primordial appropriation through relation to the issue of withdrawal.

We saw through the analysis of signs in *Sein und Zeit* that language is not to be regarded in terms of correspondence between two classes of things, linguistic

---

[54] *Ibid.*, p. xx.
[55] *Ibid.*, p. xxii.
[56] *Was Ist Metaphysik?* p. 46.

units, on the one hand, and what is meant or referred to, on the other. It is not, at the fundamental level, just a matter of words being matched up, as it were, with meanings or things, not a matter of simple correspondence. Rather, Heidegger insists that language needs to be understood in its involvement with the total meaning-context, with world which it brings to light as a whole, which it raises explicitly "into our circumspection" so as to orient us within the world.

Implicit in this analysis is a denial that language is to be regarded in terms of the concept of expression. In the later works this is explicitly enunciated: "Language is neither merely the field of expression, nor merely the means of expression, nor merely the two jointly."[57] Fundamentally, language is not a matter of expression in the sense of words serving simply as vehicles by means of which something else, units of meaning, are made conveyable, made available for exchange. It is not as though a word were, first of all, merely a sound, something sensible, which then has, in addition, a nonsensible component, a signification, so that we would need to invoke "a sensegiving act that furnishes the word-sound with a sense."[58] It is not a matter of a word, as sound, containing sense as a bucket contains water. We pass over what is fundamental in language when we say that "the word's signification attaches to its sound"[59]; even in *Sein und Zeit* Heidegger said, not that significations get attached to words, but just the opposite, that "to significations, words accrue."[60] Words are not buckets filled with sense; they are rather like wellsprings that must be dug up:

> Words are not terms and thus are not like buckets and kegs from which we scoop a content that is there. Words are wellsprings that are found and dug up in the telling, wellsprings that must be found and dug up again and again, that easily cave in, but that at times also well up when least expected. If we do not go to the spring again and again, the buckets and kegs stay empty, or their content stays stale.[61]

To speak is not simply to express, not merely to translate certain significations that we have on hand into a ready-made communicable form. It is not a matter of attaching significations to words. Indeed, there is a significance which sustains our speaking, which is taken up into it and to which our speaking must remain attached; we must "go to the spring again and again." But this taking up is no mere translating of something already on hand, no mere external attaching of significations to words. On the contrary, it is in being taken up into words that this significance first comes to light, and it comes to light not as so many discrete units of meaning through which reference to individual things could be effected but rather in such a way that it "explicitly raises a totality of equipment into our circumspection." Thus, Trakl's poem, *"Ein Winterabend,"* is no mere describing, no mere naming in the sense of distributing titles, applying words, to the various objects and events that pertain to a winter evening but is rather an invoking, a calling forth into words, which by calling is able to bring near what is called; and what it invokes are things

---

[57] *Was Heisst Denken?* p. 87. Cf. *Unterwegs zur Sprache,* p. 19. In his λογος-interpretation Heidegger writes: "Expression and signification have long been taken as the manifestations, and presented as the unquestionable characteristics of, language. But they do not reach genuinely into the region of the primordially essential determination of language, nor are they at all capable of determining this region in its primary characteristics." *Vorträge und Aufsätze,* p. 212.
[58] *Was Heisst Denken?* p. 88.
[59] *Ibid.*
[60] *Sein und Zeit,* p. 161.
[61] *Was Heisst Denken?* p. 89.

in their intimacy with the world to which they belong and from which they are granted to us [62] — just as in the context of the analysis in *Sein und Zeit* the sign "raises a totality of equipment into our circumspection so that together with it the worldly character of the ready-to-hand announces itself." To significations words accrue in such a way as to bring to light significance, that is, world in its intimacy with things. Hölderlin wrote: "But that which remains is established by the poets." [63] Heidegger writes:

> The poet names the gods and names all things in that which they are. This naming does not consist merely in something already known being supplied with a name, but rather in that the poet speaks the essential word, a being is by this naming nominated as what it is. So it becomes known *as* being [*als Seiendes*]. Poetry is the establishing of Being by the word [*worthafte Stiftung des Seins*]. . . . The essence of language must be understood through the essence of poetry. [64]

To significations words accrue, however, not only in the sense that words invoke significance and bring it to light but also in the sense that significance, first of all, calls forth words. Our words, our speaking, is sustained, is called forth, is evoked. The poet names the gods; but, Heidegger writes, "the gods can acquire a name only if they themselves make a claim upon [*ansprechen*] us and place us under their claim [*Anspruch*]. The word which names the gods is always an answer to such a claim." [65] In the context of Heidegger's λόγος-interpretation this claim is thematized as what is given to speaking so as to come to light in the speaking. Speaking as λέγειν, laying, letting-lie, gathering and keeping watch

over what is given, what is sent, is a speaking that is evoked, sustained by what is sent; speaking is ὁμολογεῖν.

We have seen that in *Sein und Zeit* discourse (*Rede*) is described as "the articulation of intelligibility." We saw, furthermore, that this articulation is not something which we simply execute but rather that it is an articulation in which we are caught up, which is always already handed over to us by virtue of our having been cast into a language —that it is an articulation already established, yet concealed, within language. It appeared then that discourse is primordially linked to the other two basic constituents of the "there," that what is designated by "discourse" is one's finding-oneself-as-thrown into a certain medium of intelligibility, into a certain already established articulation. In the later writings what was called "discourse" (*Rede*) in *Sein und Zeit* comes to be regarded as the primary sense of "language" (*Sprache*). But beneath this shift the conclusion to which the analysis of discourse in *Sein und Zeit* pointed is not only retained but explicitly elaborated. Heidegger writes that "language is not a tool" [66]; language is not something which we have simply at our disposal, of which we are master. It is not an instrument with which to master things, [67] which itself would, in order to serve most effectively, need to be mastered. Rather it is something to which we are handed over, something in which we are always already caught up, something which we are subject *to* rather than subject *of*. According to Heidegger's λόγος interpretation speaking as ὁμολογεῖν is a gathering and a keeping watch over what is given to our speaking, that is, language itself. With this we return to what Heidegger said in *Sein und Zeit*: It is the business of

---

[62] *Unterwegs zur Sprache*, pp. 21, 26–28.
[63] *Erläuterungen zu Hölderlins Dichtung* (3rd Ed.; Frankfurt a.M.: Vittorio Klostermann, 1963), p. 31.
[64] *Ibid.*, pp. 38, 40.
[65] *Ibid.*, p. 37.
[66] *Was Heisst Denken?* p. 99.
[67] *über den Humanismus*, p. 9.

philosophy to preserve the force of words.

In the same connection Heidegger writes that "we are moving within language, which," he adds, "means moving on shifting ground, or, still better, on the billowing waters of an ocean." [68] If, again, we recall from the analysis in *Sein und Zeit* that discourse, language in its primary sense, is intended to indicate our finding-ourselves-as-thrown into a way of articulation, into a medium of intelligibility, then it is clear that this movement "within language" is not just one movement among others but is rather that ground-movement through which intelligibility is already delivered up to our understanding, always already granted. But what is this understanding that is always already granted? *Sein und Zeit* gives the answer: "Understanding of Being has already been taken for granted in projecting upon possibilities." [69] This understanding which is always already taken for granted is what Heidegger calls pre-ontological understanding of Being. It is taken for granted, however, not in the sense that man as a subject is always in possession of a representation of Being, but rather in the sense that it is always granted to man in that he "stands in the openness of the project of Being." [70]

The fulfillment, the more primordial appropriation, of these issues in *Sein und Zeit* comes about in the later writings in that language is now brought explicitly into connection with the pre-ontological understanding of Being and thereby its character as "common root" made explicit. Language comes to be called "the house of Being," and Heidegger adds, "In its housing man dwells." [71] Man is housed in language, he moves within it, and thereby he is sustained in an understanding of Being. The development is explicit in a statement in *Was Heisst Denken?*: "Every human attitude to something, every human stand in this or that sphere of beings, would rush away resistlessly into the void if the 'is' did not speak." [72] Every human stand, all human comportment with regard to beings, requires — what? *Sein und Zeit* would answer: the pre-ontological understanding of Being. But now Heidegger says: that the 'is' *speak*. It is required that the 'is' speak, that Being speak. It is required, not just that Being grant itself, but that it speak, and the two are now identical: Being grants itself in that Being speaks. But where and how does Being speak? It speaks *in language*:

'Εον [Being] names that which speaks in every word of the language, and not only in every word, but before all else in every conjunction of words [*Wortgefüge*], and thus particularly in those junctures [*Fugen*] of the language which are not explicitly put in words. 'Εον speaks throughout language and maintains for it the possibility of saying. [73]

Language is the language of Being [74] — that in which Being speaks. It is in that which is hidden away in language and to which we are already subject that Being speaks, thereby sustaining man in a clearing of intelligibility, thereby sustaining him as the "there." Precisely through a more primordial appropriation of that three-fold constitution of the "there" elaborated in *Sein und Zeit* Heidegger is brought to say that the "there" takes place as language. It is now evident why "language is the clearing-concealing advent of Being itself"; this, we have seen, is the proper locus of the reversal.

---

[68] *Was Heisst Denken?* p. 169.
[69] *Sein und Zeit*, p. 147.
[70] *Der Satz vom Grund*, p. 146.
[71] *über den Humanismus*, p. 5.
[72] *Was Heisst Denken?* p. 107.
[73] *Ibid.*, p. 141.
[74] "Die Sprache ist so die Sprache des Seins, wie die Wolken die Wolken des Himmels sind." *über den Humanismus*, p. 47.

Heidegger says that Being speaks "particularly in those junctures of the language which are not explicitly put into words." Being speaks unobtrusively in language. In its speaking Being conceals itself as that which speaks; it speaks, most of all, in those junctures which remain unspoken by us. At the heart of language as the language of Being there is self-concealment, withdrawal. Heidegger writes: "If we may talk here of playing games at all, then it is not we who play with words, but the essence of language plays with us, not only in this case, not only now, but long since and always. For language so plays with our speech that it likes to let our speech drift away into the more obvious meanings of words." [75] Language is no game that *we* play; rather language plays with us and can do so precisely because we are not its master, because it withdraws its essence from us, holds itself aloof from us. It lets our speech "drift away into the more obvious meanings of words" — the meanings that have lost their connection with the unspoken, the meanings in which the unspoken lies forgotten. Yet the unspoken is, most of all, where Being speaks: "Language denies us its essence: that it is the house of the truth of Being." [76]

In the folds, the junctures, of language Being conceals itself, withdraws itself from us. To be drawn along in this withdrawal is to enter into the movement of reversal; to be drawn along in this withdrawal is also to be drawn into "a transformed relationship to the essence of language." Language and reversal belong together.

[75] *Was Heisst Denken?* p. 83.
[76] *Uber den Humanismus,* p. 9.

LANGUAGE AND TWO PHENOMENOLOGIES

Don Ihde

State University of New York at Stony Brook

Introduction.

I have three concurrent concerns in this paper. The first is to display a picturable model of some of the main features of phenomenological method. I wish in this case to clarify some of the complexities and implications of a phenomenological procedure for a philosophical context often more Anglophilic and Europophobic than not. But on the way to this end I wish also to begin the sketch of what I hope will become a considered re-interpretation of phenomenological history. I wish to differentiate two distinguishable, but often confused, lines of development from a common base in Husserlian thought. These types of phenomenology may be called respectively, existential phenomenolgy, and hermeneutic phenomenology, and are initiated in their essential forms respectively by Maurice Merleau-Ponty and Martin Heidegger. And thirdly I wish to indicate briefly how the question of language lies imbedded in these distintions. My outline of phenomenological development, then, wishes to account for the recent and increasing interest in the philosophy of language currently displayed among phenomenologists.

And since the tradition of European born philosophies of consciousness are often given to excesses of self-consciousness, I shall remain true to form and bring to public awareness some underlying polemic concerns as well. Permit me three gross generalizations: (a) Existentialism, as it has been understood particularly on this Continent, in a quasi-literary and often romantic guise is all but dead philosophically. This was the common opinion among the French professors I talked to in recent years, and although death throes may last longer just as birth pains start later in the USA, the symptoms are be-

ginning to appear here, too. Herzog in the novel of the same name (and still placing Heidegger in the existential category) proclaims that, "We must get beyond Heidegger." (b) But this is not to say that existentialism in more philosophical form is dead. Quite to the contrary, as existential *phenomenology* it is just now beginning to make its appearance. As Sartre and Camus recede, Merleau-Ponty emerges. The previous guilt by association with the cultically "very existential" is replaced by concerns with more philosophically traditional problems revolving around perception, the problem of the body, and language. (c) Despite the difficulty in dissociating the popular meaning of existentialism from its philosophical basis and the even more difficult task of removing Heidegger from that category, I would point out that today most Europeans are beginning to argue that Heidegger is actually and not just polemically correct when he disclaims ever having been an existentialist.

To counter these historical misconceptions and to construct a re-interpretation which apologetically helps to point up the properly philosophical dimensions of phenomenology, I wish to propose a new tripartite framework of understanding. Again permit me three general points: (a) Since all phenomenology in its most precise and recent formulation forms a constellation around Edward Husserl in spite of the

Don Ihde is associate professor of philosophy at the State University of New York at Stony Brook. Having received his Ph.D. from Boston University in 1964, he has published extensively on the philosophy of Paul Ricoeur and on the phenomenology of auditory experience. A book, Hermeneutic Phenomenology, *is to be published by Northwestern University Press in the spring. It will deal mainly with themes suggested in this article.*

counter-gravitational pulls of Hegel, Kant, and Descartes, not to speak of Hume, I propose that we begin to think of phenomenology as a movement from Husserl to various forms of neo-Husserlianism. (b) To date the main lines of two distinguishable directions of neo-Husserlian phenomenology are *existential* and *hermeneutic* phenomenologies. Merleau-Ponty most clearly exemplifies the first and Heidegger I now wish to cast into the second type. (c) Both of these developments have sources in the central and original phenomenological model developed by Husserl and particularly from the two sides of his notion of intentionality as the main structure of consciousness. Paul Ricoeur, one of the foremost Husserl interpreters, gives us the key from which I extend my interpretation. He says:

"In Husserl's first works . . . consciousness is defined not by perception, that is to say by its very presence to things, but rather by its distance and its absence. This distance and absence are the power of signifying, of meaning . . . Thus consciousness is doubly intentional, in the first instance by virtue of being a signification and in the second instance by virtue of being an intuitive fulfilling. In short, in the first works, consciousness is at once speech and perception."[1]

In my interpretative extension of this observation I wish to show that existential phenomenology draws its strength from what I shall call the implicit perceptualism of Husserl's concept of intentionality. Thus, although using radically different interpretations, existential phenomenology has motivations not unlike those of empiricism.

In contrast, I wish to show that hermeneutic phenomenology draws its concern from problems of language, also inherent in Husserl's concept of intentionality. This development is most clearly evident in Heidegger's work. It is a use of phenomenology which turns to problems of history and culture and which tends to read experience and ultimately perception itself in terms of a tradition of interpretation.

To outline this interpretation I turn first to a description of a general phenomenological model as a type of reflective philosophy. This type of model has its roots in the Husserlian origins of phenomenology and as a general model is the origin upon which variations are worked.

Part 1. Phenomenological models: we do it with mirrors . . .

Reflective philosophies with parentage in the line of Descartes, Kant and Hegel before Husserl, usually are described as philosophies of consciousness or sometimes as subjectivisms. But often what is involved with reflection is not clarified as a methodological notion. Reflection in our language may mean some contemplative or re-thinking activity — or it may mean more literally a reflection from a mirror or another reflective surface. My entry into a description of phenomenological reflection lies in a deliberate choice of what I would like to call *the metaphor of the mirror*. When asked how I do phenomenology, I reply, I do it with mirrors. Because, as we shall see, in both thinking as reflection and the reflection from the mirror what is arrived at is done so *indirectly*.

In fact, the metaphor of mirror may first help clarify a persistent confusion among many who first read phenomenological descriptions as if they were simply revivals of introspective psychology. The key to the difference lies not in the material dealt with, since phenomenology deals with both so-called introspective contents and extrospective contents, but with the use of reflective indirectness.

To further precise this model I wish

---

[1] Ricoeur, Paul: *Husserl* (Northwestern University Press), p. 210.

to introduce an analogy between the "I" and "eye." In relation to the history of epistemology with its play upon the subject and the object, phenomenology is a method which strictly reduces or restricts itself to a relational or bipolar understanding of the subject and the object. Husserl's *ego-cogito-cogitatum,* Heidegger's *In-der-Welt-sein,* and Merleau-Ponty's *Etre-au-monde* are all versions of this essential characteristic of phenomenological method.

Thus a rule for phenomenology is that there is no subject without a corresponding object nor is there a knowable object except for and related to a subject. This insistence upon maintaining a relational scheme is actually the functional heart of Husserl's so-called transcendental idealism. But its theoretical function serves as a normative concept which differentiates phenomenology from both the classical realist and idealist frameworks. The *epoche* or phenomenological reduction, understood in this light, is the means of strictly maintaining the bi-polarity and "bracketing" the world in relation to speculative metaphysics. The aim is to suspend presuppositions, not experience.

This suspension of belief is on one side anti-realist in the sense that phenomenology brackets the idea of an existent which exists apart from experience. But functionally this suspension merely establishes all contents of experience as "objects," or better, object-correlates *for* experience in order that they be displayed for description prior to fitting them into an explanatory or constructive schema. All cogitata or contents of experience become noema or object-correlates and are to be considered only in their relations to a subject. This means that the implied theory of evidence which takes shape in Husserl's philosophy is one which weights all immediate of fulfillable experiences as prior to constructions. In this sense phenomenology is potentially open from its very beginning to an "empiricist" direction—but an empiri-

cism which remains distinct from its British and American relations in several ways.

But if realist assumptions are bracketed by the strict reduction to relationality, the same goes for classical idealism. The ego or the I nowhere exists in phenomenology without a world or field of contents which are the object correlates. Thus Husserl's supposed idealism must again be seen as a methodological function rather than the assertion of the primacy of mind. Unlike, or short of Descartes, Husserl's suspension of the world is not an active doubt, but a suspension of presuppositions concerning how the world is given out to be. The world is always to be described as it gives itself out to be to the knowing subject.

In both these senses the first central feature of the phenomenologically reduced model is the strict maintenance of a relationality between the I and the world. Once this reduction is presupposed, the metaphor of the mirror with its analogy may be re-introduced as follows:

The eye is to the mirror
(or reflective surface)
as the I is to the World

And if we were to ask the question: how does the eye see itself or the I understand itself? The answer will be, only reflectively or indirectly. It sees itself as reflected in the mirror and I understand myself through the world.

This question, in its Husserlian context, establishes the *order* of procedure. Husserl's descriptions begin with the noematic or object-correlates of the relation. Thus in the metaphor of the mirror what is first noted is that which appears immediately or naively "out there" as the appearance in the mirror. The naive level of awareness is always first directed to what is "out there" or in the world. This choice is one which makes a certain degree of sense in relation to both the history of civilization and the history of the individual. The pre-scientific aborigine and the pre-acculturated child may not be aware of our usual inner-outer distinctions, but they are aware of a certain "objectivity" to appearances. Thus dreams and spirits as well as rocks and trees are "objective" in the sense that they are "out there" as they appear to the individual. Phenomenology takes this pre-theoretical naivete to its extreme in the description of a layer of experience later called the *lifeworld* in Husserl's writings. Thus under the restrictions of the reduction the first focus is upon the contents of experience as they give themselves out to be primitively. What appears in the mirror is first to be described.

But in the case of the metaphor of the mirror a complication is entered. The face directly before the mirror is mine and the eye reflects my eye. A turn may be made to the subject as the experiencer — but made by means of the reflection. Again the history of the individual and the civilization display in rough outline such a turn. The child at some point learns to recognize himself in the mirror, the reflection is seen as a reflection of himself in a level of awareness perhaps never attained by the parakeet. It is from the reflection, the bouncing off from the object-correlate, that the eye is to be seen, and it is from the experience of the world that the I is to be understood.

It is precisely this reflective turn which differentiates Husserl at one blow from Hume whom he admired so strongly. Husserl's critique of Hume's introspective psychology which finds itself unable to find a subject is located in the lack of a reflective turn. The ego does see itself-reflectively. From this phenomenological indirectness Husserl attempts to establish the structures of experienc*ing* and upon the experienc*ed*.

It is well known that the structure of *intentionality* became the key concept around which the understanding of experience was elaborated in the Husserlian sense. Revolving around this central concept were a cluster of other notions such as "horizons," the "ray" of attention, and passive and active syntheses. But again it is the relationality of object and subject polarity which establishes this structure. Here we may put together both moments of the metaphor of the mirror.

If I first look at the mirror and observe carefully I can note that the whole of the appearing surface is one which does not ordinarily appear with a flat or equal value. Usually somewhere near the center of the mirror the phenomena "stand out" while those on the fringe are less explicit. The eye spots the eye looking back. And if I were able to remain completely restricted to a naive and probably hypothetical level of awareness I would end up saying that the center of objects in my field of vision are "more real" or "more important" than those at the edge. But even in an ordinary context the reflective turn is already made and I say instead that my *attention* is what is focussed. It is I who "make stand out" what I will under my gaze. Permit me here to make several leaps and conclude at the risk of prematurely losing specifics that this notion of a ray of attention within a wider or surrounding field becomes a picturable model for the general structure of experience in the Husserlian context. Experience is not only selective in the normal case, but displays itself as directional or referential.

But more important in the present context is the fact that the structure of experiencing is established by means of the reflective turn, and all experiencing is to be read via or upon the world of appearances. There is no subjectivity, phenomenologically speaking, apart from a world. But what is initially taken as a reflective surface makes a great deal of difference.

Part 2. Multiple "Worlds" or the Hall of Mirrors.

From a description of a general model based upon an interpretation of

Husserl, I move to its variants with the neo-Husserlians. Husserl himself evolved a number of ways towards phenomenology and he characterized himnomenology, and he characterized himof his days. At least three of these ways to phenomenology have become watermarks in traditional Husserl interpretations. The so-called "early Husserl" found his way to phenomenology by means of *eidetic* sciences, i.e., mathematical and logical questions, and in this period he belongs to the set of philosophers who were concerned with the problems of logicism and psychologism at the turn of the century. The "middle Husserl," particularly of the *Cartesian-Meditations* tried for a while to describe phenomenology as a type of egology modeled in certain respects upon a Cartesian paradigm — but with some essential differences. It was during this period that the questions of solipsism were at their height. The "late Husserl" began to take a third major direction, increasingly perceptualistic in its form, in the concept of the *lifeworld*. It is here that he comes closest to what was to become an *existential* phenomenology.

I shall not enter into the various arguments in current Husserl scholarship which now often revolve around this enigmatic period other than to make two suggestive indications about possible relations to the neo-Husserlians I shall momentarily examine. First, it is possible and perhaps even likely that Heidegger, already published and working out his own phenomenology, may well have influenced Husserl himself in relation to the *lifeworld* concept. Secondly, it is demonstrably the case that Merleau-Ponty concentrated his work upon the so-called "late Husserl" and took the lifeworld as a primary concept in the development of his own version of phenomenology.

Rather I shall return to the struc-turally generalized model I have suggested and indicate how the neo-Husserlians began to vary this model to their own uses. The differentiation into an existential and a hermeneutic phenomenology depends upon which of the dual foci of consciousness is taken as primary, perception or signification, upon which serves as a "world." Thus, if I maintain my mirror metaphor, what is taken as the reflective surface is of great importance. I shall argue that although there are obvious overlaps between existential and hermeneutic phenomenologies that Merleau-Ponty makes use of a "perceptual mirror" and Heidegger a "linguistic mirror." I shall, however, deal with these variants in an order inverse to their actual history since I believe that in some respects Merleau-Ponty comes closer to an extension of Husserl than Heidegger who couples phenomenology with a quite different set of problems than those motivating Husserl.

A. Existential phenomenology as a perceptualist philosophy.

Merleau-Ponty began with the "late Husserl" who had already turned increasingly to problems of perceptual experience. It was a turn which, accelerated in Merleau-Ponty's thought, formed the possibility for existential phenomenology. Merleau-Ponty put it bluntly: "Far from being, as one might think, the formula for an idealist philosophy, the phenomenological reduction is that of an existentialist philosophy." [2] But in turn, an existential philosophy is one which focusses upon and makes more explicit the perceptualist side of Husserl's basic model. The distance to the world of the "early Husserl" becomes the presence to the world (Etra-au-monde) of Merleau-Ponty.

But a perceptualism was implicit from the beginning in Husserl's theory of evidence. For one thing the very use of language in Husserl drew its

---

[2] Merleau-Ponty, Maurice: "What is Phenomenology?", *Cross Currents*, Vol. IV, Winter 1956, p. 65.

strength from perceptual metaphor. The phenomenological process was described as "viewing phenomena"; experience was focused as a "ray of attention"; things appeared in "perspective variations"; and even introspection was termed "inner perception." But more essentially, the whole reduction was one which as a theory of evidence increasingly weights immediacy or concrete experience as primary. Only that which is "bodily present" or which can be fulfilled in the intuition (experienced) shall be accepted as evident.

In Merleau-Ponty this direction becomes more apparent so that he makes the claim that "perception is primary." This phenomenological "empiricism," now known as existential phenomenology, is one which attempts to understand all human behaviors upon the basis of or in relation to phenomenology of perception. Of course the theory of perception which Merleau-Ponty developed was one in keeping with the reflective model I have described. It is the use of this model which differentiates his "empiricism" from its Anglo-American cousins. He rejected all sense-data theories and systems of causation as constructions rather than descriptions of perception and turned to a description which was closer to gestalt psychology and perspectivism as the basis for his understanding of perception.

I would note, however, that Merleau-Ponty's existentialism *is* this version of perceptualism. His use of phenomenological reduction is one which attempts to reach a level of pre-theoretical experience, the experience of the (perceptual) lifeworld. He says, "By these words, the primacy of perception, we mean that the experience of perception is our presence at the moment when things, truths, values are constituted for us; that perception is a nascent *logos;* that it teaches us, outside all dogmatisim, the true conditions of objectivity itself; that it summons us to the tasks of knowledge and action." [3]

This theory of evidence, regressive in its drive towards primitivity, remains in line with its Husserlian sense. To gain the perceptual lifeworld the suspension or critique of all merely taken for granted interpretations or presuppositions is to be undertaken. In this process Merleau-Ponty's arguments against the empiricists attack the doctrines of sensation as merely constructs which falsify primitive experience rather than explain it.

But, as Merleau-Ponty notes, the reduction is never complete because what it arrives at is always the essential assumption of being already in a world and it is this assumption which the phenomenologist wishes to explicate. The regressive direction of Merleau-Ponty's use of phenomenology nevertheless retains the bi-polar model which remains essential to its Husserlian understanding.

To this point, Merleau-Ponty may be seen as essentially phenomenological in his use of a basic model. What differentiates him from Husserl is in what he takes as the world and what it reflects as a subject. His "mirror" and his "eye" are distinguishable. The world, for Merleau-Ponty, is the perceived world. It is presumed to be concrete, expressive, and rich in its contents. It is also a "natural" world rather than the strictly bracketed world of Husserl's formal ontologies. In this sense Merleau-Ponty tends towards a realism more strongly than did Husserl.

The same pattern is repeated when the reflective turn is made. If the perceptual lifeworld is the object-correlate for Merleau-Ponty, one would expect a symmetry in relation to the subject who must be thought of as a concrete perceiver. And this is the case. The problem of the body takes on a central role for the reflected side of existential

---

[3] Merleau-Ponty: "The Primacy of Perception," *Existential Phenomenology* (Prentice Hall), p. 41.

phenomenology. The *embodied* or incarnate subject is the perceiving counterpart to the perceived world. *Le corps vécu,* usually translated as the lived body, is the perceiving subject in a perceptual world and the concrete finitude of the body corresponds to the perceived presence of the world. Merleau-Ponty retains the bi-polar Husserlian model, but interprets it through perception.

One could argue, however, that this extension of Husserl is legitimate and that existential phenomenology is but carrying on the program of the "late Husserl." But that is not quite the case. By the selection of a "perceptual mirror" Merleau-Ponty chose only a partial aspect of Husserlian intentionality as basic. The perceived world and the perceiving embodied subject selects as primary the experiential side of intentionality as its basis and tends toward making signification secondary.

This becomes more apparent when one examines Merleau-Ponty's view of language. Even if his theory of language never attained the degree of development that his theory of perception did, it remains the case that it embodies a direction which is necessitated by his perceptualist base. It is also the case that as he turned more and more to the problems of language that this perceptualism was called into question.[4]

At first the Pontean theory of language seems to parallel clearly his theory of perception. Just as perception begins with gestalts and unitary wholes, so the world is seen as primitively expressive. And just as the perceived world is always understood only in its relation to a subject, so is language considered only in relation to the existant, speaking subject. In contrast to attempts to deal with language as if it were an empirical object, Merleau-Ponty insists that one begin with phenomenological speech.

But as this theory of language develops, a second meaning to Merleau-Ponty's phenomenological empiricism begins to emerge. His use of phenomenological reductions was one which always attempted to move back towards the perceptual lifeworld which at base becomes unspeakable. In return, speech becomes the counter-movement from the "silence" of the perceptual world to its expression in language. Thus Merleau-Ponty argues that language arises out of silence, out of gesture, and even that it is metaphorically a kind of music. This theory of expression parallels the aim of a phenomenology of perception to a pre-theoretical world. The theory of expression is one which seeks a *pre-linguistic* basis for expression. Thus the whole weight of the Pontean theory of language concentrates upon the birth or coming-into-being of expression, the movement from silence to speech.

I shall not here try to show how this theory of languages follows from certain aspects of phenomenological investigation nor make complaint of some of the problems which I believe Merleau-Ponty raises. But I would point out that it is because he takes the perceptualist base as primary that this theory of language follows.

B. Hermeneutic Phenomenology as Linguistic Philosophy.

But here I abruptly leave Merleau-Ponty, suspended as it were, and turn to the second main neo-Husserlian direction as it takes shape in the thought of Martin Heidegger. My interpretation parallels that which I used with Merleau-Ponty and continues the metaphor of the mirror. The mirror which Heidegger uses is the world of language in a broad conceptual and historical sense. And the side of intentionality which is developed is that which begins with problems of signification and meaning. Heidegger's pre-

---

[4] There is even some question about a possible hermeneutic direction in the late Merleau-Ponty, *cf. LeVisible et l'invisible.*

sumptuous *fundamental ontology,* to my way of thinking, is a phenomenology of language. And it is from this phenomenology of language that Heidegger ultimately reads experience itself. This reading of Heidegger which sees him as hermeneut emphasizes aspects overlooked in interpretations which would make Heidegger an "existentialist." [5]

I begin by pointing up the frequent use of linguistic-historical metaphors in Heidegger's writing. For Heidegger, man is discourse *(Rede)*; he is called *(Ruf)* to listen to the voice of Being; the famed destruction of the history of ontology is to be by means of a violent examination of philosophical language, etc. In his backward or regressive aim at phenomena, hermaneutics or interpretation becomes the vehicle to be used. Heidegger explicitly claims: "Our investigation itself will show that the meaning of phenomenological description as a method lies in *interpretation.* . . . The phenomenology of Dasein is a *hermeneutic* in the primordial signification of this word, where it designates this business of interpreting." [6]

The essentially linguistic or conceptual strategy is revealed from the very beginnings of *Being and Time.* Instead to turning to Husserl or announcing in strictly Husserlian fashion a program and a method, Heidegger formulates his phenomenology by his own version and translation of Greek terms. The phenomenon becomes "to let that which shows itself to be seen from itself" (the manifest). And logos, again translated in Heidegger's sense, is *discourse* or language in a primary and broad sense.

But for Heidegger phenomena are mostly covered over, hidden, and the task of phenomenology is to let these phenomena appear. On closer reading, it becomes apparent that what covers over the phenomena is *the history of interpretation,* the way in which language is used. Thus to recover one's hearing of the voice of being one must loosen up and rework this covering. It is here that the long task of the "destruction of the history of ontology" begins and takes the long and varied detours via Kant, Descartes, Aristotle, and the pre-Socratics. Hermeneutics has as task the re-opening of language to its fundamental or "original" possibilities. For Heidegger the categories of thought we employ have become hardened and prevent us from seeing, or better, from hearing, what underlies our catagories as basic phenomena.

The whole context of interpretation which appears therapeutic in some respects is one which, through the distinctions of authenticity and inauthenticity, discourse and idle talk, seeks to uncover phenomena by hermeneutics. Heidegger wants us to "get back to" discourse, but to do so we must recognize and break through idle talk or mere abstraction. But what is important in this outline is to recognize that the way this is done is to take for the surrounding element which constitutes the world the element of language. It is from this recognition that we may understand the mirror Heidegger uses.

The functional outcome of choosing a linguistic mirror has more than one result. But it also changes the context of phenomenological questions. The substitution of a language world for a perceptual world moves what forms worldhood from the natural world to the cultural world. The field of silent objects is replaced by the field of human expression, the world of subjects. Secondly, the language world is one which re-locates the focus upon intersubjectivity from gesture to the fullness of language. Intersubjectivity here is the necessary given from which one begins for there is no private language to be found.

---

[5] In certain respects, Heidegger is actually closer to a philosophic version of "symbolic interactionism" (Mead) than to existentialism.
[6] Heidegger, Martin: *Being and Time* (Harper & Row), pp. 61–62.

Thirdly, one may expect to find, as Heidegger has already so well emphasized, that I am used by language as much as I am able to use language. But this is recognizable in the phenomenological context most precisely if one turns first to the language world as it gives itself out to be. One may expect to find that in certain respects, just as the concrete positionality of an embodied subject is constituted by the perceptual world, so will the hermeneutic subject be constituted by his language world and the task becomes one of specifying in what ways and to what extent this occurs. Secondly, one may expect to find that the subject changes and has a history in relation to the language world. We are already aware that subjectivity is differently understood today than it was at the birth of our culture and that the "self" of a child is quite different from that of the adult. There is a history to the subject just as there is a history to the culture. In fact, one may expect to find with this mirror, historical considerations playing ever stronger roles as the language world is noted in its subtle changes.

But thirdly, one may expect to find in a counter-fashion something about the way language (or thought, if you will) changes what is perceived. The world may be potentially expressive — but what it expresses is different for us than for others in certain respects. The reflective model applied to language has not yet been exhausted. All of this lies within the scope of Heideggerian hermeneutics. For my purposes here, however, it is sufficient merely to point up the differences in problems and directions implicit in the difference between existential and hermeneutic phenomenologics.

Part 3. Mirrors and Ontologies.

If the neo-Husserlians seem to take different "mirrors" from which the subject is reflected and if, as both seem to claim, what is arrived at is an ontology of human existence, it would seem we are back to a hall of mirrors.

And although a series of mirrors may, by their very selections and exaggerations reveal possibilities previously unexpected, each remains partial and short of finality. It might seem that phenomenologists now must choose between existential and hermeneutic directions, between what is taken as basic: experience or language? immediacy or history? And it might seem at worst that this is a return to sheer metaphysics with resurrected, if modified, empiricists and idealists again dividing up.

I would suggest that this is not quite the case. And I return to a comment of Paul Ricoeur whose notions began this paper. Ricoeur argues that phenomenology of speech and a phenomenology of language are two quite different matters and focus upon quite different aspects of the whole linguistic phenomenon. And it is precisely this difference of task and focus of attention which holds the key to at least some of the differences between Merleau-Ponty and Heidegger.

By beginning with the "silence" of perceptual experience and by viewing language as expression, as the coming-into-being of significance, Merleau-Ponty in effect begins a phenomenology of speech. The subject struggling with language, to say the new, to ex-press himself, is the focus of the perceptualist's immediacy. But by beginning with what has been said and by showing how we are used by our language and our interpretations, Heidegger begins with a phenomenology of language.

The phenomenology of speech and the phenomenology of language belong together. Immediacy without history is silent; history without speech is empty noise. And if the issues meet in a question of language, however differently that question is formulated on the Continent than in Anglo-American circles, it is not mere historical accident. The "linguistic turn" now belongs with the hedgehogs as well as to the foxes and the philosophy of language animates

Paris today just as it does Oxford. And phenomenology through or in spite of its excursion through existentialism is returning full circle to Husserl. But this is a response to our time and I close with a comment by Ricoeur whose earlier comment suggested this line of interpretation.

Today we seek a broad philosophy of language which would be able to account for the multiple functions of human signification and its mutual relations. Now is language capable of such diverse useages as mathematics and myth, physics and art? It is not by chance that we ask this question today. We are precisely the ones who use symbolic logic, exegetical science, anthropology and psychoanalysis, and who for perhaps the first time are capable of embracing as a unique question that of the reconstitution of human discourse. In effect the progress of the disciplines as disseparate as those mentioned have at the same time manifested and aggravated the dislocation of this discourse. The unity of human speech is a problem today.[7]

---

[7] Ricoeur, Paul: *De l'Interprétation* (Editions du Seuil), pp. 13–14.

THE WORK OF ART AND OTHER THINGS

HAROLD ALDERMAN

Sonoma State College

Introduction

In the *Ion* Plato writes:

a poet is a light and winged thing and holy, and never able to compose until he has become inspired, and is beside himself, and reason is no longer in him (534b).

From the argument of the *Ion* and from material in the *Apology* (22c) it becomes clear that Plato means to say that the poetic (i.e., artistic) vision is an essential one which is completed only when it becomes the object of philosophical reflection. In other places, however, Plato clouds the issue by condemning the poet's work as a kind of idle, untruthful play (*Republic* 599a).

Modern philosophy has to a large extent resolved this ambiguity in Plato's thought by adopting his condemnation of art. The work of Martin Heidegger, however, in one of its most important phases, tries to re-new the first, positive interpretation by arguing that art is a way through which a people discover themselves within their world. Like Plato, Heidegger believes that the work of art is essentially innocent—that it becomes complete only when seen as part of a movement of thought toward some more comprehensive mode of cognition which grounds and renders intelligible the work of art.

In this paper I shall clarify Heidegger's important conception of art by showing how his rediscovery of the work of art is a fundamental move in his retrieval of *das Denken des Seins*—a retrieval necessary because western philosophy, again following one direction in Plato's thought, has neglected to appropriate a genuine thought of Being. I shall proceed in this clarification by first elaborating

Heidegger's mature statement of the nature of the thing, and shall then show how the work of art is the most thingly of things. By fulfilling its clarificatory obligations, the present essay enacts—however modestly—the role of the thing as a work of thought. The paper is divided into four main sections: (I) "The Thingliness of the Thing," (II) "The Thing as a Work of Art," (III) "The Adventure of Poetry," and (IV) "Summary."

I. The Thingliness of the Thing

In *Being and Time* Heidegger considered the possibility of a thought which could take the worldly conditionality of beings as its theme, but he did not at that point engage in such thought. Yet it is precisely such thought which is the thought of Being; and it is precisely such thought which yields an owned (*eigentlich*) thinking and an owned way of being-in-the-world for the thinker.

The essay "Das Ding," in attempting to think Being, is the necessary complement of *Being and Time*, for it seeks to think in the way that *Being and Time* merely recommends as a possibility. Obviously, it is only with the actual undertaking that the possibility or impossibility of a way of thought gets demonstrated. In "Das Ding" Heidegger's argument that the thinker can take over the *experience* of the worldly character of beings is thus exemplified. Since the thought of Being is designed to lead the thinker back to experience, it is an evocative

Harold Alderman is at present Associate Professor at Sonoma State College, Rohnert Park, California. He received his Ph.D. from Tulane University in 1968 and has published a number of articles, several in the field of phenomenology.

thought, and its language is thereby necessarily evocative rather than re-presentational.[1] In "Das Ding" we watch Heidegger attempt to occupy thoughtfully the dwelling of Being.

Heidegger begins "Das Ding" with a consideration of the meaning of nearness and its relevance to the concept of 'thing.' He first argues that the technological overcoming of temporal and spatial distances is irrelevant to a genuine experience of proximity. For example, although we can record the total life cycle of a flower by means of time-lapse photography, we do not thereby get any nearer to the actuality of the flower. Knowing about a thing is not at all the same as knowing a thing itself. Heidegger's examination of technology reveals that we are in danger of forgetting what it means to be intimately near something. Yet if we are to achieve a grasp of Being we must understand what nearness means. Being after all is nearer to us than anything else.[2] In "Das Ding" Heidegger uses the term 'thing' to denote any being which serves the explicit role of directing man back to his world and back to an owned encounter with Being. Things bring us into nearness, that is into close proximity to our world.

1. The Word 'Thing'

The justification of etymological analysis in the work of Heidegger derives from two factors: in the first place, old definitions of words give us an insight into their meanings before they became complicated by years of linguistic inheritance; in the second place, to understand these simpler meanings is to appropriate a different experience. It is this appropriation of an earlier, simpler experience that is crucial, for through such an appropriation we are committed to a way of

thinking. If Heidegger utilizes an archaic meaning he does not, then, merely imitate a time past; and the warrant for the utilization will depend on the general warrant for the thought of which the etymology is only one aspect.

According to Heidegger both the Latin 'res' and the old German 'thing' signify "that which concerns man, the matter in question, the argument."[3] If we look at each of the elements of the definition separately, we see that a thing is that with which a man is involved (concerned); it is something undetermined—an issue (question); and it is a center of conflict (argument). These dynamic elements of the meaning of both 'res' and 'thing' are even clearer in the phrase 'res publica.' The res publica was not simply the state of the nation, but was the open place of concern within which a people assembled to deal with matters of common interest. In Anglo-Saxon the term 'thing' signified the council within which the ealdormen gathered to confront the problems facing the people. As such, the word 'thing' signified not only the gathering and facing of an issue, but also the resolution of the issue since the ealdormen represented the wisdom of the clan. The Oxford English Dictionary gives an identical meaning to the old Norwegian word 'ting.' As Heidegger observes, we find some of this archaic sense of 'thing' still present in contemporary English. In English we say, "He knows how to handle things," meaning "He knows how to deal with matters which concern him." Likewise, contemporary argot advises us to "do our thing," again meaning to confront the matters which are of real importance to us.

We must take such etymological clues as Heidegger intends that we

[1] Martin Heidegger, Vortäge und Aufsätze (Pfullingen: Neske, 1954), p. 182. Hereafter VA.
[2] This nearness is the universality spoken of in Being and Time, tr. J. Macquarrie and E. Robinson (New York: Harper and Row, 1963), pp. 22–23. Hereafter BT.
[3] VA, p. 172.

take them: as signs which point to new directions of thought. The clues from language are then simply attempts to uncover *depth meanings* of privileged words which can evoke a sense of Being. Yet the uneasy suspicion remains that it is more than coincidence that many of these privileged names of Being are old ones. We can make additional sense of Heidegger's etymological appeals by observing what the archaic names of Being have in common with Being itself.

The past, Heidegger argues in *Being and Time*, is not something which merely lies behind us. Rather, it is itself present as the ground of the present. Like Being, the past is always close to us even though we might be unaware of its proximity. In trying to appropriate archaic names we are thus involved in the same kind of effort required to think Being itself: we are forced to abandon the everyday (the present) and focus our attention on something which underlies what is present. Being then is analogous to archaic meanings in that it lies before beings in the same way that past meanings lie before present ones —as their archē. By directing our attention to old, venerable words we thus gain not only simpler definitions, but we also learn to look through that which is present toward its ground (toward the possibility of its presence). With these reflections we turn to Heidegger's analysis of a particular thing, remembering that a thing is that which manifests concern, issue, and conflict.

2. The Thing and the Foursome (*das Geviert*)

Heidegger's search for a mythopoetic language of thingliness begins with a critique of those *Gestell* modes of language which are used to objectify 'things' as if they were ob-jects

merely present before us and passively awaiting our theoretic interpretation.[4] Things are closer to us than objects and we can never understand the thingliness of things by considering the objectivity of objects. If we are to grasp a thing in its Being, we must let it be what it is, that is we must learn to speak phenomenologically. Heidegger's attempt to restate the Being-beings relation in terms of a Foursome-thing relation is then an attempt to develop a genuinely phenomenological language. Let us see how he uses this language to describe a simple everyday utensil like a pitcher.

According to Heidegger the pitcher must be understood in terms of its function of storing refreshing liquids. But storing cannot be understood in terms of the filling of an empty physical space which is bounded by the impermeable walls of the pitcher. Such talk, Heidegger says, commits us to talk about objects. Nor on the other hand can we reach the thingliness of the pitcher by regarding it as a product produced by a potter. If we would understand this thing, the pitcher, then we must get closer to it than we do when we regard it as either a scientific object or a manufactured product. In order to achieve this closeness Heidegger describes the pitcher as a focal point which manifests the unity of a world.[5]

The storage capability of the pitcher must be seen in its essential unity with its ability to pour forth that which is stored. According to Heidegger, it is the ability to yield, to pour, which defines the retaining emptiness of the pitcher. The empty space of a pitcher is not simply a neutral geometrical space and cannot, therefore, be described fundamentally in terms of geometrical coordinates. Rather we must learn to see the emptiness of the pitcher as a significant space, and if we would talk about it in appropriate

---

[4] VA, pp. 163–170.
[5] VA, pp. 169–172.

terms we have to first abandon the mode of discourse which is appropriate only to geometrical spaces. But how does one talk about significant spaces? Obviously enough, in terms of significances. By 'significance' here Heidegger means both something which is of concern and something which is a signifier, a pointer. The space of the pitcher is, then, a concernful space and a pointer.

Heidegger's point here is that before we know the space of a warehouse or a church, for example, as of such and such geometrical dimensions, we know it as a significant space. It is for this reason that he refuses to discuss the pitcher as an object which only incidentally has some significance. To talk about objects and their significance is to assume the ontological priority of objects and the logical priority of talk about them. In Heidegger's thought geometrical space is simply one kind of significant space. Such spaces are significant only within a scientific and technological world. Obviously one can talk about a multiplicity of spaces that are significant within different worlds (for example, theatrical spaces, classroom spaces, etc.). And just as obviously there is no *prima facie* reason to presuppose that the world within which geometrical spaces are significant is the fundamental world.

If the emptiness of the pitcher is not merely a geometrical absence of a volume of liquid, then neither can the liquid itself repose in the pitcher's emptiness as a mere metrical volume. We have seen that it is the pouring in and out of the pitcher which defines the pitcher and its emptiness. Now Heidegger cautions us to understand that what is poured in and out is not a mere objectified liquid, and that the pouring in and out is not a mere changing of the location of an objectified liquid. For Heidegger, the fundamental sense of pouring lies in the meaning of gift giving; in the

pouring out of a liquid, for example water, the pitcher gives the gift of thirst quenching. The essence of the pitcher lies in the gift of what is poured, and the pitcher's empty space concerns us in that it makes possible the quenching of thirst. But the pitcher gives the gift of water and shows its thingliness only within a context (i.e., world) which Heidegger analyzes as a foursome consisting of earth and heaven, mortals and gods.

In the water that is poured from the pitcher there sojourns (*weilt*) the spring from which the water comes. In the spring itself there sojourns the earth which contains the spring. And in the earth itself there sojourns the heaven which gives us rain and dew. In the spring water the earth and heaven are united and in the pouring out of the water earth and heaven are brought to stand for the first time in their essential unity. The gift giving of the pitcher brings together this mutual sojourn of earth and heaven. Thus the pitcher signifies (i.e., points to) the complementary presence in it of the earth and the sky. In giving the gift of water the pitcher quenches the thirst of mortal man; or the event of pouring may also bring men together into a sociable gathering. With such gatherings those who drink together honor what is ideal and in so doing they call forth the presence of a god. Thus, according to Heidegger, human activity points, however elliptically, toward some ideal human committment; and such a commitment is, in the pre-Socratic sense, a god. Thus in every out-pouring or filling of the pitcher each member of the Foursome is brought to presence. Some occasions of course may not emphasize the presence of all the members; nonetheless it is only when we grasp the pitcher as that which retains and pours by presenting heaven and earth, gods and mortals that we know it as a fully concrete thing. We can better understand what is to be gained by discussing the Being-being relation in this new vocabulary of Foursome-thing if we examine more fully what Heidegger means by each of the terms of the Foursome.

3. The Foursome: Mortals and Earth, Gods and Heaven

By mortal (*Sterblicher*) Heidegger means the being which dies; and by dying he does not mean merely ceasing to be. To be able to die signifies being able to understand the possibility of death, and thus *be* toward death. Although Heidegger means by mortal what he meant by Dasein in *Being and Time*, the term 'mortal' is not simply a synonym; it is, instead, part of Heidegger's move into an evocative language. The term 'Dasein' is appropriate to the early and re-presentational discourse of *Being and Time*, but when one seeks to occupy an owned dwelling in the world, language which objectifies this world must be abandoned. One must take over the world not in a theoretical stance by talking, but in a real appropriation in which one dwells in the source of his ownness, which is mortality. The use of the word 'mortal' is then a fundamental appropriation of what Heidegger earlier meant by Dasein.

As for the earth, Heidegger says that it is that which "constructively supports; it is the nourishing bearer of fruit; it is that which guards and preserves waters and stones, plants and animals." [6] Here we have an obviously naturalistic, although non-objectified earth; it is an earth within which man dwells prior to any theoretical reflection. As the foundation (i.e., constructive support) the earth is the from-which of the directioned dwelling of man. It is only on and out of the earth that man can dwell at all. Heidegger's earth is then not the scientific earth of minerals, geological formations, and earthquakes; it is something darker and richer than this.

Darker because the earth has not been lit up as the objectified scientific earth, and richer because the earth has exhausted its potential if it is already interpreted in terms of a scientific object. On the earth man constructs his dwelling; such an earth is pure, uninterpreted foundation, and it is only within a particular world (i.e., within a particular mode of dwelling) that the world receives a content. By earth in this context, Heidegger means essentially what he meant by *physis* in such works as *Plato's Doctrine of Truth* and *An Introduction to Metaphysics*. If we recall that the word '*physis*' is usually translated by 'nature,' and at the same time remember that by nature we do not mean scientific nature, then something of the sense of earth becomes clearer. The earth is nature in its primeval wildness; it is nature as profuse abundance, as an untamed and endlessly rich chaos; it is nature as the endless, brutal, destructive, and creative upsurge of beings. In *An Introduction to Metaphysics* Heidegger says that Being is the play of *physis* and *logos* in which *logos* binds that which is thrown forth by *physis*. As we shall now learn, Being is conceived as the play of the earth and gods in which the gods bind the wildness of the earth.

The gods themselves are hidden messengers who give signs and directions to mortals. If the earth is the from-which of the dwelling of mortals, then the gods are the toward-which of that dwelling. Just as the earth is dark and unfathomable, the gods are themselves the source of illumination; they light up the darkness of the earth. If the earth is pure potentiality of Being, the gods are the realization of Being in terms of bringing it to stand in a particular way; they are the *telos* of the earth. Let us be quite clear about what is meant here by recalling something of the Greek sense of the gods. The Greek understanding of the gods

---

[6] VA, p. 176.

is expressed in such phrases as "love is a god," "beauty is a god," "intelligence is a god." The appearance of a god is thus, for example, a manifestation of love, beauty, or intelligence. When a god appears to a people, his presence is felt as a call which moves them in a given direction. A god is then the shaping of the destiny of a people; with the appearance of a god the earth comes to stand in a definite way as a definite mode of dwelling. A people dwells out of the earth toward its gods, and thereby achieves its own way of being-in-the-world. It is in this sense that the play of the earth and gods brings Being to stand forth.

The fourth member of the Foursome, the heaven, is "the path of the sun, the course of the moon, the splendour of the stars, the seasons of the year, the light and dusk of the day, the darkness and the clarity of the night; it is the hospitability and indifference of the weather; it is the clouds and the blue depths of the sky." [7] The first insight to be gained from this description of the heaven is that it is not the scientific heaven which is of interest to astronomers and astro-physicists. To describe the heaven of the Foursome he employs not the laws of celestial mechanics but the imagery and metaphor of the poet. Such a heaven is the dwelling place of the gods: from it man awaits the arrival of the sacred, of the ideal. Heaven like the earth, remains pure possibility until a god dwells in it and defines it as his dwelling place.

From this discussion of the members of the Foursome, we see how Heidegger attempts to move away from a *Gestell* mode of representational language. In the first place each member of the Foursome is described in terms of what might best be called a naturalistic

pantheism. Such descriptions are part of his effort to wrench thought free from metaphysical language. In the second place, his talk about the Foursome has an archaic flavor, quite reminiscent of mythological talk. This is not mere coincidence since talk about the Foursome is, indeed, mythological. If we remember the archaic sense of *mythos* as a mouthing, or laying of foundations, then we see quite clearly that we have here a mythology —an attempt to lay a foundation for discoursing about Being.

4. The Play of the Foursome

Heidegger describes any worldly manifestation of a Foursome as a mirror-play (*Spiegel-spiel*),[8] by which he means that each member of the Foursome manifests and is at the same time manifest in, the other three members. When the "thing things the world," the "world worlds" and a human dwelling is enlightened and made secure.[9] With the cryptic notion of the thinging of the thing Heidegger describes its coming into its own as a thing; thus the verb 'to thing' refers to the activity by which a thing is grounded in its Being. For the thinker, the thinging of the thing involves the thinking of the thing in its Being; thus the thinker must play his role if the world in which he and his fellow mortals dwell is ever to be manifest in its full concreteness as "the mirror-play of the earth and heaven, god and mortals..." [10]

The thinking which brings the thinking of the thing about is always initiated by the summons of the thing. In such thought the thinker is literally be-thinged (*Be-Dingt*) and leaves behind all non-thingly thinking which talks about causes and explanations. In this context we must understand that by 'be-thinged' Heidegger means

[7] VA, p. 177.
[8] VA, p. 178.
[9] VA, p. 179.
[10] VA, p. 178.

162

what he earlier meant by letting things be, or by going to the things themselves. Instead of imposing the human *logos* on things, we become be-thinged; we spare the thing in its Being. In sparing the thing we dwell in the near and come to understand that it is in sparing that we enter into the mirror-play of the world itself. We become players in the game of Being when we let things be.

How then do we become be-thinged? Not simply by remaining inactive. The sparing, getting near the thing, requires a watchful vigilance—the first step of which is to go beyond the merely representational thinking of metaphysics. We make part of this step by inquiring into the nature of metaphysical thinking as Heidegger does in his studies of Plato and Nietzsche, for example. But after this analytical preparation we must wait silently and thoughtfully for a summons from things. In this respect we see that the thinking of Being is similar to the arrival of Grace in Christian thought. One prepares, and then one waits. What one waits for is the moment when the world worlds as world, and the bond of thing and Foursome shines forth in all its splendor; at such a moment we learn that the thing is itself the focal point of world and Foursome. Reference to the concept of dread (*angst*) will help make clear how this new mode of thinking yields an owned existence.

In *Being and Time* Heidegger shows that the attunement of dread provides a privileged mode of access to the world. In "Das Ding" we learn that a non-representational thinking of the thing in its role of world bond provides another mode of access. We recall that the attunement of dread throws us up against the world and thereby reveals the ultimate conditionality of all beings. The thought of Being serves the same purpose in that through it man encounters himself as a being amidst beings whose Being derives from the play of the Foursome. The thinker takes over this insight as he contemplates the minimal structural possibilities of there being any such thing as a world; the poet takes over this insight by working to name the gods of his own world. That is, the poet's naming of a god is the original evocation of the holy and the lighting up of a world out of the dark obscurity of earth.[11]

II. The Thing as a Work of Art

The most general statement Heidegger makes of the nature of art is found in the 1935 article "Der Ursprung des Kunstwerkes" which has been translated as "The Origin of the Work of Art."[12] A long section of this essay is involved in an elaborate and inconclusive search for the meaning of 'thing'. Our preceding discussion of the 1959 essay "Das Ding" which contains Heidegger's mature conception of the thing makes it possible for us to avoid that section and get to the heart of the matter.

Heidegger concludes "The Origin of the Work of Art" with a general reflection on the work of art and on

[11] Heidegger makes several other major attempts to describe the foundations of human worlds. One of the most important of these is the 1935 essay *Gelassenheit*, published in English under the title *Discourse on Thinking*. That essay, like 'Das Ding,' provides both a statement of the contemplative nature of the thought of Being and an exercise in that thought. Utilizing a new name of Being—'the region of regions'—to emphasize that no worldly manifestation of Being is exhaustive of Being itself, Heidegger labors to show that it is exactly this 'region' which lies beyond any particular gathering together of the Foursome. The 'region of regions' names Being in its difference from worldly beings, whereas the Foursome names Being in its worldly aspect. It is the thinker's task to render possible some apprehension of both these faces of Being. Martin Heidegger, *Discourse on Thinking*, tr. John Anderson and E. Hans Freund (New York: Harper and Row, 1966).

[12] Martin Heidegger, 'The Origin of the Work of Art,' tr. Albert Hofstadter, *Philosophies of Art and Beauty* (New York: Modern Library, 1964). Hereafter OWA.

the special function of poetry within the arts. We will examine these two matters first because they provide a necessary context for his discussion of a Greek temple and a van Gogh painting. To begin, "*All art,* as the letting-happen of the advent of the truth of beings, is, as such, *essentially poetry (Dichtung)*." [13] In this context Heidegger uses the word "poetry' as a synonym for art in order to express the fundamental importance of this linguistic art within the whole of the arts. The medium of poetry is language, and it is for this reason that poetry is the privileged art. As Heidegger says, "Language brings what is as something that *is* into the Open for the first time. Where there is no language, as in the Being of stone, plant, and animal, there is also no openness of what is ..." [14] We learn immediately, though, that Heidegger is using the word 'language' in a special way: 'language' is "projective speech"—a lighting-up of what is. [15] 'Language' as Heidegger uses the term here means any opening up of a realm of Being. Such an opening might, for example, be accomplished in a painting or a piece of sculpture. In this sense, then, the opening by a painting would be established within the language of graphic discovery.

Within what we call ordinary language, there resides the possibility of that privileged opening which is language in the fundamental projective sense. Since in Heidegger's analysis 'poetry' is a synonym for 'art' or 'projective speech', what we ordinarily mean by poetry Heidegger indicates with the term poesy (*poesie*). Poesy is, then, the art which establishes a world by making ordinary language extra-ordinary. Because it is the fullest expression of the day to day language wherein Being is mani-

fest for the first time in the life of a people, poesy occupies a privileged position within the arts. It is in poesy that a people first fully discover the truth about themselves.

Such discovery is the essence of a work of art which "thrusts up the extraordinary and at the same time thrusts down the ordinary ..." [16] Thus the work of art accomplishes the difficult shift from the everyday mode of existence to the extra-ordinary mode in which it is possible to take the world itself as a datum of thought. With this shift man as creator (or as participant) in the arts takes over the play of beings against their non-Being; and this play is what Heidegger means by truth (i.e., *alethia*). Unlike the ordinary beings with which we are for the most part pre-occupied and which tend in the course of their daily use to hide their thingly character, the work of art is a being which always forces its thingliness upon us. It is in this overt thinglines that its privileged position among beings consists.

To make this privileged position clearer we refer to the way Heidegger describes tools in *Being and Time*. Tools as beings which are ready-to-hand fail to disclose the world itself precisely because, as tools, they disappear into the activity for which they are designed. It is only when a tool breaks or, for one reason or another, is not immediately ready-to-hand, that it points us toward its world. But this is the extraordinary situation for tools. The situation is just the opposite for works of art, for it is the ordinary nature of such beings to serve as signs of their world—as *things*. When works of art fail in this dislocative, unsettling function then we say that they fail as works of art. The ordinary situation for art is then itself extra-ordinary. Thus, it is Heidegger's view that the work of art confronts man

---

[13] OWA, p. 693.
[14] OWA, p. 694.
[15] OWA, p. 695.
[16] OWA, p. 696.

with the conditionality of his Being and provides the foundation for existential truth, that is for the owned encounter of man with himself as Da-Sein.

The question that Heidegger asks himself, in his analysis of Van Gogh's painting of a peasant's shoes is, "How does the painting present the worldly character of the shoes, and thus the world of the wearer of the shoes?" [17] In the first place the shoes which appear in the painting first come to be what they are when they are worn by the peasant in walking through the fields. The less obtrusive the shoes are, the more they fulfill their role of binding together the peasant's world. The lack of obtrusiveness of the shoes stems from their reliability (*Verlasslichkeit*), and it is this which guarantees them their essential equipmental, world-binding character. The painting however by displacing the shoes from the fields to the aesthetic space of the painter's canvas insures that their equipmentality is destroyed. With this destruction the character of the shoes as a signifying bond comes to the force in much the same way that it would if the peasant simply mis-placed the shoes. The painting then is a deliberate, dis-placing enshrinement of the thingly, world evoking character of the shoes.

Now whereas a painting may name the gods of a world, it is in their temples that a people discovers most explicitly that which is sacred to them. A temple gathers the space around it, and by sanctifying that space as a place of worship, is itself a prayer calling for the presence of the god. Thus the environing temple is a projective language which lays the foundation for the dwelling of the god. The presence of the god in the temple is what delimits the space of the temple as a holy place. But what is this temple itself other than a bond between heaven and earth? It is made out of the stone of the earth and stands on the earth at the same time that it reaches out to the heavens as a summons to the god. Between the dark earth and the light of the heaven the temple manifests a world through the presence of the god in the temple. "The temple, in its standing-there, first gives to things their look and to men their outlook on themselves." [18] Like linguistic works in the plastic arts, the temple functions as a work of art which "transforms the people's speech" and gathers them together into a world.

In Heidegger's analysis of the Greek temple the worldly character of a work of art becomes perfectly explicit: a work of art is a thing which evokes the sense of a world. Thus it is clear that if we remove a work of art from its world and place it, for example, in a museum, we thereby destroy it as a work. A painting or a sculpture in a museum becomes an object that can be analyzed into its form and content by aestheticians and critics and viewed on Sunday afternoons by tourists. In the same way many of the churches of Europe are no longer houses of the Christian god, but are now museums containing the antiquities which represent another world. Thus when we take such works as the Elgin marbles and place them in the neutral space of a museum we desanctify them, destroy their role as worldly things, and thus destroy them as works of art. Part of the task of the thinker is to protect the work of art from such destruction.

III. The Adventure of Poetry

By poetry Heidegger means what Plato meant by "poetry in the true sense of the word—that is to say, calling something into existence that was not there before ..." [19] As we have already

---

[17] OWA, p. 662.
[18] OWA, p. 670.
[19] *Symposium*, 205b.

seen, the poet issues this call into existence by naming the gods of a people. According to Heidegger, the main problem of the modern epoch—dominated as it is by technology—is that no god has been made manifest and consequently there is no consecrated assembling of world. The modern epoch lacks gods as measures, and it is the task of the poet in this "needy time" to respect in his work the traces of the absent gods.[20] Because modern man is in need of the poet, the poet's role becomes a crucial one. Modern man in this view of things wanders the earth as technician and has forgotten the thingly, worldly character of his beings. The poet must sing to such a man, and thus show him the way back into his owned dwelling as a mortal creature who lives beneath the heavens and on the earth.

To dramatize this need for the poet, Heidegger tells us that man's being-in-the-world is essentially poetic: "man dwells poetically on the earth."[21] By this Heidegger means that the owned being-in-the-world which we have been seeking to elucidate is itself a poetic mode of being-in-the-world. Being toward Being and poetically dwelling on the earth are the same thing in the sense that it is the poet, as the namer of the gods, who is the Da of Sein in the most illuminating way. Let us, however, be clear about what is meant here. Heidegger does not intend to say that it is only the writer of verse who is authentically Da-Sein. On the contrary, he means to say that the man who dwells in the fullest openness to Being is himself a poetic namer of the gods. Yet the man who dwells on the earth as the maker of poetry (i.e., poesy) fulfills this most open of dwellings in a crucial way

because he is the caretaker of language.[22] We can clarify all this by examining the two essays "Remembrance of the Poet" and "Holderlin and the Essence of Poetry."

The essay "Remembrance of the Poet" deals with Holderlin's poem "Homecoming"[23] and its primary contribution is the idea that the poet is he who is *always* in the process of coming home. Through his homecoming the poet gets near the source of his world by naming the gods of that world.[24] But for whom is homecoming a possibility? Surely not for those who do not leave the home, those who remain in the protective environment of the everyday world and are never thrust up against the conditionality of that world. Homecoming is a possibility only for the wanderer. The poet is the wanderer who like Odysseus tempts his fate; he is Odysseus coming home.

As the pre-eminent wanderer the poet is also a minstrel through whose song the people of his world really come together as a people for the first time. The poet then wanders for all of us and his homecoming is the full appropriation of what it means to be at home; it is the living of an owned existence. We have seen all this before, though the expression of the poetic task in terms of a wanderer's return home adds something new to our understanding of poetry: the poet, like all wanderers, runs the danger of losing his home. Like geographical adventures, the poet in his voyage of discovery risks himself in risking the loss of his world. Heidegger provides no suggestions as to why there are such adventures. His interest lies in showing that it is only because there are such poet adventurers that any of us can

---

[20] Martin Heidegger, *Holzwege* (Frankfurt: Klostermann, 1957), p. 251.
[21] VA, p. 192.
[22] Martin Heidegger, 'What is Metaphysics?', *Existence and Being*, ed. Werner Brock, tr. R. F. C. Hull and Allan Crick (Chicago: Henry Regnery, 1949), p. 360.
[23] 'Remembrance of the Poet,' tr. Douglas Scott, *Existence and Being*, ed. W. Brock (Chicago: Henry Regnery, 1949). Hereafter RP.
[24] RP, pp. 258, 233.

understand what it means to be at home in a world. Thus, unlike Thomas Wolfe who writes, "You Can't Go Home Again," Heidegger believes not only that we can go home again but that we must if we are to rediscover our selves. The trip toward the home is, indeed, the original *telos* of all human activity; it is the primal search for the point of origin. And it is a trip we are all always on; a trip which, if completed, takes us back into the source of our Being.

In "Holderlin and the Essence of Poetry" Heidegger shows us something more of the poet's risks.[25] The essay is based on five suggestions that Holderlin gives on the nature of poetry, but because these suggestions cover points we have already examined, I shall refer to the essay only in order to make clear the dangers of the adventure of poetry. Poetry, Heidegger says, is a matter of play; but its field of play is language, our "most dangerous of possessions."[26] In creating the open place where beings become manifest to man, language at the same time founds the possibility of man's forgetfulness of Being.[27] In *Being and Time* Heidegger discusses this mutual promise and threat in terms of language as mere prattle (*gerede*) and language which names and founds (*rede*). Thus the poet as the caretaker of projective language must play with our foremost possibility in such a way that in his very play, his creation—the poem—does not hide its thingly character from us. The danger of the poet is that he may become the artful technician of language and thus lose the innocence so essential to genuine play. The artfulness in which the poet loses his innocence at the same time destroys that silence which makes it possible to hear the message of the god. With the loss of innocence the poet's language no longer attempts to evoke the god, but at best only to represent him.

There is however another danger for the poet in his naming of the god, for he works under a two-fold responsibility: he must be silent before the gods, yet he must *speak* intelligibly to his fellow mortals about that which he learns in this silence. In a very real sense the poet is then the man between —neither at home nor not at home. We learn then of a third danger. In standing silent before the gods the poet presumes to be able to endure what the gods have to tell him. This risk of the poet in waiting for the sign of the gods is really the risk of madness. Heidegger suggests this risk most dramatically in quoting Holderlin's "King Oedipus has one/Eye too many perhaps." It might be better for the poet if, unlike Oedipus, he were really blind and could not see so much; but surely such blindness would not be better for those of us who await the poet's return.

IV. Summary

What then may be said of those of us who wait for the poet in our needy time? In the first place it is quite clear that Heidegger's description of the modern world is accurate. We have grown so busy and so noisy in our technological production that we no longer have either the time or the quiet to attend to the play of the poet. Yet if we are to listen for the poet's message, it is also clear that we must listen as the men we are within the situation into which we are thrown. We cannot look for our own complex world by trying to find some other simpler one. Thus it seems that it is only within the technological world itself that *our* poet can speak to us modern men—we are, after all, all

---

[25] Martin Heidegger, 'Holderlin and the Essence of Poetry,' tr. Douglas Scott, *Existence and Being*, ed. W. Brock (Chicago: Henry Regnery, 1949). Hereafter HEP.
[26] HEP, p. 273.
[27] HEP, p. 276.

technicians.[28] It is therefore *here* and *now* that the poet must discover the thing which will re-establish the community of men.

If all of what I have said is accurate then it follows that Heidegger's own attempts to be the poet of his Heimat in *Der Feldweg* or the poet of the philosophical world in *Aus der Erfahrung des Denkens* are necessarily incomplete. For the gods we await in our need are not the gods of peasants, fields and farms. To yearn for the arrival of such gods is simply *nostalgie de la boue*. Thus in his poetic attempts to evoke the world of his Baden childhood, Heidegger functions as a poet qua archaeologist: He takes the poem of another world and displaces it to our own. In this archaeological displacement, the poet of the modern technē can of course discover in the rural world the archē of silence: but then in order to be himself he must return to the polis of technology and discover there the sort of quiet appropriate to his own world.

From Heidegger's own work we get then only the most general clues as to what may distinguish the poet for whom we modern men are waiting. We know from his discussion of the Van Gogh painting and the Greek temple that the *thing* which fixes and illuminates a world may be either the most profane—a peasant's shoes clogged with the dirt of the fields—or the most sacred—the dwelling of the god himself. Yet we live, do we not, in a dark time with only an obscure glimpse of our own world. Thus there is no sacred dwelling toward which we can turn, expectantly awaiting the poet's message. It is no accident, I think, that Heidegger can discern a god only in a *Greek* temple. Thus it is necessary for us to expect a first intelligible message from a poet who rediscovers the sacred in the profane.

The wanderer's search for the visage of a god can after all be successful only if he has first seen the traces of that god in the things of his world. Otherwise the incredibility of a demon may seem the illumination of a god.

Yet despite its very general and only suggestive character Heidegger's analysis does indicate what we must demand of the poet. He must re-establish the things of our world in their own time and in their own place. He must teach us that we have a history and that our possibilities are real only when they are projects from our past—a past which does not itself exhaust our possibilities of Being. When we, as thinkers, insist on this demand, then we responsibly play our own roles in the poet's homecoming by requiring that the poet give nothing less than what we need, nothing less than what he can give: a clear view of our world, and of ourselves.

Thus, this paper shows how we can take up for ourselves the problematic and poetic task of enlightening the human realm by fulfilling the Socratic dictum to "Know Thy Self!" An essential part of such knowledge is, according to Heidegger, to be found outside the domain of philosophy in an inquiry which must ever be permeated with the phenomenological attitude of letting things speak for themselves. Such an inquiry pursued rigorously and consistently leads to the question of the transcendental ground of human being. At the point where this question is asked, the phenomenological inquirer can affirm his commitment to his method only if he is willing to face the nothing which is the ground of his being. Thus with this question the inquirer discovers his point of origin and, if he speaks at all, finds he can say only "nothing."

---

[28] VA, p. 13. For a clarification of this point, see my articles 'Heidegger's Critique of Science' (*Personalist* vol. 51, Autumn. 1969), 'Heidegger: Technology as Phenomenon' (*Personalist*, vol. 51, Autmun, 1970).

Heidegger's originality consists in directing us back to this point of origin. Along the way toward that point we leave the busy talk of philosophy and the sciences, pass through the quiet and worldly domain of art, and come to rest in a silent and contemplative experience of the nothing which lies at the heart of human existence. It is then that we reach home and can begin to be what we have been all along: rational animals who are also mortal.[29]

---

[29] VA, p. 177.

TWO HEIDEGGERIAN ANALYSES

F. J. Smith

Kent State University

The philosophical world would be a sorry one without its "international vocabulary," which is heavily dependent upon Greek and Latin loan words. Some of these words have a very long history. Boethius put such words as form, nature, substance, etc., into the history of philosophy.[1] Other words like idea, physics, metaphysics, etc., came directly from the Greek. Husserl's *eîdos* is the restitution of the primary form of the word, idea. And of course, "synthesis" and "analysis" are also loan words direct from the Greek. The word, analysis, conjures up the vision of the studious chemist, the music theorist, the news commentator, and even the philosopher. But in philosophy there can be any number of approaches to analysis. It is obvious that a "Heideggerian analysis" presupposes the principle points of departure of Martin Heidegger. It is not our present purpose to enter into a dialogue with philosophical analysts of the Oxford school.[1a] A Heideggerian analysis includes more than an examination of ordinary language in the sense understood by philosophical analysis, as a contemporary school of thought. However, though Heidegger leads from the ontic to the ontological level, understood in the sense of SZ, the analysis of sentences can also be of import here. But since Heidegger writes and thinks in German, we have to undertake an analysis also of the translation process. For translations may often stand in the way of an understanding of the original text. For this reason we shall examine two statements. The one is from SZ, "Being-there is in truth and untruth"; the second is a Pre-Socratic fragment, "Man's character is his destiny." The first statement is on the surface a good example of a typical "nonsensical" Heideggerian pronouncement; the second sounds like an adage written by some fine English stylist. They are both translations. The first statement is a translation of "Dasein ist in Wahrheit und Unwahrheit"[2]; the second is a rendition of Heraclitus' fragment, ἦθος ἀνθρώπω δαίμων.[3] We shall attempt to analyze

F. Joseph Smith received the Ph.D. in music and philosophy from the University of Freiberg in 1960. He is professor of philosophy and musicology in the College of Fine Arts at Kent State University, Kent, Ohio. He has written for The Journal of Value Inquiry, Revue de métaphysique et de morale, *and other journals. Contributing to several books and authoring a three-volume commentary on the* Speculum Musicae, *he has edited* Phenomenology in Perspective *(Martinus Nijhoff) and is co-editor of* Heidegger and the Quest for Truth *(Quadrangle, 1968).*

[1] Grabmann, M.: *Die Geschichte der scholastischen Methode* (Berlin, 1957), I, p. 157. Cf. 1a (b. 17).

[1a] It is the present writer's pleasure to be in the midst of a thorough study of H. Khatchadourian's *A Critical Study in Method* (Nijhoff, 1967), to be reviewed for JVI. At the conclusion of this fine work (p. 248) Dr. Khatchadourian leads the philosopher beyond the analytical framework to experiential phenomena and to "the thick of actual life and action." For a Heideggerian this sounds like attempting to get beyond the ontic dimension.

[2] Heidegger, M.: *Sein und Zeit* (Tübingen, 1960⁹) p. 222. The statement in this essay is a composite from the following passage: "Der volle existenzial-ontologische Sinn des Satzes: 'Dasein ist in der Wahrheit' sagt gleichursprünglich mit: 'Dasein ist in der Unwahrheit'." It is obvious that our present analysis is not an exegesis of Heidegger and goes beyond his intent at this point.

[3] Kirk, G. S., and J. E. Raven: *The Presocratic Philosophers* (Cambridge, 1960 p. 213, no. 250. "Man's character is his daimon"; p. 214, "δαίμων here means simply a man's personal destiny; this is determined by his own character . . ." It is obvious that the authors had some difficulty translating the simple (?) word, δαίμων.

both statements as we try to translate them. We shall then see what relationship there exists, philosophically, between these pronouncements of two "obscure" philosophers. In all this we shall bear in mind the background of both SZ and the recent ZS.[4]

1. "Being-there is in truth and untruth."

What is the meaning of this phrase taken from Heidegger's SZ? Let us conduct an "analysis" of this single statement from Heidegger's masterwork. This is not a linguistic analysis in the ordinary sense. Rather it is more along lines indicated by philosophers who see phenomenological possibilities in ordinary language.[5] Ordinary language is definable as that mode of speaking which is not distorted by formal philosophisms; it is the language of the ordinary person. Yet, for all its ordinariness, common idiom may hide some rather uncommon truths (often called "folk wisdom," which may at times exceed the wisdom of the formal philosopher in his frantic pursuit of "truth"). "Ordinary" language often originates some perplexing problems, even with regard to the nature of language itself. What does the word, ordinary, mean? Webster defines it as what is customary, the usual, the normal. Does this mean that what is not immediately customary is unusual or abnormal? The ordinary dictionary meaning of the word, music, is "the science or art of pleasing, expressive, or intelligible combinations of tones." This definition would eliminate a good deal of twentieth century music, which is neither pleasant, expressive, nor "intelligible." Such music thus becomes extraordinary in the sense of unusual or abnormal.[6] The dictionary definition of words leaves much to be desired, to say the least.

"Ordinary" means what is arranged in orderly fashion, if we take philologists at their word. Yet it is not enough merely to arrange things in orderly fashion. Grammarians often become too absorbed in arranging, re-arranging, and analyzing words, paradigms, roots, phrases, and sentences. The word, ordinary, does not have to mean merely being arranged in neat and tidy order, with the result that "ordinary" can even be synonymous with the commonplace, the usual, the taken-for-granted, i.e., what is so well ordered that one can dispense with thought and originality. Most of all it does not have to mean being arranged in mere logical (or theo-logical) order, since such ordering hits but one facet of the ontological order — and certainly not the most important one at that. The ordering of such words as ordinary and origin implies not mentalistic order but an "existential" originating. In this sense common language can have a good bit of uncommon meaning, inasmuch as it is frequently in more fundamental contact with life, with life-world, and with the "existentiality of Being." For language expresses in gesture and in speech who man *is* and what he is doing, i.e., how he comports himself *as* a doer. "What he is doing" means primarily what he *is* as doer of deeds rather than that it merely indicates an activity.

---

[4] Heidegger, M.: "Zeit und Sein" in *J'endurance de la pensée* (Paris, 1968 with transl. by Fédier, pp. 12–71. Cf. the present author's comments on ZS in "Being and Subjectivity: Heidegger and Husserl," in *Phenomenology in Perspective* (The Hague, 1970), p. 141f.

[5] Wild, J.: "Is there a World of common ordinary language?" in *The Philosophical Review*, 1958; cf. also D. Ihde, "Some Parallels between Analysis and Phenomenology," in *Philosophy and Phenomenological Research,* June 1967; G. Küng, "Language Analysis and Phenomenological Analysis," in *Akten des XIV. Internationalen Kongresses für Philosophie*, II (Wien, 1968) pp. 247–253.

[6] The present author has the good fortune to have as chairman the scholar who wrote the definitions of music for the unabridged Webster's dictionary. The definition used here is from the new collegiate dictionary, the one ordinary speakers more frequently consult. Dr. Merrill is in substantial agreement with the present author's restlessness about too much reliance on dictionaries for definitions and too little on the actual musical experience.

Being lies at the basis of language beyond mere communication.[7]

Heidegger writes, "Dasein ist in Wahrheit und Unwahrheit." And we translate this "Being-there is in truth and untruth." But can we really achieve an understanding of this extraordinary and unusual statement by such a literal translation? Is this not quite nonsensical? Perhaps and perhaps not. The trained philosopher will be able to grasp the difference between truth and *Wahrheit;* but most people would call the translation a good one, an ordinary one, since ordinarily *Wahrheit* does mean "truth." Hence being-there (*Dasein*) is in truth or is true. But, to repeat the classic question, what is "truth?" Does this mean veracity, the verity of an object, or the truth of a proposition? Truth is quite ambiguous. In addition to this, does *Wahr-heit* mean exactly what "truth" means in English? The word, *wahr,* and the word, true, come from different linguistic families. To translate the one by the other without further ado is to ignore the history of these words, i.e., to pretend they have no individual past at all, as we force them into an artificial present where they are coerced into meaning exactly the same thing. This, of course, is part of the story of philosophy's "international vocabulary": coercion and the ignoring of history as such. Actually, the word, *wahr,* is much closer to our word *ver-*ity, from the Latin *ver-*um. But this root has a much wider meaning than propositional truth. English is a complex language with many loan words. While it is true that it gives loan words its own historic meanings, a good bit of the central and sometimes of the peripheral meaning of the original words still perdures. And thus the word, verity, still carries Latin meaning, i.e., it witnesses to the history of historic meaning. Not so the word, truth, which comes from an Anglo-Saxon stem, *treowth.* In translating *wahr* as

"true" we ignore sources completely and settle for an artificial and homogenized vocabulary. Granting momentarily that this procedure is a valid one, though it hardly touches on the issues it raises, let us see what happens if we try to get at an English word which is closer to the Saxon stem. The closest we can get is the word, aware, which comes from the Anglo-Saxon, *waer.* To be aware means to be cognizant, conscious, wary, etc. Suppose we substitute this word for "truth," just for the sake of seeing what happens, independently of what grammarians or logicians we mortally offend by so doing. Thus we have the statement, "Being-there is in awareness and unawareness." For one thing we have gotten rid of one more truism, as it were, by eliminating the word, truth. But what extraordinary and uncommon thing have we done instead? We have made bold to do the unpardonable thing; we have introduced the word, awareness, as a translation of *Wahrheit.* It is obvious that knowers of truth need no awareness of reality, since they belong to a truth system which automatically explains all things in categorical and logical terms. Hence this word, awareness, is unpardonable and unphilosophical. Theologically, of course, it is simple heresy. How can *Wahr-heit* be a-*ware*-ness? The answer is that it may be already. Our word, aware, connotes the same experience described in the German phrase, "etwas wahr-nehmen." When we become aware of something, we do not immediately interpret it in terms of some truth system: we simply become aware, conscious, and perhaps also wary of something that has presented itself to us in perception. Perhaps the latter word is the key. Awareness is a question of perception; truth is a historic question of cognition. The ancient metaphysical dualism of mind and body comes through in this distinction. But becoming aware does not mean becoming conscious only in the

---

[7] Kockelmans, J. J.: "Language, Being, and Ek-sistence," in *Phenomenology in Perspective* (The Hague, 1969), p. 94f.

sense of a historic dualism, especially when the latter is much more a question of indoctrination than of experience. We learned that we were made of mind and body; we did not necessarily experience it. Thus even perception need not be restricted only to sense perception as over against intellectual cognition. Phenomenologically, perception is prior to both. To become aware does not entail merely the psychological act of a thinking or sensing subject. It can be interpreted in terms of phenomenological consciousness and perhaps even in terms of an existential encounter with being, as it presents itself to us, as it "gives" of itself.

If this be true, then "Being-there is consciousness and unconsciousness (of Being)." One can become aware or conscious of Being even to the point of dread and anxiety! It is apparent that this is all considerably broader in scope than preoccupation with truth propositions, however important and fascinating that can be. *Dasein* is thus "aware of Being": its own Being, all of which it would like to become, in the sense that one would like to be able to actuate all one's potential. Yet man is finite, and one can never become all the possibilities one is aware of. One of the reasons for this is that most people are too wary of their truer potential. They would rather settle for less — for a truth system? Man, as one who "is there" (*Dasein*), is one who-is-aware or conscious of his potential to be. He owes it to himself to become his authentic self and to unfold his potential, to stand-out (eksist) in the sense that he raises himself from the level of the automaton who only does what "one does," thinks what "one thinks," or says what "one says." Thus as one who "is there," man is aware of the potential and the invitation of Being and at the same time he becomes aware of what Heidegger has called "the One" (*das Man*). As man becomes increasingly aware of his true potential he becomes increasingly dis-

affected from the One, which dictates what one is to think, say, do, and be. The One freezes man in a state of unawareness or forgetfulness of Being, as it forces him to use language only as "one speaks." The One is the great Lexicographer, the great Giver of Words, who in order to maintain control over mankind, enforces the use of words in accord with meanings and patterns that will guarantee his own vested interests. Thus the maker of dictionaries runs to the theologian to get his definition of God, to the scientist to get his definition of science, to the logician to get his definition of truth. And so vested interest rules through the anonymity of the One. And man is asked to repress his natural potentialities in favor of some truth system which seeks to perpetuate itself rather than truly ask "What is truth?"

Thus far we can say that "Being-there means becoming aware of one's own Being." Or one remains unaware in submission to the One. What about *Unwahrheit?* In un-truth, which we are now going to translate as "unawareness," man is unaware of his potential, of the possibility of his becoming, thinking, doing, being something else than he already is. He is entirely absorbed in the world of the One, its obedient servant, a firm believer in its truth. But to the extent that this connotes being entangled in the essentially irrelevant, even banal or trivial facets of existence, man is not in fact himself. To the extent that this entails being the servant of one's fears rather than of one's convictions it is a dangerous unawareness. "Being-there is in the state of awareness and unawareness." So far with our translation! Even when *Dasein* is aware of its potential to be, it is nevertheless in danger of doing nothing, or rationalizing everything, of interpreting things only in terms of a safe truth system, or even of falling back into a state of unawareness — be it now with a "guilty conscience." Hence one must be wary in another sense. One must beware.

The English sentence is still by no means satisfactory. What is *Dasein?* The German means "There-being," which is perfectly nonsensical in English. "Being-there" is better English. We even have English idioms that make use of these words. We say someone "is not quite all there," meaning he is not quite fully in possession of his faculties, i.e., he may not be fully conscious. When some one "is there" it means he "comes alive." It need not mean he is merely located in some particular place. (The literalist might be tempted to answer the question, "Are you all there today?" with the plaintive query "Where?".) "There" (*Da–*) does not mean only a physical place: rather it can mean the scene of our being-there in awareness of Being. It is the drama of existential encounter with "all that is," as it tries to give of itself to us. It is confrontation with the world within us, the "inner self" that our ontic ego has suppressed. It is an encounter with eros. But this going within oneself, to recoup one's genuine self and liberate it from the servitude of the One, is not a Wundtian introspection, which isolates from the world and focuses on an ego that is more like a vanishing point than a substance. Introspection looks within and finds nothing; it banishes world. It ends up with solipsistic ego. But to "be there" means to be outgoing even as one goes inward. Unless we go within to meditate alone, we cannot find our world, and thus even when we are with others we remain "worldless." And yet we do not go within like the classic misguided ascetic who cuts himself off from reality and becomes the pawn of a theo-logical truth system. We go within to discover and awaken our truer self. And this discovery is a dis-closure, i.e., a kind of liberating from closure, a kind of unlocking process in which the self emerges from the cloister of ego. But

to unlock ourselves, to unbind Prometheus, we must decide and resolve to do so. Implicit in this "resolve" is the dissolution of ego as the inauthentic expression of the self. But the condition for all of this is a basic awareness, in which we are "all there." In going within we "take a stand"; but taking a stand makes one "stand out" in more senses than one. Yet only he who can take a stand with regard to his authentic being can stand with the other in friendship or love, and at the same time withstand the other, lest he in turn take over the authentic self. This postulates a mutual wariness, a mutual awareness. It entails being true to one another, whatever truth system one had belonged to. Awareness of one's truer self and of the other is suppressed in the classic truth systems we have known, whether religious, political, or philosophical.

This may all be well and good, but we are still not satisfied with regard especially to the phrase "being there." Everyone knows that being is an empty word, since the One gives everyone to know this. The Being of being-there (*Da-sein*) is a mere link-word and an empty concept. It took Martin Heidegger and Johannes Lohmann (who has written a monograph on the origin of music, dedicated to Heidegger[8]) to begin to recover the original richness and concreteness of the word, being.[9] Being could once more become the richest word we have, unless we are to accept the hollowing out of historic words as an irreversible event in language. The roots of the various words that go to make up the verb, to be, are quite fascinating. While we could never merely restore an archaic meaning, there is nothing wrong about examining a historic model and learning from it. In Indo-European to *be* meant to live, to grow, to dwell. (The Anglo-Saxon *eardan* meant to dwell, i.e., to

[8] Lohmann, J.: "Der Ursprung der Musik," in *Archiv für Musikwissenschaft,* (Trossingen, 1959) 1/2; 3, pp. 261–291, "M. Heidegger zum 70, Geburtstag gewidmet (26, IX, 1959).
[9] Cf. M. Heidegger, *Einführung in die Metaphysik* (Tübingen, 1953), cf. esp. ch. II, pp. 40–56, "Zur Grammatik und Etymologie des Wortes 'sein'."

live on-the-*earth*.) The root *es* (to live) gives us the form "is." The stem, *bhû,* means to grow, to flourish, to come forth; and from this comes our form, to "be." "I have been" meant I came forth, I grew in such and such a manner, I flourished. From the same stem came the Greek, φύσις, which with the help of Boethius we translated as "nature." The third root, *ves,* means to abide or dwell, and from it comes our form, "was." History has taken these three originally "unrelated" meanings and blended them into one verb system. Being (*bhû*), as representative of all the stems, thus means to live, dwell, abide, come forth, grow, and flourish. There is a richness of meaning here that belies any logical attempt to level everything out. The modern meaning of being, as an empty concept or as a mere auxiliary verb, is a degeneration that may well reflect the decline of language and culture as such. One sees everywhere the tragic effects of this historic leveling out process, this inflation and devaluation of words. But it is nowhere more evident than in the word, to be. Language has grown pale and colorless; and thus meaninglessness and "nonsense" is indeed a problem for contemporary philosophy, but not in the way it understands it. Certain strains of contemporary philosophy would simply accept the devaluation of language symbols, thereby joining the forces that have brought about the degeneration of language. At least this is a way of looking at the situation. Much can be said against Heideggerian methods, but at least he does not simply settle for "what is." There seems to be a vacuum at the center of "what is" in modern life and language. We have not yet succeeded in coming out of the metaphysical period of civilization. Metaphysics, which took away concrete meanings and substituted abstract and hollow ones for them (*cf.* even the early Carnap!), is still with us in many a covert and even overt form.

"Being-there means to be in a situation of awareness and unawareness." This must be our "final" translation of Heidegger's statement. The German sentence is, of course, a legacy from Hegel and is further elaborated on by Heidegger himself in later works, such as *Der Ursprung des Kunstwerkes.* In this essay I do not pretend to give a scientific exegesis of Heidegger himself, but merely to engage in the "free play of imagination," if I may be allowed to borrow a phrase from Kant. Hence nothing is claimed for what results, but then philosophy is in a poor condition to claim much of anything these days. Our present translation is not such as to arouse the admiration of an exact lexicographer, but it may strike closer to the heart of the matter, in that it gets at certain latent possibilities in language. It has the advantage of lifting the statement out of the perils of becoming merely a logical proposition. It has no logical meaning at all. There is little here to satisfy the objectivist or the scientific thinker. To be-there as aware or unaware seems to mean that man, as one who "is there," has or has not found his place, his abode, his inner dwelling in the world and on the earth. He has been enabled to find himself because he has become aware of his potential, and he resists the impositions of all those forces which would keep him unaware of the possibilities latent within himself and within language as such. For man is the shepherd of the word. Man is not the "rational animal" of the classic tradition but rather the living being ξῶον who is himself a fleshly "word" (λόγος). As λόγος man experiences his own ingathering (λεγειν) and he gathers others into his embrace. It is from this basic experience that language is born. All "logic" comes not only historically but also experientially from the primordial λόγος that man himself is, as one who "is there" in awareness of his truer self and that of the other. And thus "man is in truth and untruth," a puzzle and a paradox to himself and others. This is his basic ethos or character: to fathom his own destiny in the awareness of his full potential, even though he realizes his finitude.

2. *"Man's character is his destiny."*

Heraclitus, the Puzzler ('ο αἰνίκτης), has left us a fragment, "The ethos of man is a daemon." This has been translated into better English as, "Man's character is his destiny." [10] Yet, however beautiful the English reads, to translate ἦθος as "character," especially as "moral" character, does not necessarily render the original properly. (A similar anomaly is translating *lógos* as "reason.") The word, character, is far too moralistic and psychological a term to render the quite unmoralistic Greek word ηθος. It is also dubious to state that δαιμων is "simply a man's personal destiny . . . determined by his own character." [11] We cannot translate Pre-Socratic fragments using nineteenth and twentieth century concepts. We are entitled to our own concepts; but we are not to read them into the words of another era, when its whole literature speaks to the contrary. Instead of trying to translate this at all, let us simply ponder the meaning of the "demonic" in man and then return to Heraclitus with hopes of giving a more adequate interpretation of the fragment.

Heraclitus is said to have written a book, entitled Περὶ Φύσεως, which he placed in the temple of Artemis. He was not a philosopher of "nature" nor a "physicist" but someone who thought and wrote about φύσις, which is closer to growth and "being" than to metaphysical "nature." (Actually to *be* and φύ-ω may both derive from the same root, *bhû.*) Heraclitus' book was divided into three parts: 1) on everything (!), 2) on "politics," and 3) on "theology." But it would be rash for us to expect three systematically arranged chapters in a book that we interpret as giving the complete thought of the thinker. A true philosopher's thought is never complete and very often is far from systematic. How can the reality of Being be encountered systematically, i.e., with the patterns of traditional and scientific intellectual categories? Such categories seek to impose themselves on reality, but Being gives itself only to the truly receptive spirits who can disengage their prejudices. Whatever the case, Heraclitus apparently wrote a book; but he hid it in the temple of Artemis, to keep it from those who "are glutted like cattle on straw." [12] The Dark One ('ο σκοτεινός) would take a dim view of contemporary efforts to popularize philosophy. He was a misanthrope, a kind of religious prophet; he was no intellectualist. Fragment two from Diogenes Laertius tells us he wrote his book in a rather unclear and obscure manner, in order that it would not be accessible to one and all but would be read only by the serious few, a remnant that was able to grasp and appreciate its message. [13] But this does not mean the book was "esoteric." Rather it was meant for those who were serious of purpose and intent. Heraclitus did not want "truth" to be easily grasped by the multitude, which turns with equal indifference to this or that. In an allied sense, this may be true also of Heidegger's writings, which require more than the ordinary seriousness and concentration. But this is an offence against the public mind which pretends to philosophy. Nietzsche wrote that the philosopher was and should remain a rare species; Kierkegaard decried "storekeeper philosophy." In all this we walk a dangerous path with snobbery on one side and banality on the

[10] Cf. footnote 3. This translation is taken from Kirk and Raven by substituting "destiny" for "daimon" as explained.

[11] *ibid.,* p. 214.

[12] Kirk, G. S., and J. E. Raven, *op. cit.,* p. 213; "οἱ δὲ πολλοὶ κεκόρηνται ὅκωσπερ κτήνεα·"

[13] *ibid.,* p. 184.

other. In Heraclitus the demarcation is quite clear.

The book Heraclitus is said to have written must not be conceived according to modern standards. There was no market and no demand, since there was no market-place mentality among thinkers. Heraclitus wept when he came into the market-place, Seneca tells us. Democritus laughed. Perhaps they were both doing essentially the same thing. Heraclitus' "book" was probably simply a random collection of unrelated sayings proffered in oracular or prophetic manner. Thus they are "fragmentary." And they are quoted and paraphrased by such writers as Diogenes Laertius, Plutarch, Themistius, Hippolytus, etc. He was not so much a Presocratic philosopher or "scientist" as a religious prophet. As such, loving but few words, he probably came out with short enigmatic statements rather than in involved chapters and the prolix prose common in our era. He was called the Enigmatic One (ὁ αἰνίκτης), and he lived up to his reputation for puzzles and paradoxes. In an age that seems to have a compulsive demand for clear and distinct truth concepts, Heraclitus and Heidegger are a distinct offense, i.e., in the original sense of the word, a stumbling block. For they make the merely curious, the dilettant, the merely professional philosopher stumble over their thinking. These philosophers force one to confront shallowness and superficiality; they carry the thinker to the edge of darkness and in a sense this is the "demonic" element in their thinking.

What is the "demonic"? Leaving Freudian connotations to psychologists, let us investigate the philosophical implications. Among modern writers it was Kierkegaard that gave us perhaps the most authentic description of the dimensions of the demonic in man, though we must be careful not to read even this existential interpretation into Heraclitus. In *The Concept of Dread,* to which Heidegger owed much, Kierkegaard treats of the demonic in man under the title, "Dread of the Good." [24] This, of course, is already a post-Christian interpretation of the demonic as implicated with the evil and the inauthentic in man. The word, δαίμων, means simply a "divinity," which can be either good or bad. It is the rough equivalent of the Latin *numen,* which is literally a "nod" (*nu-o*) from the gods in the sense of their approving presence. (This is the probable meaning of the *dii consentes* of which Heidegger writes in *Einführung in die Metaphysik,* where he derives *consentes* from the same stem as *Wesen.*) By virtue of their presence the gods are not only present and consenting but present and approving. The word, consent, means the presence of the numinal deities.

The δαίμονες are not θεοί but rather somewhat ambiguously intermediary divinities, perhaps even, as Hesiod put it, the shades of the departed who are the "guardians of men" by grace of Zeus. The numinal deity was a kind of world power to be confronted in personal manner. Primitive and pre-rational man addressed himself to this personal power in a kind of I-Thou relationship, a kind of communing or encounter. This attitude is not "animistic" but rather reminiscent of what the Greeks meant by "cosmozoic" world, i.e., a world in which everything was somehow alive. Thus Thales spoke of the world νοῦς, but hardly in the sense of a Hegelian *Weltvernunft.* All things were "full of gods" and everything had "soul life." This ensouled universe was full of δαίμονες, according to Aetius' account concerning Thales. [25] For Thales "soul" ψυχή

---

[24] Kierkegaard, S.: *The Concept of Dread,* trans. W. Lowrie (Princeton, 1957). Cf. p. 105 ff.
[25] Kirk, G. S., and J. E. Raven, *op. cit.,* pp. 95–96; "Θαλῆς νοῦν τοῦ κόσμου τὸν θεὸν, τὸ δὲ πᾶν ἔμψυχον ἅμα καὶ δαιμόνων πλῆρες." He goes on to say that this is a "divine power" (δύναμις θεία).

was conceived as the "movement" of φύσις, as the source of "all that is," and this under the mythological designation of water. (Water is thus not just H_2O!) He mentions that the "soul" is "kinetic." But this has little to do with physical motion and much to do with "movement" conceived along much broader terms. Everything has this life-movement (τὸ πᾶν ἔμψυχον). This is a truer translation than the usual one according to which the whole universe has a "mind." By virtue of this life-movement everything that exists is "full of daemons," i.e., of personal powers which move us. This is hardly a question of "animism"; rather it is "animal" power in the sense of *anima,* which is the Latin equivalent of ψυχή. It is not an "entirely unphilosophical animism" except to a British rationalist.[16] It is no more a case of animism than Martin Buber's I-Thou or Rilke's "person-thing." It is no more a question of animism than Francis of Assisi's "Brother Fire" and "Sister Water."

It was Christianity that in its battle with a superior pagan intellectual tradition fixated on the evil side of the δαίμονες. It is from this theological tradition that Kierkegaard's concept of the demonic stems. For him the demonic was dread of the Good, understood in the sense of Christian faith. The individual, as "sinful," is in dread of the good, in that he is in an unfree relation to it. The demonic man is in bondage, but even in the best of men there is a demonic dimension. More specifically, the demonic has to do with a basic closure (in Danish *indesluttedhet* as being "shut," as unfreely revealed). Whereas freedom is expensive, the demonic closes off and shuts in. It is a self-prisoner. The "daemon" is mute and does not speak to or commune with the other. Yet in the presence of the Good the "daemon" is forced to reveal itself; thus the mute demon calls out "What have I to do with you?" In

this confrontation of good and evil anxiety comes to the fore. But we must guard against reading psychological meanings into *angst.* Both Kierkegaard and Heidegger (*Angst*) reject phychological interpretations of dread or "anxiety." Kierkegaard writes of anxiety as a radical Christian theologian, Heidegger as a post-Christian ontologist, who has detheologized Kierkegaardian concepts.

Angst is badly translated as "anxiety." It is not just a question of psychological uneasiness or alarm, though that, too, can become a part of the spectrum of dread. Dread is first and foremost a kind of primordial awe or wonder, a sense of mystery and adventure, even of joy, i.e., the courage and confidence of one who faces his own ontological potential and the meaning of death. "Dread" is anxiety in the encounter with Kierkegaardian good. The demonic in this sense is like a Mephistofeles, appearing suddenly on the scene. The suddenness of dread is stressed by Kierkegaard. One is tempted to quote Boito's *Mefistofele,* where the demon says, "Io sono il No al mondo . . ." Demonic suddenness is brought out in Berlioz' *La damnation de Faust,* when the demon interrupts the chorus of angels. Amidst all the angelic reveries and dream choruses the demon comes suddenly onstage, announcing his displeasure and annoyance with the good. Despite the humor of the scene in Boito ("Questi angeletti mi spiacciono . . ."), the discontinuity and sudden emergence of the demonic is made graphic. This discontinuity is what Kierkegaard stresses in his interpretation of Faust. Amid the sweetest dreams of virtue there is always the possibility of the sudden intrusion of the demonic. The negative of unfreedom is present in all men, Kierkegaard writes, in the mocker, in him who lacks "inwardness," in the Roman Christian who makes a fetish out of good works, and in the rigidly orthodox who make

---

[16] *ibid.,* p. 95.

an idol out of one order of things and live in dread of any other. This very otherness and its possibility is of the essence of dread. In Danish, the word *altereret,* to alter, to become other or change, has the ordinary meaning, to fear, to become frightened. The demonic element is present in all who resist change and refuse to acknowledge the collapse of the old order of things.

Heidegger detheologized the Kierkegaardian concept. In SZ anxiety is neither theological nor psychological but existential-ontological. It is connected with a basic finding of oneself (*Grundbefindlichkeit*) and with a primordial unlocking of the self as "being there" in the world. Anxiety is thus connected with a basic expansion of awareness, and now one might interpret the "demonic" in the sense of dread at the thought of being truly "there." In Sartre this becomes *angoisse,* too easily taken as "anguish." *Angst* is one special kind of unlocking. The "there" of any "being there" is the unfettering of the potential to *be;* the "there," as the scene of becoming aware of one's potential, is one's existential "place," one's basic ethos which comes before any "ethic." Man's existential place is related to the demonic dimension of dread — a possible interpretation of the Heraclitan fragment. In anxiety — to be distinguished from an ontic fear that identifies its fear-object — the trusted world of ontic realities sinks away into meaninglessness (and this includes logical categories). Man sees he cannot be his truer self in this "real" order of things, with its deities, rules, regulations and clutter of categories; and thus he is confronted with the possibility of *being* himself. He therefore rejects the proposition, "Everyone is someone else and nobody is himself." He rejects ontic "realism."

Anxiety is "nothing and nowhere," i.e., it is not an ontic thing and it cannot be found in any ontic place. It cannot be experienced psychologically. It can only be sensed ontologically, for

it has no definite object that we can identify. Hence *Angst* is not a question of psychological anxiety, i.e., "anguish." It is a question of ontological meaning and non-meaning, sense and nonsense, sensing and non-sensing, caring and not caring, being aware and unaware. Anxiety opens the dimension of freedom and choice. It loosens the hold of the ontic world and dissolves an all too easy trust in the ontic order of things. It is thus mephistofelean, for it throws *Dasein* back upon its ontological potential, its authentic being in the world, its being unto (not "toward") death. Ontological "evil" threatens the ontic "good." This, of course, is a transformation of Kierkegaard's conception of the demonic. Perhaps Being is "beyond good and evil."

Death, which man, as one who "is there," confronts, is not to be understood as mere physical demise; and anxiety, as ontological, is not merely fear of it. Rather, death is an anticipation of authentic life and existence. We "run ahead" to encounter death as the fulfillment of life, but it is a life not projected on some mythical Beyond but lived on the earth and in the world of the awakened awareness of *Dasein.* "Media vita in morte sumus," a medieval àntiphon tells us. Luther translated this as the hymn, "Mitten wir im Leben sind, sind wir all' im Tode." But this sentence has little to do with the usual Christian meditation on death, in which the burden is thrown on another, i.e., on a historical personage of religious myth. Rather, it has to do with an awakened awareness of death in the midst of life, of the possibility that a certain order of things can die and another take its place. It is not involved in the construction of an artificial other-world as abode of the dead, nor does it postulate the pathological religious history of another's death. It is a question of one's own being and one's own death, which western man has sought to evade through devious philosophical and theological means. Now, finally, modern man is asked truly to confront himself and death-in-life. It is here that anxiety is engaged and the "demonic" discovered.

Traditional western man tried to avoid this confrontation with the demon of death by the construction of theological and philosophical truth systems, that suppressed a true emergence of Being and put a myth in its place, thus assuaging the basic anxiety with metaphysical comforts. And so there is a forgetfullness not only of Being but also of the truer meaning of death in western culture. Paradoxically, western man is fixated on physical demise and on some sort of afterlife, as a substitute for the authentic life that was never led when the chance was given. The ancient world by and large did not seek to evade the basic problem of ilfe and death. The Stoics recognized an anticipation of death-in-life in recommending "suicide." This meant taking one's life into one's own hands, rather than simply taking one's life, though the latter could also be entailed. Kierkegaard understood this when in *Entweder Oder* he tells of the man who could not die. Thus it is best, he claimed, to die at the height of life as a young man, rather than be condemned to life as mere duration and the bleak existence of merely hanging on. Mere duration is meaningless. Indefinite duration of a disembodied soul after death is merely a pathetic theologism. The Greeks were made of stronger stuff than our Christian metaphysicians. And the secret of life-in-death is contained in another Heraclitan puzzle, "Immortal mortals, mortal im-

mortals, living their death and dying their life." [17]

Anxiety before the fact of death means awe and wonderment in the midst of life, the joy of becoming truly oneself in encounter with the other in the absence of any petty deities and willfully constructed truth systems. But what does all this have to do with the "demonic"? What does it have to do with the "daemon" that is "an ethos to man"? From a Kierkegaardian viewpoint the demonic might now be interpreted as a dread of authenticity. The demonic in man would be his dread of having to become his authentic self as opposed to his artificial ego; thus there is a dread of dying to the self-of-the-One (*Man-selbst*) with its apparent certitudes and securities. It would amount to a dread of Being. It would mean a decision against a new ethos and for the old ethic. And thus man's character, as formed in the old ethic, would be quite demonic, in that it would represent a definite closure of spirit. But the demonic as ontological is not delimited by biblical meanings that are an inherent part of the Kierkegaardian conception. It is not a question of good and evil which are ontic ideas. In this case the "demonic" might well be viewed as the numinal power of Being, as living presence, as the gift which is sent to man as his "fate." Being sends itself and gives itself to man. It is a man's δαίμων, which can inspire a Socrates or arouse dread in the metaphysician.

The linguistic roots of anxiety are to

---

[17] *ibid.*, p. 210; "Ἀθάνατοι θνητοὶ, θνητοὶ ἀθάνατοι, ξῶντες τὸν ἐκείνων θάνατον τὸν δὲ ἐκείνων βίον τεθνεῶτες." The Greek is far more subtly nuanced than the English; thus: the immortal mortals live and experience their death during life (ζωή), but they die completely with regard to their "biological" existence (βίος). "Living one's death" is expressed by a present participle (ζῶντες) but "dying one's life" is expressed in the finality of the perfect participle (τεθνεῶτες). English is an impoverished language as compared with classic Greek, and ordinary language theorists would apparently keep it so. None of the above is to be found in Kirk and Raven, who settle for a more or less simplistic translation of this and other fragments. Cf. Heidegger-Fink, *Heraklit* (Frankfurt/M., 1970), pp. 158f, esp. p. 161. Here another but similar interpretation is given, stressing ἐκείνων i.e., the death of *others*. The problem is referred to philologists.

181

be found in the Greek ἄγχω and the Latin, *angere.* Inasmuch as anxiety is related to man as a bodily being, or rather is actually bodily man as "anxious," it has to do with his struggle to throw off the tyranny of the ontic order and the stifling embrace of the One, that he may breathe freely. The One stifles a man's soul. But "soul" is not to be understood as some hypostatized entity apart from man as a bodily being.(μλαή)is the "life breath" of man. Anxiety is experienced as a feeling of being stifled. This stifling and struggling in anxiety is a sign of life. Man wants to die to the self-of-the-One and live anew. He wants to be resurgent as a full human being. This is his resurrection from death and his "immortality." [18] And this resurgence is nothing less than eros, as a bodily *"surgissement,"* i.e., as the *surging forth* of his whole being toward a fuller life, one in which his fullest possible potential is released. The breath of life which breathes life into man is not some transcendent deity but rather the numinal voice of Being which in-spires man, as did that voice which spoke to Socrates. This "voice" is not the voice of deity or the preachy voice of moral conscience which attempts to dictate character. Rather it is the call of Being, and man as ek-sistent must become aware of this voice, if he is to "be there" in the world and on the earth. Awareness is not a question of psychology but of a phenomenological awakening; man becomes increasingly aware of ontological "truth" (*gewahr, Wahrheit*). Man "is there" in truth, i.e., in an expanded awareness of Being, as it is relieved of its seven veils. The call of Being comes suddenly, like some demon, in the midst of our stifling ontic situation. It is "il No al mondo," i.e., the negation of the purely ontic order of reality.

The Heraclitan fragment reads "ἦθος ἀνθρώπω δαίμων." We cannot translate this enigma. It has little to do with character or destiny. Ἦθος has little to do with "ethics" and a good deal to do with one's situation, as the "place" where one "is there." [19] It is the setting in which one becomes aware of Being, the "seat" upon which one sits. It is the place where one posits self authentically. This is not a moral posture or an actual place but an "existential position." It is no mean coincidence that Rodin portrays the *Thinker* in a sitting posture. Here is a man in deep recollection, naked and despoiled of all that is not himself. He is in a position of ingatheredness and inwardness. He is naive and naked in his openness to Being. His existential ethos is unethical; this is the "demonic" in man. This ethos is a demon to man. It torments him until he throws off his shackles and becomes aware and free. "Being there is in truth and untruth"; "Man's character is his destiny." Two fascinating statements indeed. But perhaps they say the same thing.

---

[18] Tillich, P.: *The Courage to Be* (New Haven '52), p. 169, has a pertinent passage with regard to the Christian corruption of the existential notions of immortality and by implication of resurrection: "The popular belief in immortality which in the western world has largely replaced the Christian symbol of resurrection is a mixture of courage and escape. It tries to maintain one's self-affirmation even in the face of one's having to die. But it does this by continuing one's finitude, that is, one's having to die, infinitely, so that the actual death will never occur. This, however, is an illusion and, logically speaking, a contradiction of terms. It makes endless what, by definition, must come to an end. The "immortality of the soul" is a poor symbol for the courage to be in the face of one's having to die." This is, of course, a very Heideggerian passage with its emphasis on finitude and confronting death as part of the courage to *be.*

[19] Boelen, B.: "The Question of Ethics in the Thought of Martin Heidegger," in *Heidegger and the Quest for Truth,* ed. M. S. Frings (Chicago, 1968), pp. 76–105.

ON THE PATTERN OF PHENOMENOLOGICAL METHOD

by

EDWARD G. BALLARD

Tulane University

History often appeared to the ancients to move in cycles, for· their imaginations were dominated by seasonal periodicity and by the eternal return of life everywhere. St. Augustine, however, was directed by his faith to belief in a steady and straight advance from creation, through the coming of Christ and the New Law, to the second coming, which would be the perfection and end of time. This cumulative and progressive model was later secularized and exercised a profound influence upon certain aspects of modern scientific and technological thinking. It will be interesting to follow up these two leads and to determine whether either has anything to say or to suggest about philosophical thought in history, in particular about the ways of phenomenological thinking. Geometry was once defined as those problems which could be reduced to circles and straight lines by manipulations of compass and ruler. Perhaps an analogous simplification and definition by method will serve to delimit kinds of philosophy.

After some further brief mention of progressive versus cyclical thought, I shall consider Husserlian and Heideggerian methods in philosophy and then shall elaborate the latter by relating it to the dramatic tradition.

I. *Straight Edge and Protractor*

It is rather easy to be persuaded that the Christian linea plan for history offers a model which dominates other kinds of thinking. All sorts of progressive thought may seem to move along such a line. Long ago mathematicians conceived of their doctrines as moving outward step by step from an axiomatic base to prove a succession of theorems in a progress toward the rationalization of the whole of space. Ideally, according to some philosophers, an empirical theory moves likewise in this step by step fashion toward demonstrating the detailed and complete subordination of the observable to the theoretical. When the Christian model was purged of religious content by certain Nineteenth century philosophers, it was used to reflect their convictions concerning the infinite and cumulative advance toward the perfection of technological civilization and the complete control by technicians of the world, life, and society. Many other sorts of perfectionist plans and systems of millenial thinking have followed similar linea schemes involving, in outline, a series of cumulative steps directed toward an end. The model is not complex and persuasively suggests a general and apparently useful mode of procedure prior to the encountering of particular problems.

This kind of progressive thought is typical of all that is most advanced in civilization. Civilization, I take it, is the attempt expressed in the dominant mood and type of actions of a people over a considerable time to mould human character according to a definite ideal and toward a definite (though usually unconceptualized) end. However, a great danger may be invited by the success of Western progressive civilization. For its aim is evidently to de-

Edward G. Ballard is professor of philosophy at Tulane University. Educated at the College of William and Mary, Harvard, Universite de Montpellier, the Sorbonne, and the University of Virginia (Ph.D., 1946), he has been past president of The Southern Society for Philosophy and Psychology. He is presently a member of the Editorial Board of SJP. Among his publications are: Art and Analysis (Martinus Nijhoff, 1957) and Socratic Ignorance (Martinus Nijhoff, 1966). Professor Ballard is co-editor of this special issue of The Southern Journal of Philosophy on Heidegger.

velop devices, machines, which at all levels — action, thought, and decision making — will perform more and more of the functions earlier performed by men. When this goal is fully achieved, then even the function of inventing such machines will have been willingly relinquished by men to the machine. At that moment, civilization will have reached its end, and so will man since at this end point he will have nothing further, in terms of the values of that civilization, to perform.

An alternative to this progress may be opened up by a return to a cyclical model for thought. Cyclical thought, however, is puzzling. Where does it begin? Where does it end? Heraclitus observed that every point of a circle was both beginning and end. There is at least the relevant truth brought out by this analogy that any next point on the historical cycle does not promise unequivocal progress. Rather it is inextricably bound up with that which has preceded. The way this analogy applies in cyclical philosophical thinking is to observe that the use or elucidation of any principle, even any proposition, changes to some degree the context of thought, and thus it eventually alters the meaning of the principle or proposition in question. Hence, the new meaning of the principle or proposition must again be thought through— and so on for another cycle. No doubt this cyclical movement is illustrated in the Platonic philosophy where the journey out of the Cave of the Republic is completed only by the philosopher's return to the Cave with an insight which to some extent renews and enlightens the life within.

Probably, however, the illustration which would most spontaneously spring to the mind of a modern philosopher would be the Hegelian method. The Hegelian dialectic, impelled by internal contradictions, moved through cycles to the elimination of contradiction and thus toward the freedom of absolute spirit. This end achieved, it would seem, all movement ceases. In this in-

stance, cyclical dialectic is explicitly combined with linea thought to produce a combination which might be described as spiral progress, a circuitous evolution. It is progressive and moves toward a final point; but it moves thus by way of continuous cycles. Let us consider this to be a third pattern of thought.

Now, phenomenological thinking seeks, first, so far as possible, to discover and exhibit the object of its interest, viz., being, as it is experienced for itself and prior to the accretions of specialized disciplines and the accidents of idiosyncratic viewing; it then seeks to discover within these purified phenomena the origin and growth of world, of self, of science, and of societies, and it seeks the meaning of these developments. We may turn now to the question which of these models just mentioned is exemplified in phenomenological thought. Does phenomenological method guarantee a progress, an evolution of philosophical insight? Does it do so by way of a circuitous route? Or is it content merely to move in circles?

II. *Husserl and Heidegger*

Upon first glance Husserl's manner of doing philosophy may appear to be progressive in type. He certainly honored above all the ideal of Western rationality, the ideal of rigor, and considered that philosophy, no less than the special sciences, came into its own only to the extent that it approached this ideal. However, there are circular patterns in his thinking. These are present owing to the requirement of presuppositionlessness placed upon philosophy by the ideal of rigor. This necessity rationally to examine one's philosophic starting point forced him to turn back to include within his developed philosophy the presuppositions with which he had begun, at least presuppositions of which he was aware. For instance, use of the technique of epoche in volume one of the *Ideen* issued in a vision of the purified phenomenal world;[1] then these purified phenomena recur in the later developed philosophy as the neutrality modification of noemata (*op. cit.*, §§ 109f). Again, *Ideas* begins by accepting the task of understanding objects (material things) and their place in a schema of objectivities (§§ 16ff). Empirical objects are initially assumed to be a recognizable division of beings within experience. Then after pursuit of phenomenological clarification, *Ideas* ends with a return upon this objective with an elaborate description of the region material thing (cf. § 142), a circle which is recapitulated in the final chapter of *Ideas*.

It is uncertain, however, whether Husserl's mode of thought is properly to be classified as cyclical. For in the first place, as just observed, he clearly regarded the highest developed thinking—i.e., Western scientific and philosophic thinking — as progressive and linea in character.[2] Secondly, the circles which I have noted stem from the self-reflective nature of philosophy in its attempt to become completely rational, scientific, and confidently progressive. They are not a repeating pattern characteristic of all philosophical thought, rather they are to be executed by those who would activate their grasp upon the beginning of scientific thought. Thus, for Husserl, cyclical thought belongs only to first philosophy.

If Husserl's philosophy marks something of a change-over in mode of thinking from that characteristic of the mathematician and natural scientist toward that characteristic of the Greek humanist, then this change is partial only; its cyclical character refers only to the initial steps in phenomenological clarification.

Heidegger's thought, on the other hand, is quite thoroughly and self-consciously cyclical. Heidegger first presents the cyclical nature of thought in terms of a movement from the pre-ontological to the ontological, from that which is "closest" to us to that which, in an everyday sense, is "farthest." Philosophy, then, is the project of bringing close that which is remote. Thereupon, that which once was remote, now being close, requires and enables a renewal of a similar project. Two such transitional cycles are discernable in his philosophy. The first moving from the everyday or average self (*Das Mann*) to one's own individual being or Dasein, and the second turning from the latter to Being itself. It may be supposed that this philosophic account can be given a formal expression which can be seen to hold generally. The particular way, however, in which alterations in the self are experienced and expressed will no doubt change from individual to individual, and more sweepingly from epoch to epoch.

The relevant account springs from the analysis of Being-in-the-world and its changes. The cyclical nature of the changes to which Heidegger's thought seeks to conform can be indicated by a brief excursus into his formal descriptions. Being-in-the-world is exhibited first as *Befindlichkeit* and concretely experienced in some dominant mood or atunement which has its own way of understanding. This understanding is interpreted initially in some sort of action or praxis and subsequently in discourse ("the articulation of intelligibility").[3] That language should be humanly possible, Man's being must possess a characteristic a priori structure derived from the structure of understanding. That is to say, the "forestructure" of understanding is mirrored

---

[1] *Ideas, General Introduction to Pure Phenomenology*, tr. W. R. Boyce-Gibson (New York: Macmillan, 1st ed., 1931), cf. §§ 50, 136.
[2] Cf. Husserl's "Philosophy as Rigorous Science," tr. by Quentin Lauer in *Phenomenology and The Crisis of Philosophy* (New York: Harper Torchbook, 1965), esp. pp. 71, 77.
[3] *Being and Time*, tr. John Macquarrie and Edward Robinson (London: SCM Press Ltd., 1962), p. 203f. (Hereafter BT.)

in the "as" structure of assertion (BT § 32). Three factors are discernable in this structure; these become the three points, so to speak, which determine the circular character of this thinking (cf. BT p. 194). The first such factor is *that* which is already possessed (the *Vorhabe*). This prepossession consists, for example, in funded interpretations of the past which provide the basis for the present. The second factor is the *way* of understanding with which one is endowed by reason of membership in a particular world or culture. This membership determines in advance a point of view (the *Vorsicht*) which in in turn delimits or determines in general *how* the interpretation may proceed. The final factor, (the *Vorgriff*) is the specific concept(s) or categoreal structure which is used, within this point of view, to yield an account of *what* something is. Elsewhere, as I understand the matter, Heidegger refers to these prior concepts as "the mathematical."[4]

This tripartite fore-structure is expressed, for illustration, clearly enough by the three kinds of a priori in the Kantian philosophy. Kant points to the aesthetic a priori which imparts a certain initial form to the matter of experience whose intelligibility is to be articulated. In addition, the Newtonian world refers to the way in which this material, received via the forms of space and time, is to be rendered intelligible. This world is the point of view, which Kant presupposed and of which the twelve categories define the conceptualizable form, the possible essences, which the understanding can properly entertain. This articulation is elaborated in the Principles where their unity with the aesthetic material is worked out. It is, however, difficult to see a continued circular movement in the kind of thought for which Kant's philosophy provides, unless it be the mind's repeated reflective disclosure of its own formal-categoreal structure

within its (Newtonian) experience. But these disclosures, considered apart from reflection, develop progressively toward the perfection of the science of objects. Heidegger, on the other hand, being preoccupied with the possibility of becoming and remaining human, discovers this three-fold structure within the essence of humanity (or of care, *Sorge*) as revealed by *Angst*.

That of which care is already possessed (its *Vorhabe*) is the facticity to which it is thrown. Its foresight, expressing its characteristic movement beyond itself, is its existence. And its fore-conception is the basic stock of concepts by which it manages objects of concern in the world delimited by its foresight or its current possibilities of existence. These basic concepts give the intelligible structure to the world in which a man lives (e.g. *Zuhandenheit* and *Vorhandenheit,* BT §§ 15f.). Heidegger is not much concerned with the task of developing the categoreal structures of these worlds but rather in exhibiting their function and effect in man's existence. For example, the existential effect of accepting and using the technological world-structure is rather important for the current Dasein to understand.

The general and essential consequence of the use of such concepts in the interpretation of human existence is some mode of falling. This fallingness is a necessary element determining the cyclical nature of Heidegger's philosophical method.

Falling is inevitable and ironic. Its inevitableness is manifested most clearly in relation to the finite, and hence in some sense always inadequate, character of the fore-conception. For instance, Dasein is inevitably concerned with objects in the world. A usual outcome of this concern is the identification of oneself as some sort of object (BT p. 361). Yet that to which objects or facts appear and are truly identified can not

---

[4] *What is a Thing?,* tr. W. B. Barton, Jr., and Vera Deutsch (Chicago: Henry Regnery Co., 1967), pp. 69–111.

be merely another such object. So to identify the self is to distort it. This existential tendency is also ironic, for since falling is an aspect of care, any care to understand it or to compensate for its effect is itself an instance of falling. Thus, any attempt to understand oneself must begin with the self one already has, and this self is in fact seen as an object, a fact among facts. Now although the non-objective self is distorted when treated merely as an object and subjected to the concepts used to manage objects, this distortion can be successful. At least, as measured by common standards, object-concepts have been used with striking success to understand, predict, and control men's behavior. Thus, it is scarcely likely that this way of understanding will be abandoned. Even so, this success appears to be altogether desirable and progressive only if one does not turn back in cyclical fashion, and attempt to glimpse the possibilities and qualities of human being which these concepts are not designed to express. It is, though, exactly the function of philosophy to turn back in this manner and to bring the human being into question.

The anxiety arising from recognition that the self may be lost or destroyed in the world which it itself has made leads thought back to question its existence. Heidegger holds that the tradition provides certain clues for renewing self-understanding, although they may not yet have been used effectively. These clues may lead one back to a contemplation of Being, the source of one's existence, unencumbered by naive acceptance of the current fore-conception. Heidegger's use of these clues led him to characterize Dasein's unified and authentic Being in terms of present silent acceptance of the call of conscience to be just its finite, given self, anticipating its death as its own individual end (BT. p. 357). Here the usual concept of the self, the content of its past, and the way these are commonly viewed have undergone a sea-change (BT. p. 358). This change

in the way Dasein can experience itself is then shown to be possible, not if it occurs in a time conceived to be a progressive series of nows, but rather if it is or becomes temporal, where concrete temporality is conceived (schematically) as a present, developing out of its future, which has taken over its past. That is to say, that which one experiences in the present is determined primarily by the way it emerges from the future as it repeats or takes responsibility for what emerges from the permanent factors exhibited primarily by the past. The meaning, then, of Dasein is concrete temporality, which is to say that time thus conceived provides the context within which it makes sense to speak of the project of becoming one's owned self. The present day alternative is to become a standard self, a self which easily and willingly identifies itself with an assigned technological function that can be performed almost automatically, with minimum reference to past or future.

Here one cycle of thought is complete; it has moved by way of reinterpreting the three points determining this circle, from the pre-ontological context of everydayness to the ontological context of concrete temporality. It has, as one might express the matter, come into possession of its own time.

Still another such movement would seem to be possible. Although Heidegger does not put the question so baldly, one might next ask, why become one's authentic self? The response could be "for the sake of Being." Here Heidegger's execution of the *Kehre* does not quite clearly, it seems to me, follow the circular path described so far. He appears to be led by the conviction that the elements of care, the extases of temporality, find their unity in Being and originate there. Accordingly, he attempts to take the point of view (a renewed *Vorsicht*) of Being. Perhaps, then, that which is given for interpretation is *Sein im Ganzen,* Being as a whole. But the concepts which he brings with him to effect this interpretation are not exactly easy to extract from their poetic embodiment — nor perhaps should they be. Perhaps not three points but *Das Vier* determine the circle for this thinking of the question of Being. In any event, sufficient points have been made to substantiate my immediate thesis: that the method chracteristic of the Heideggerian phenomenology is essentially cyclical.

In this respect, Heidegger is one with with an important part of the philosophic tradition. The cycles through which his thought weaves its way are not, however, to be construed on analogy to a spiral. They have no progressive characteristic. But neither are they by any means mere routine repetitions of the same circle. The movement from one cycle to the next seems to be discontinuous. His circles are suggestive of the movement taken by the wayfarer in Dante's *Purgatorio*. In this part of the Divine Comedy the transition from one circle to the next is marked by an instantaneous leap. The end of one circle is a transmutation into the next. There is in addition, in Heidegger's philosophy, a kind of experience which accompanies, or perhaps *is*, this transmutation. Anxiety is the experience which can initiate or accompany the transition from the daily round of inauthentic life into the anticipatory resolution of authentic or owned being. The second turn is marked by a sort of poetic experience. Perhaps a part of this experience finds expression in *Das Ding*.[5] Paul Ricoeur has described it as the gift of poetical life. Thus, the first circle is a turn away from the inauthentic being of the everyday world toward oneself, and the second is the owned self's turn toward Being, toward an influx of poetic and creative life.

III. *Further Identification of the Phenomenological Circles*

Heidegger himself indicates the connection of his thought with the Aristotelian search for archai or principles.

There are, as Heidegger quotes Aristotle, three archai[6]: the what (η $\varepsilon\sigma\tau\iota\nu$) which is to be discovered, the that (η $\gamma\iota\gamma\nu\varepsilon\tau\alpha\iota$) which is inquired into, and the how (η $\gamma\iota\gamma\nu\omega\sigma\kappa\varepsilon\tau\alpha\iota$) or truth, the disclosedness or $\alpha\lambda\eta\theta\varepsilon\iota\alpha$ which determines or limits the kind of *what* (*Was-sein*) which can be discovered. This latter, the initial disclosedness of Being, is commonly neglected, for it is supposed to be obvious in the West that truth is nothing more than a precise correspondence of statement to its referents (which are already disclosed). No small part of Heidegger's contribution to philosophy is his insistence that truth lies primarily in the initial disclosure rather than in correspondence of fact to statement, and that the disclosing or uncovering process can occur in many ways. It occurs in one way for the man who thinks poetically, in another way for the man who thinks scientifically. These, indeed, are two of the ways of existing historically and to each corresponds its own view of the *that* which is to be experienced and thought, and to each corresponds a characteristic *what* or kind of essence which is disclosed. That, how, and what, thus, correspond to facticity, existence, and falling as the most formal and abstract expressions of the points determining the circle of this phenomenological thought. This much was considered, apart from its origin in Greek thought, in the preceding section.

In addition, the Greeks offer another mode of considering human existence, its determining factors, and its development. Their dramatists achieved an extraordinarily concrete grasp upon human life and its unfolding, and any later attempt to deal with this life does well to test itself by their understanding. This dramatic experience and especially its form of presentation will now be considered for the purpose of determining whether phenomenological thinking retains any analogy to the forms in

---

[5] *Vorträge und Aufsätze* (Pfullingen: Neske, 1954), pp. 163–181.
[6] *Meta.* D 1, 1013a–17ff. cited in *Vom Wesen des Grundes,* translated as *The Essence of Reasons* by T. Malick (Evanston: Northwestern University Press, 1969), p. 5.

which this understanding has been preserved. The following comments, referring to this drama, are not offered as an exercise in scholarship; rather they advance certain hypotheses which define a possibly useful point of view for reading this drama, one which does in fact develop a concrete illustration of the mode of philosophic reflection being considered here.

That very puzzling yet universal kind of human activity called 'play' may with some generality be regarded as a struggle—or a mimic struggle—between protagonist and antagonist. This definition admittedly eliminates such excessively general usages as are exemplified in the proposal to term any language a game. Of course, there are games, mimic struggles, played with language; but to call any sort of speaking a game or a form of play is to use these terms so broadly that they can refer to virtually any activity; hence, they lose their specific meaning.

In naive play (e.g., children's games) protagonist and antagonist are usually clearly identified. For instance, in Wildwestern films the good men wear white hats, and the bad wear black. With maturity, however, an ambiguity comes increasingly into play. It may, for instance, not be quite clear who the protagonist and antagonist are, nor what their respective values may be, nor just what victory in the struggle may signify. Where this ambiguity becomes a dominating element and approaches irony, then the play begins to become dramatic. The ancient and beguiling tale of reversal of role, illustrated in Twain's *The Prince and the Pauper,* was actually played by members of the French Aristocracy during the eighteenth century. Perhaps this play was suggestive. At any rate, the events of 1789 intimate that it was so, and thus lend a certain ironic tone to the Aristocratic game. In Sir James Barry's drama *The Admirable Crichton* the reversal of roles between master and servant, enforced by a change of circumstance, issued in a change of character which might almost undermine one's confidence in the validity of British class distinctions. Let us say that a drama is a play wherein the protagonist — and perhaps the antagonist too — undergo some sort of change in identity or reversal of role as the consequence of the struggle in which they are engaged. In this change, which may become a basic alteration of personality structure, lies the irony of mature play. Drama, then, is an ironic struggle.

The difference between tragedy and comedy is determined, I believe, by that against which the hero is struggling. In tragedy, the struggle may initially appear—especially to the hero—to be between the hero and another personage or group or situation; however, it turns out in the end really to be a struggle against fate or against a decree of the gods (the relation between fate and the will of gods was not clarified by the Greeks). Thus, Oedipus of Sophocles' *Oedipus Rex* at first believed himself to be struggling against the ambitious Creon, but he came to see in the end that he was struggling against the powers who had inspired the utterance of the Oracle at Delphi. Tragedy, if we may generalize, is a struggle against fate. But furthermore, this is the same fate which so determines situation and circumstance that Oedipus discovered his mistake concerning his identity. In struggling against this fate, Oedipus was opposing the way to self-identity. Herein lies the irony of the struggle. More fully, then, tragedy is an ironic struggle with fate.

It is characteristic of comedy, at least of a great many comedies, that society, its taboos, and its more or less arbitrary regulations, take the place of fate. Now the hero whether he thinks so or not, is indefeasibly a part of society. Hence, in struggling against society, the comic hero is fighting against himself. In defeating that element of society which the comic hero took to be his adversary, he often discovers that he has foolishly defeated himself. Comedy, thus, is an ironic struggle with society. This social basis of comedy is well illustrated by Aristophanes' *Birds* where the judgments and customs of men, transferred to the empire of the birds, come to be manifested in all their captiousness and silliness.

In both tragedy and comedy, irony is exhibited in the change which the hero undergoes in consequence of his participation in the struggle. Drama is play in which those who engage in it, perhaps those who witness it, are changed in unforeseen ways. Moreover, the change is manifest both in tragedy and in comedy when the protagonist comes to recognize his altered status. He achieves insight into his changed identity or altered role. According to Aristotle a dramatic action is a complete action. Its completeness, I suggest, is marked by this fact; that the insight reached in the final event returns to the initiating event and throws a new light upon it. Thus the insight is an essential element in dramatic action.

A dramatic insight evolves quite naturally from a logically linked series of events. The initiating event will have been the decision on the part of the hero to assume a certain identity or to play a certain role. The consequence of this decision precipitates the struggle (with fate or with society); this struggle, the central portion of the drama, runs its course to the final event, which is marked by the insight. This is the insight which is directed back upon the initiating decision, interpreting it as distorted or foolish, reached arrogantly or blindly. This movement through decision, subsequent struggle, to insight is the movement of drama. Of course, irony permeates the whole, for the initiating decision concerning the hero's identity is perforce made in the semi-darkness of the hero's limited understanding; then follows the ambiguous struggle which terminates in somewhat greater yet always limited insight.

The limited character of the final insight, perhaps a consequence of the fundamental obscurity of fate, guarantees that one dramatic action must be followed by another. Hence the composers of tragedies tended to write trilogies or to return to the same theme, as Sophocles returned to the Oedipus legend in *Antigone* and in *Oedipus at Colonus*.

Still another variation on this dramatic movement can be imagined. It may be indicated in this way: what if the tragic hero were mistaken about that which he took to be fate? What if a supposed fate were merely the reification of local taboos or social customs. The possibility of this confusion is suggested by the tradition that Dike, Justice or Fate, is the daughter of Themis, who presided over the Olympic banquets and is often identified as the personification of social custom. When it becomes evident that the hero has indeed mistaken some social force or habit for the extra-human opposition of fate, then the tragic hero becomes comic. Conversely, social custom need not be so arbitrary as it may at first appear. It may have a deeper origin in something which suggests fate itself, as Pentheus, hero of the *Bacchae*, discovered to sorrow. In both these instances it is not merely the identity or role of the hero which is in doubt and which changes; rather that against which he struggles is not only obscure initially, it becomes and remains conspicuously ambiguous or may even seem to change. It is as if the two kinds of opponents, the tragic and the comic, themselves come into conflict. We may call the dramas which exhibit this kind of conflict tragi-comedies. They often display with particular clarity the limited character of man's insight and power. Shakespeare's "The Tempest" offers a typical illustration: Prospero's expulsion from Venice and his shipwreck intimate that he is the victim of a tragic fate; but then he sets up an order — social and magical — which seems to dominate events and even to entrap his enemies; finally, though, he recognizes the dream-like quality of all these constructions and evaluations; and

190

he sees that he is limited by non-human powers —

> We are such stuff
> As dreams are made on, and
>   our little life
> Is rounded with a sleep.

My conviction is that these three patterns of human change, gathered by poets and imaginative writers from their contemplation of human life and its changes, offer concrete illustrations of the kind of thought which is used and described formally by Heidegger upon contemplating the same life and changes. These patterns become perceptible in his philosophical method, perhaps determine it. This conviction is based upon other factors than the obvious cyclical patterns evident in both drama and the philosophy. For one thing it is also based upon observing that the same pre-possessions are discernible in the drama to which I have referred as in Heidegger's philosophy. For another, it is based upon the relevance of the spheres of drama to the contexts of Heidegger's philosophy. These two points of similarity need to be elaborated briefly.

The Dasein whose being is recognized by the philosopher to be intrinsically in question is, I hold, embodied in the dramatic protagonist who discovers himself in a situation requiring a decision concerning his identity or role. In order that Desein should deal with his self-questioning by making a decision and following through the consequent dramatic action, he must clearly be possessed of certain powers. In these powers we recognize the existentials of Dasein. Dasein must, for instance, be thrown; that is, he must already be possessed of a world, a language, a history. Indeed, his decision is precisely an interpretation of himself, a visualization and management of himself as a definite, functioning human being within an already given world. His grasp of himself as having been such and such, hence able to perform in a definite way, expresses his grasp upon facticity, or upon the fate which

seems to arise from the past and may threaten to tyrannize over him. Thus the prophesy, the plague, the civic responsibility, the characteristic inclination to make sudden and over-confident decisions were elements which Oedipus unavoidably had already at hand. They are the concrete embodiments of facticity, of that which was given him to use.

In addition, the dramatic hero is also already possessed of a stock of concepts and habits of thought which enable him to assemble evidence and the recognize familiar patterns, instantiations of certain concepts. He may also be receptive of inspiration by reason of which he might be led to the recognition of change, even of a radically new turn in his life. We recall, for example, how Oedipus attempted to force data which came his way to yield certain desired and exonerating conclusions. But then he was also possessed of the heroic courage to see the reversal of events, to recognize and to accept the almost total change in identity to which circumstances drove him. This end brought him back to correct his initiating decision; it was as if he saw in the end *what* he was for the first time. His categories were sufficient to express this renewed insight into his essence.

The least obvious element, yet the determining one, of which the tragic hero must be possessed is foresight (*Vorsicht*). This element refers to the general way in which the world is unveiled to the hero and specifies how he tends to see the world, events, himself. It refers to $\alpha\lambda\eta\theta\epsilon\iota\alpha$, the truth, in which the hero currently exists. The kinds of decision, the possible sorts of identity initially open to him are limited by this primitive unveiling of the world. Similarly, the identity of the opponent he may face and the kind of struggle in which he may engage are limited by the way in which the world is disclosed to him in advance. Thus, at one time a disagreement over rights was envisaged as naturally requiring a physical combat

191

by means of which justice would be done, the gods appeased, the order preserved. Subsequently another truth dominated; the combat was transferred to the verbal and legal plane. This transition provides the theme for Aeschylus' *Orestia*. At issue, then, in this trilogy, is the nature of the world, and the kind of *Vorsicht* which predominates. In Oedipus' case the foresight included a certain vision of kingship and of himself as ready and obligated to take over its responsibility; there was also the awareness of dangers to which kingship is subject in the courts of men; finally, there was the obscurer awareness of the gods, of fate, and of the sometimes indirect ways in which they work. Thus, upon identifying himself as the one designed to rid Thebes of the plague, he concluded at first that his struggle was against those who were jealous of his position and power. Only later did he recognize the irony: he had made his own fate into his antagonist.

Although pre-possession, fore-sight, and prior concepts are undoubtedly determinative at every step or moment of any human action or speech, my methodological suggestion is that the functional differences among the beginning, middle, and end of a drama are differentiated through their domination primarily by one of these elements respectively. Thus a cycle of dramatic action, the means by which human beings become themselves and mature, exhibits the same existential components as a cycle of Heideggerian phenomenological thought. We may say, then, that the method of this thought is to imitate dramatic action. As dramatic action mimics and interprets a complete cycle of the human struggle, so this philosophic thought mimics and interprets dramatic action.

Another drama-related factor is the spheres in which this philosophy moves. We observed that the ironic struggle which is dramatic action is diversified by the kind antagonist envisaged. In the Western tradition, this antagonist

has most frequently been taken by comedy to be society or some social factor, by tragedy to be fate, and by tragi-comedy to be an ambiguous opponent whose identity seems to shift between these latter two. Now there is a certain rough analogy, at least a relation of suggestiveness, between these three spheres, the comic, the tragic, and the tragi-comic, and the three realms within which — and among which — Heidegger's philosophic method moves. Thus the first division of *Being and Time* elaborates the existential analysis of everydayness and concludes with a sketch of *Das Man,* who evades his own being by way of a sort of superficial sociality, curiosity about contemporary events, and impersonality. Such a context is the air breathed by comedy. In particular, we recall that a function often played by high comedy is to enliven awareness of the artificiality and inauthentic values of such a social atmosphere.

The second division of *Being and Time* moves to an analysis of authentic Dasein, who is individualized by accepting and making his own the inalienable traits of his existence: his indebtedness for his own being, his response to the silent call of conscience, and his anxiety in the face of his finitude. Here I think, is something like the realm of tragedy, where the hero is aware of his own being and freedom, concerned about his identity, and anxious concerning his fate. It is the realm of high seriousness, resignation, and self-sacrifice.

The relation of tragi-comedy of the Being with which Heidegger is more directly occupied after his *Kehre* is, perhaps, more tenuous. But so is the fate—which after all may not be fate— with which the tragi-comedian seeks to make his peace. And Heidegger's effort to listen to the silent voice of Being and to think in imitation of the event of Being must inevitably have about it, we may suspect, something of Prospero's cloud-capped towers and gorgeous palaces which fail before the final sleep. We understand him when he says the old gods have departed and the new ones not yet come. Dasein may be the shepherd of Being, but it is not altogether clear whether man is in fact Dasein, or a sheep, or even a wolf. Remembrance of the irony of fate and of the ambiguity of falling should make us wary of leaping quickly to possibly comic or tragic identifications.

Someone has remarked that the "there" of "Being-There" (Da-sein) is the scene of the dramatic encounter between the self and all that is.[1] If so, then the method of this encounter, the way of achieving it, may properly be thought on the same dramatic model as that which guided Oedipus to his fate. Consequently, I have tried to show how Heidegger's method deals with a philosophico-dramatic circling through the three realms familiar to tradition. More particularly it is concerned to effect the transition from one of these realms to the other. By corresponding with or by thinking more fully through the tradition, the method seeks to think with the Being which is to eventuate. Thus, the method expresses a longing for a change of Being. And though Heidegger disclaims practical ends, it sometimes appears to seek to accomplish this change. We must ask, therefore, whether in fact it does accomplish this change. And we must answer that it does not— a correct answer if the earlier assimilation of his method to the circles of Dante's *Divine Comedy* rather than to the spiral movement of the Hegelian dialectic was appropriate. Any single cycle of this methodical thinking does not lead necessarily to a next realm. One may undergo *Angst* or desire to become one's authentic self, but without success. Many an anxious patient has been returned by his physician to the everyday world; many a depressed business man has been helped by family and friends through a disturbing crisis and returned to his job and to his familiar personality. And no doubt many a resolute and tragic individual

has listened for the voice of Being and has failed to hear its silent response.

What, then, does the method accomplish? Surely it does not offer any of the fruits of modern progressive problem-solving thought. It does not provide any tools by which the environment may be mastered and possessed. It is concerned only with an inner change of the self. But perhaps even there it merely sharpens awareness of a possible passage from tradition and the contemporary world to new horizons. Perhaps also it prepares one for this passage. As Dante might have said, the discipline of one circle of Purgatory prepares one to receive the Grace which will enable passage to the next. But the discipline does not produce the Grace. No more does Heidegger's philosophical method produce a change of Being. Hence much of Heidegger's later writing emphasizes the receptive aspect of Dasein, a corollary of its finitude. The method prepares one for a change of Being, but the change itself is effected only upon the initiative of Being.

In this respect again, Heideggerian phenomenological method exhibits a dramatic trait. Sometimes personages undergo quite catastrophic struggles without being deeply affected thereby. They end with no new insight into themselves or their fate. On the other hand the genuinely dramatic personage often undergoes a rather radical change in a manner difficult, sometimes impossible, to account for in terms of the rationality of the times. These are the heroes, leaders of their world, the *dramatis personae*. Others remain the everyday victims of circumstance or calamity, or they are sometimes merely amused onlookers. But Oedipus was changed by events; he was not merely horrified by his violation of taboos. Blinding himself signified the acquisition of inner vision. And in his last play he met his end quite mysteriously in the thunder and lightning of Zeus.

---

[1] Cf. F. J. Smith, "Being and Subjectivity: Heidegger and Husserl," in *Phenomenology in Perspective,* ed. F. J. Smith (The Hague: Nijhoff, 1970), pp. 122–156.

HEIDEGGER SEEN FROM FRANCE[1]

JEAN BEAUFRET

Lycée Henri-IV

Since the responsibility for the pre-amble has been allotted to me, I presume that I may treat the theme, *Heidegger Seen from France,* freely.

But what is France? Perhaps it is the land where, when in May of 1968 the student man-in-the-street manifested, as elsewhere, some unrest, one could, it seems, read on a wall of the august Sorbonne: " 'God is dead' — signed Nietzsche." The next day one could read just below: "Nietzsche is dead' — signed God." To tell the truth, neither of them is really dead. Both have left Complete Works. And the edition of the *Nachlass* poses as many problems in one case as it does in the other. One can say, though, that the Complete Works of one benefits from a much more wide-spread printing than does the works of the other. God's superiority over me, Nietzsche thought — and this delights the French — can be formulated thus: "I have never written anything but the best German. But on the other hand, this is a refinement which the Greek god learned when he wanted to become an author, and he learned it no better (es ist Feinheit, dass Gott Griechisch lernte, als er Schriftsteller werden wollte, und dass er es nicht besser lernte. [Jenseits #121])."

Here we are then in France — with Nietzsche. But now a question arises: In what fashion could the French people, if they have such a spiritual disposition, react to Heidegger's appearance? I will not atempt to provide a history of this question from 1927 and even before, for such a history could only be anecdotal and tedious. But it is a fact that some people in France are becoming attentive to his thought for purposes other than merely adding to a collection of foolishness. And so the question recurs: Who is Heidegger for them? Though the French pretend to cordially ignore geography, they still have the habit of encountering him geographically — having sometimes seen pastoral images of him. And they do this through one of La Fontaine's fables, "The Peasant of the Danube." But who is the Peasant of the Danube? La Fontaine has scarcely explained himself. One has to go back to Pindar. The French have learned from Pindar that the Peasant of the Danube belongs to the race of those Hyperboreans, friends of Heracles who visited them twice and brought back from their land — the land of the shadowy sources of the Ister — the olive tree which he lodged in the Grecian lands. In Greek thought then, the Peasant of the Danube is the donor of the olive. Thus, the olive is not indigenous to Greece.

If we go from there to Phenomenology, many differences between Husserl and Heidegger will be clarified, particularly the change of meaning of this strange word, Phenomenology. Husserl, a citizen of the land of the sciences, presents Phenomenology as a *new science,* though he says it was already for more than three centuries "the secret longing of all modern philosophy (die geheime Sehnsucht der ganzen

Jean Beaufret, a professor at Lycée Henri-IV in Paris, is one of the leading French interpreters of Heidegger and the addressee of Über den Humanismus. *In addition to several works of his own, he is the author of the introduction to the French translation of* Vorträge und Aufsätze *and* Der Satz vom Grund.

---

[1] Delivered in June, 1969, in Heidelberg, Germany, at a colloquium honoring Heidegger's 80th birthday. Translated by Bernard Dauenhauer. Subsequently published in *Die Frage Martin Heideggers, op. cit.*

neuzeitlichen Philosophie)." ² Many
Frenchmen have stayed with this mod-
ernism which has irremediably cut
them off from Heidegger for whom
Phenomenology is much more the natural method and "self-evident" way of
Greek philosophy than it is the secret
aspiration of modern philosophy. This
is what has happened in the case of
Sartre and even of Merleau-Ponty,
though the latter did have a presentiment both of the possibility of a different approach from that which he
followed and of another dimension of
the Phenomenon than that which he
tried to measure in *The Phenomenology of Perception.*

But there is much more. Only
gradually and belatedly has it become
clear to the French that Phenomenology in Heidegger's sense, even prior to
being characterized by a "return to the
Greek (Zurück zu den Greichen)," a
return still so enigmatic for many, was
already distinguished by a totally different experience of the Phenomenon
than that which Husserl had. Unquestionably the guiding maxim is still
Husserl's "to the thing itself (zur
Sache selbst)." But Heidegger immediately adds, borrowing from Kant,
"in the field in which the thing itself
is heavily shrouded (in dem Felde, wo
die Sache Selbst tief eingehüllt)." ³
And there that which very soon appears to come center stage is the enigma
which the participle eingehüllt
(shrouded) — which only refers to a
state—conceals. Why is such the case?
Why is "the thing itself (die Sache
selbst)" heavily shrouded (tief eingehüllt)? Kant does not raise this question. Nor does Husserl. It seems to
them that "the thing itself" is shrouded for simply the same reason that the
equality between two right angles and
the sum of the angles of a triangle is
not immediately evident. No more.

With but a little patience we will reach
the proper conclusion.

In Heidegger's thought, on the contrary, we see the outline of a movement
which recalls in its own way the critical position of Leibniz with reference
to Descartes. Faced with the Cartesian
evidence of the piece of wax as an *extended thing* (extensum quid) Leibniz
asked himself: Why is it an *extended
thing?* His answer can be formulated
thus: It can only be an *extended thing*
because it is more essentially a thing
extending *itself* (sese extendens). One
could say analogically that for Phenomenology in Heidegger's sense what
is in question is not *heavily shrouded*
(tief eingehüllt), except to the degree
that it is *self enshrouding* (sich einhül-
lend). The concealment (Verborgen-
heit), which is critical to the Phenomenon, is not a simple state. It is *to be
in hiding* (sich verbergen) ; it is a *concealing* (Verbergung). The significant
point here is clearly expressed in paragraph 7 of *Sein und Zeit* (p. 35).
Question: "What is it that phenomenology should let us see (Was ist das,
was die Phänomenologie sehen lassen
soll)?" And the answer: "Something
which proximally and for the most part
does not show itself (offenbar solches
was sich, zunächst und zumeist, gerade
nicht zeigt)." The peculiar characteristic of the Phenomenon then is to
be essentially the bearer of a *Not*
(Nicht) which is not exclusively that
of the logical negation. Phenomenology
in Heidegger's sense shows precisely
what does not show itself. One could
even say that what it shows is, more
accurately, in that which does not
show itself, as a refusal to show itself.
This is perhaps what Heraclitus was
alluding to when he said enigmatically,
"the real constitution of things is accustomed to hide itself" ⁴ — to which,
after more than two millenia, some remarks of Schelling dealing with the

² *Ideen*, p. 118.
³ *Sein und Zeit*, p. 27.
⁴ G. S. Kirk's translation is being used here. Cf. G. S. Kirk, *Heraclitus, The Cosmic Fragments.* Cambridge, 1962, p. 227. Trans.

Essence of Human Freedom reply in their own fashion.

If such is the "in no wise spoken" (ουδαμωζ ρητον), the unformulated of Heidegger's thought, then this is what so profoundly distinguishes the *Source of the Work of Art* for example from what Husserl wrote during the same period, a work to be published with the title: *The Source of Geometry*. Without the experience of this unformulable, Heidegger's thought remains opaque. It even risks seeming altogether arbitrary — whether it is a question of the *Kantbuch* or the *Satz vom Grund*, the *Frage nach der Technik* or the interpretations of Hegel and Nietzsche.

The best example of this way of going to "the thing itself" is perhaps found in the conference published under the title of *Die onto-theologiche Verfassung der Metaphisik*. Some thought that they could see here an exercise in structuralism. The onto-theological structure however is not related to metaphysics as the equality of two right angles is related to the sum of the angles of a triangle or as refraction according to the law of sines is related to the nature of light. It is much more a question of that in which metaphysics is not showing itself (sich gerade nicht zeight), lying hidden (sich verbergend). Thus there is question of a phenomenological interpretation of metaphysics. Borrowing from Aristotle, one can define metaphysics as the study of the first principles and the first causes. The interpretation then seeks to express that which secretly escapes notice. The investigation prior to the disclosure is a search for what is undisclosed, *unnoticed*, or better, in speaking more in the middle voice than in the active voice, but not in the passive, what is *escaping notice*. Henceforth, the onto-theological structure appears as the *undisclosed harmony* of metaphysics itself. But this structure is in its turn not at all clear, no more than Being itself is clear, even when thought under the horizon of

time. Being clarifies itself no less than it makes itself, and time with it, an enigma. Cezanne said: "When color is at its richest, then form is at its fullest." Perhaps one could dare say, following the same "Cezanne way,": "When the manifestation is at its richest, the non-manifest is at the fullest of its secret unique character.

When I speak thus with my students, they are less astonished than attentive, unless they have already had too much philosophy, that is, unless they have learned too much without having read anything, or have read too much without having learned to read. If they have had too much, then of course they refute Heidegger as easily and as learnedly as a worthy professor emeritus could do, whether he be a rationalist or an existentialist, or as could a beginner in the trade, whether he be a Marxist or a structuralist. At least they do not go beyond merely performing another stylistic exercise.

But now to conclude, there is Nietzsche. It is impossible to speak of Heidegger seen from France without speaking of Heidegger's Nietzsche. France is in its second discovery of Nietzsche. The first, at the end of the last century, came from the translations of Henri Albert in *Mercure de France*. Gide and Valery read them. But since then the French, a mobile people, have had time to forget Nietzsche. They are rediscovering him today in the most astonishing disorder, as one could see on the occasion of the Nietzsche Congress held in 1964 at Royaumont. Heidegger's *Nietzsche* is not yet translated, or at least the translation has not yet been published. But *Holzwege* has been in French for several years, and the fourth of the *nonways* which this singular book proposes to us is precisely that of Nietzsche. One of the questions, *the* question perhaps which Heidegger poses a propos Nietzsche has not failed to awaken in its turn some further questions. We can put Heidegger's question thus: In Nietzsche's enterprise of

rejecting Platonism, does Nietzsche
merely make Platonism return or does
the rejecting not free itself, by the
turning movement, from Platonism so
that the so-called turn from Platonism
(sogenannte Umdrehung des Platonismus) would in reality be a turning
out from Platonism (Herausdrehung
aus dem Platonismus [N. I, p. 233])
and thus Uberwindung, a surpassing of
Platonism?

I do not know whether many Frenchmen have dealt with this issue. I believe that most of them, whether they
refer to Heidegger or not, rather consider the philosophy of Nietzsche as a
philosophical going-beyond of Platonism, presupposing that philosophy
would be capable of such a going-beyond. Heidegger, as we know, is more
reserved. Unquestionably Nietzsche
ends by reducing, in the last months
of his lucid life, the Platonic opposition of *true world — apparent world*
(wahre Welt-scheinbare Welt) to the
more radical opposition of *World*
(Welt) and *Nothing* (Nichts). Henceforth it is no longer the ον but also the
μη ον in Plato's sense which is now
nothing but an ουχ ον, and the World,
that which truly concerns us, no longer
allows for any division, so that the
putative turning back is a surpassing.
But, says Heidegger, is this surpassing
not in its turn a re-establishment of
Platonism itself in a new shape? For,
as we read in *Vorträge und Aufsätze*
(pp. 122-123), if the profuseness to
which the Grand Nostalgia, with which
Zarathustra is concerned, aspires is ultimately the appearance of becoming
itself in the guise of the Eternal Return
of the Identical, then Nietzsche himself would be nothing but the *Zügel-
loseste Platoniker,* the most unbridled
of the Platonists, and thus perhaps the
last metaphysician (der letzte Meta-
physiker).

It is astonishing, Heidegger continues,
that Nietzsche's philosophy in no way
lacks the trait by which Nietzsche
characterizes all previous metaphysics,
and which he calls in French *"l'esprit*

de ressentiment" (the spirit of resentment) and in German *"die Geist der
Rache."* The new is what this resentment with its "venomous glance" or its
"evil eye" now has for its object beyond Platonism which, according to
Nietzsche, is its popular version. Thus,
it is in a *Gegen* (an against) that Nietzsche sums up his whole philosophy.
"Does anyone understand me? Diony-
sius against the Crucified (Hat man
mich verstanden? Dionysos gegen den
Gekreuzigten)."

Is this the speech of surpassing? Is
it not once again devotion to the "black
serpent" whose head had supposedly
been bitten off in *Zarathustra* by a
young shepherd? Heidegger writes in
Vorträge und Aufsätz (p. 72): "Metaphysics does not let itself be settled like
a finished view (Metaphysik lässt sich
nicht wie ein Ansicht abtun)." Perhaps one could echo back "the spirit
of resentment does not let itself be dis-
missed with a mere snap of the fingers
(der Geist der Rache lässt sich nicht
mit einem blossen 'Beiss zu' abschaf-
fen)." Perhaps to overcome the hatred
it is necessary that there be *Gelassenheit,* that untranslatable word, so dear
to Heidegger, which he took from Master Eckhart with a slight change of
meaning. This is what some in France
have thought or at least had a hint of,
if they have not yet meditated on it.

The word Gelassenheit is untranslatable. It has, however, been translated by "serenity." This translation is
none too felicitous. If one would want
to retranslate serenity into the German,
one would rather use *Heiterkeit*. A
more careful reader has proposed another word, acquiescence, where the
Latin *quies* corresponds rather to ap-
peasement which in effect is involved
in *Gelassenheit*. But here again acquiescence would be translated rather
by *Zustimmung* or *Einwilligung*. That
was already the Latin sense of the term
it seems that Cicero valued highly:
*tu cum es commotus acquiescis, assen-
tiris, approbas* (When you are moved
you acquiesce, agree and approve).

Heidegger, it is well known, is none too Ciceronian. When I read *Gelassenheit,* I say to myself — silently to be sure — still another word, one which passed from Latin into French through Italian, a word which enchanted Ernst Junger, the word "désinvolture" (graceful bearing and demeanor). This word is hard to grasp. If one wanted to translate it into German, perhaps one would come to something between *Unbefangenheit* (candor) and *Ungeniertsein* (uninhibitedness). A French friend said to me one day, "la désinvolture, that is an elegant way of being homely." Heidegger, to tell the truth, like the Peasant of the Danube, is neither elegant nor homely. Will we be shifted to *Unbefangenheit?* Yes and no, if désinvolture can render *Gelassenheit.* For *lassen, gelassen* (release) in Heidegger's sense does not exclude *gefangen* (being held) in the sense of *umfast* (enclosed), *umzäunt* (hedged in), *angefangen sein* (to be begun). *Gelassenheit* is in effect also Umfängnis (embrace). "For the essential condition of the poets is not grounded in the thought of the gods but in the embrace by the Holy (Denn der Wesensstand des Dichters gründet nicht in der Empfängnis des Gottes, sondern in der umfängnis d u r c h das Heilige)."[5] Hölderlin named this condition "the lighthearted embrace (das leichte Umfangen)."

Can *Gelassenheit* then be rendered by *désinvolutre?* Perhaps the French think of désinvolture too subjectively. In Heidegger's thought, what is essentially *désinvolte* is less man than it is Being itself. Like the Rose of Angelus Silesius, Being has no why (das Sein ist ohn' Warum). And it is from this "without why" which Being is that, as bearers of history, its epochs "suddenly spring forth like buds (jäh aufspringen wie Knospen)."[6] The *Gelassenheit* would then be from man's side: to open himself to the désinvol-

ture of Being. It is Being's business, not ours, that it has been able to be for so long and to be us — the Being of being.

Open to the désinvolture of Being, such was perhaps, in a remoteness which nevertheless remains extraordinarily close to us, the thought of Heraclitus. Perhaps we are still drawing life from him, as Braque said of the great artist: "Everybody exploits him without knowing that it is he whom they exploit." Heraclitus' closeness — it was Hölderlin who first experienced it to the degree of being a destiny, then Hegel, then Nietzsche. Heraclitus, Nietzsche said in *Ecce Homo,* "is the one in whose vicinity I feel warmer and more comfortable in spirit than anywhere else (in dessen Nähe überhaupt mir wärmer, mir wohler zu Mute wird als irgendwo sonst)." Heidegger does not seek either to re-animate himself or to cheer himself by contact with Heraclitus. He is no longer one who chooses Heraclitus as his hero, as Hegel does. Closer to Hölderlin than to Hegel or Nietzsche, Heidegger tries to hear with a Greek ear, not for love of the Greek but "to go back to the Greek and to come out beyond the Greek period (zurück zu den Greichen und über das Greichische hinaus)." And perhaps it is thus that Heidegger is, in the sense some Frenchmen have of it, the man of the grand *désinvolture,* the *désinvolture* of Being itself, such that, since the Greeks, it unceasingly opens itself in the clearing within being. Such a désinvolture spreads itself out within the appearance of Being as the Being of the being which is but one of its epochs, though it is only through this epoch of Being beyond whose termination we live that a future is perhaps destined for us, if the history of Being preserves within its tradition "the quiet power of the Possible (die stille Kraft des Möglichen)."

These are only nuances. But as Hus-

---

[5] *Erläuterungen zu Hölderlins Dichtung,* p. 67.
[6] *Satz vom Grund,* p. 154.

serl said, it is such nuances which make the difference for philosophy between what is a path and what is an impasse. If there is one of Husserl's lessons to which Heidegger has always been resolutely faithful more than any other, I believe that this is the one. One sometimes evokes the power of Heidegger's speech or of his thought, and this is undoubtedly correct. Weakness, I would say, slightly parodying Valery, is not his forte. Into the asthenia in which that inconsistent hubbub, the so-called contemporary philosophy, collapses, Heidegger brings anew to issues the sobriety of the "athletic gaze" which Hölderlin honored among the Greeks. But the secret of power in the domain of thought is to culminate in a liberty whose law is the sense of nuances. Pascal speaks in this regard of the "spirit of finesse," or better of the "spirit of the precise." Perhaps it is through such a spirit that Heidegger will little by little become in the land of Pascal, if not a popular author, then at least a master in the most difficult of tasks, that of distinguishing when others confuse, by thinking and by teaching us to think Identity as Difference. *Identität und Differenz.* Thus the green-gold of the olive crown which came to the Greeks from the Upper Danube is still radiant. Thus appears the ov η ov, the being-to-be. Thus speaks Philosophy, a secret speech and a doubled simplicity, nuance and only nuance. But then the French will find themselves on a higher plane in opening themselves to an art of speaking whose destiny is perhaps to pass through France. They are listening. For as one of our poets, who knew how to recognize your great poets, has said, while marveling at the saying of it:

For we still want the nuance
Not the coloring, only the nuance.
The nuance alone betroths
The dream to the dream and the flute to the heart.[7]

---

[7] Beaufret is here quoting from Paul Verlaine's "Art Poétique." Trans.